Taking Child Abuse Seriously

Contemporary issues in child protection theory and practice

**The Violence against Children
Study Group**

London and New York

First published in 1990 by Unwin Hyman Ltd

Reprinted 1993
by Routledge
11 New Fetter Lane
London EC4P 4EE

Simultaneously published in the USA and Canada
by Routledge
29 West 35th Street, New York, NY 10001

© The Violence against Children Study Group 1990

Printed and bound in Great Britain by
Biddles Ltd, Guildford & King's Lynn

British Library Cataloguing in Publication Data
Taking child abuse seriously : contemporary issues in
    child protection theory and practice. (The State of
    Welfare)
    1. Children. Abuse by adults
    I. Violence Against Children Study Group   II. Series
    362.7'044

Library of Congress Cataloging in Publication Data
A catalogue record for this book is available from the Library of Congress.

ISBN 0–415–10480–7

Contents

Contributors: Members of the Violence against Children Study Group

Eric Blyth holds a joint appointment as Senior Lecturer in the Department of Behavioural Sciences at Huddersfield Polytechnic, teaching sociology and social policy of social work and health-related courses, and Development Officer with Wakefield Social Service Department. He is also Director of the Centre for Education Welfare Studies at Huddersfield Polytechnic. His main research interests are in interdisciplinary work with school-age children. He has published extensively on the subject of child sexual abuse in social work and education journals and conducted workshops with junior headteachers, education welfare officers, and social workers. He has also published articles on stress and infertility and is co-author (with J. Milner) of *Coping with Child Sexual Abuse: A Guide for Teachers* (Longman, 1988).

Yvonne Channer completed her BA and CQSW in 1978. Since that time she has worked for local authorities as a generic case worker and also worked on a project aimed to assist and enable parents (mainly young single mothers) and their children within the Afro-Caribbean community in areas of welfare benefits, child care, counselling, etc. Her current post as a lecturer in the Social Work Section at Huddersfield Polytechnic gives her the opportunity to develop and share views on important issues such as service delivery to black clients and the deskilling of white professional carers when working within black communities. Her Afro-Caribbean origin has heightened her interest in counteracting the pathological view of black communities, which has been reinforced by much of the current social work literature, and in the unresearched areas of strength within black communities.

Barrie Clark is a qualified social worker and currently a part-time lecturer in behavioural sciences at Huddersfield Polytechnic. He has recently been engaged in research concerning social workers' perceptions of cases referred to a Family Centre.

Harry Ferguson studied and qualified as a social worker at Bradford University. He has worked as a social worker, for a number of years specializing in child protection. He is currently researching a PhD on the history and theory of child abuse and welfare practices, and is based at the Faculty of Social and Political Sciences, University of Cambridge, where he is a member of Clare Hall.

Nick Frost is currently a Development Officer with responsibility for childcare services in a social services department. He was formerly a lecturer in social work at Bradford University and for eight years was a local authority social worker. He has published on social work and social policy issues and is co-author (with Mike Stein) of *The Politics of Child Welfare* (Wheatsheaf, 1989).

Jeff Hearn is Senior Lecturer in Applied Social Studies, University of Bradford. He has published widely on organizations, gender, and social policy, including *Birth and Afterbirth* (Achilles Heel, 1983), *'Sex' at 'Work'* (St Martin's/Wheatsheaf, 1987; co-author), *The Gender of Oppression* (St Martin's/Wheatsheaf, 1987), *Studying Men and Masculinity* (University of Bradford, 1988; co-author). During 1988–9 he was Hallsworth Research Fellow of the University of Manchester, researching into men and masculinity.

Michael Horne is a qualified social worker who has worked mainly in residential social work, before studying for a first degree and then undertaking research into social work values for a master's degree. He is Research Associate at the Hester Adrian Research Centre, University of Manchester. He was previously a lecturer in the Social Work Section at Huddersfield Polytechnic, teaching mainly on the CQSW course. He has also taught on CSS and In-Service courses. His publications include *Values in Social Work* (Wildwood House, 1987).

Helen Masson is a Senior Lecturer in the Behavioural Sciences Department of Huddersfield Polytechnic. She is mainly involved in teaching human growth and behaviour to social work and health visitor students and family therapy to CQSW students. She is particularly interested in exploring the applications of family therapy. She is a qualified social worker, having worked as a generic social worker and as a senior practitioner specializing in work with adolescents in a social services department. During the year 1987–8 she undertook a full-time secondment with Rochdale NSPCC Child Protection Team. Her publications include *Applying*

Family Therapy: A practical guide for social workers (Pergamon Press, 1984; with Patrick O'Byrne).

Judith Milner is a Senior Lecturer in Social Work (part-time) and Tutor in Education Welfare at Huddersfield Polytechnic. She is qualified in teaching and social work. She is an adviser in staff appointments at a special school and occasional adviser to child protection workers in Bradford. She has published extensively on the subject of child sexual abuse in social work and education journals and conducted workshops with junior headteachers, education welfare officers, and social workers, and is the author of *Social Work and Sexual Problems* (Pepar, 1986) and co-author (with E. Blyth) of *Coping with Child Sexual Abuse: A Guide for Teachers* (Longman, 1988).

Patrick O'Byrne is Senior Lecturer in Social Work at Huddersfield Polytechnic, where he is also Probation Tutor on the social work course. His special interests in teaching are social work values, a task-centred approach to casework and the use of 'paradoxical' methods in work with individuals and families. His practical experience includes ten years in the probation service, working especially with multi-problem families. He has maintained his links with that service, still taking cases as an accredited volunteer, mainly with a view to offering family interventions. He is co-leader of a family therapy support group within the probation service, is interested in a systems approach to conciliation work with couples who are separating or divorcing, and is also a consultant to a Family Centre. Publications include co-authorship (with Helen Masson) of *Applying Family Therapy* (Pergamon, 1984).

Wendy Parkin has experience of social services area work including crisis, short-term, and long-term work of a generic nature with an emphasis on work with families and mentally ill people. She has taught on CSS and In-Service courses. Currently she holds a half-time Senior Lectureship in Social Work/Sociology at Huddersfield Polytechnic, teaching social workers, health visitors, district nurses, and on degree courses. She is also a half-time social worker in a Family Centre, where sessions work is undertaken with families where abuse has occurred. Her research interests include gender and sexuality in relation to leadership, organization, and social theories. She has published several journal articles on these areas and is the co-author (with J. Hearn) of *'Sex' at 'Work'* (St Martin's/Wheatsheaf, 1987).

Christine Parton is a qualified social worker. She has worked in local authority social service departments and as a lecturer in sociology and social work at Huddersfield Polytechnic. She is currently a social worker in a social services department. She is particularly interested in feminist social policy theory and in developing a feminist perspective to social work theory and practice. She has researched and published on the history of maternity services in the early twentieth century and on contemporary policy developments in child protection.

Nigel Parton is a qualified social worker who previously worked in a social services department. He is Principal Lecturer in the Social Work Section at Huddersfield Polytechnic. He has been researching, teaching, and writing on child abuse for ten years. He has published numerous articles in professional and academic journals and is the joint editor (with Bill Jordan) of *The Political Dimensions of Social Work* (Blackwells, 1983) and the author of *The Politics of Child Abuse* (Macmillan, 1985).

Martin Richards is currently employed in a Family Centre as a senior practitioner. Following qualification, thirteen years ago, he worked as a generic social worker in area teams in three local authorities. He has a particular interest in working with children and families.

Series editor's preface

Over the past decade the postwar consensus on the welfare state has been undermined by economic crisis and the growing appeal of right-wing social policies. In all Western countries public debate has focused on the burden of public spending, particularly on welfare, and on the measures necessary to reduce it. Austerity policies have squeezed welfare provision under governments of the right in Britain, West Germany and the USA, and under socialist governments in Greece, France and Spain.

In Britain, all sides are dissatisfied with the old system of welfare. The right denounces the profligacy and inefficiency of public services while feminists and the left insist that social welfare provision must be transformed to establish new democratic forms of socialized welfare provision. After forty years of consensus, the debate about welfare is in a new phase.

In practice, the attempts by governments in Britain and abroad to restructure welfare services have encountered difficulties. Welfare professionals, trade unions and substantial bodies of public opinion have opposed drastic cuts in welfare services. In general resistance has been most effective in relation to health provision, where established facilities tend to enjoy considerable public popularity, and least effective in social security and council housing, where unpopular state services have been the targets of hostile media comment and political propaganda.

However, despite some successful delaying tactics, the general trend towards retrenchment and piecemeal privatization is unmistakable. The increasingly defensive position of the welfare agencies and their supporters, and the growing reliance of welfare on charitable and voluntary initiatives, large and small, reflects the growing success of government pressure in transferring the cost of caring away from the state. The 1989 White Paper on the National Health Service signalled a major extension of market principles into the area of welfare provision which had most successfully resisted the pressure of Thatcherite austerity over the previous decade. Meanwhile the Conservative government's social security 'reforms' threaten to deepen and widen the scale of poverty in Britain.

In addition to the pressures resulting from public expenditure cuts and threats of privatization, state practice has shifted in favour of a more authoritarian approach to social problems. A series of moral panics around issues of law and order, the family and sexuality have contributed to a generally more coercive climate. Social workers, teachers, doctors and other welfare professionals have been expected to play a more interventionist role in dealing with a range of problems including crime, poverty and juvenile delinquency.

The issue that has placed the most intense and the most conflicting pressures on social workers and others in the field of childcare is that of child abuse, especially child sexual abuse. This is the theme of the third book in *The State of Welfare* series. As the Violence against Children Study Group note in their introduction, the spate of public inquiries that began with the report on the death of Jasmine Beckford in Brent in 1985 put the issue of child abuse at the centre of national attention. In these reports social workers were criticized – even scapegoated – for trying to support and work with the family, rather than invoking their statutory powers to remove children from situations of risk. The recommendation was that social workers should be more prepared to use their repressive powers and take children directly into council care.

Events in Cleveland in 1987 produced a public backlash against a more interventionist approach to child protection. Here social workers and paediatricians were vilified for taking just the sort of direct action that had been recommended in the earlier reports. When large numbers of children were taken into care on suspicion of having been sexually abused, some from middle-class homes, the angry response from parents, backed by a local campaign and the media, revealed the potentially destabilizing effects of the child abuse panic for the most ardent defenders of conventional family values. Welfare professionals were caught in the middle, accused in London of not taking child abuse seriously, and in Cleveland of taking child abuse too seriously. Written in the heat of these contradictory pressures, by people actively engaged in working and teaching in this controversial field, *Taking Child Abuse Seriously* provides a balanced assessment of the current state of the debate.

Mary Langan

Guest preface

PROFESSOR LINDA GORDON

In the past few decades we have come to understand that child abuse is a *social* problem, not merely an individual crime. The cause of the abuse cannot be located simply in particular psychopathologies; rather a number of social factors, such as poverty, isolation, and overwork combine with individual propensities to produce mistreaters of children. In parallel, understanding the problem as social means that law enforcement and professional psychotherapy alone cannot provide solutions; social services are required as well. This understanding has been a very important breakthrough. It represented a break with the Victorian legacy of romanticizing family life and mythologizing 'normal' relations between parents and children as respectful and harmonious. This denial of the conflict that is so often at the heart of intimacy led to embarrassment and shame about family violence. The result was often to punish doubly the victims of family violence by hiding their problems and sometimes even blaming the victims. The rediscovery of the widespread incidence of child abuse since the 1960s, and its redefinition as socially constructed, have led to new public programmes aimed at helping victims and abusers, even preventive programmes. In the US, for example, schools have incorporated a kind of 'assertiveness training' for children, encouraging them to trust their instincts, not to blame themselves, and to seek help against abuse. Child abusers have also benefited from this new understanding that they are not unique because it allows them more easily to ask for help.

Another aspect of child abuse has been less well understood: that it is a *political* problem. I mean this in two ways. First, the very definition of what constitutes unacceptable violence against children developed and then changed according to political moods and the force of certain political movements over the last century. This is best seen historically. For example, child abuse has received most attention when feminist movements have been strong, bringing with them a willingness to challenge the sacredness of family relations. In more conservative periods child abuse has been alternately denied or redefined in victim-blaming ways.[1] Indeed, while the concept of child abuse exists in all societies – i.e., certain treatments of children are defined as bad, there is always a distinction between acceptable punishment and abuse – the definitions of what counts as child abuse vary widely, and reflect politicized, culturally specific, and historically shifting notions of what counts as good childraising. In modern societies with heterogeneous populations, child abuse has always been defined amidst contested family values.

Second, family conflicts are political with respect to familial power relations. By and large domestic violence grows out of intrafamily power struggles in which material resources and benefits are at issue. In cases of wifebeating men usually fight to obtain material goods and services or to enforce their dominance and privilege; women resist and often counter with their own desires for autonomy and control. It has perhaps been harder to see these power struggles in cases of child abuse, in part for fear that any acknowledgement of children's agency in family conflicts might lead to victim blaming. This difficulty is created in turn by myths of childhood 'innocence' (as contrasted with adult evil), maternal selflessness, and paternal authority. Innocence and evil, self-sacrifice and selfishness – these are simply not the right categories. To see the intrafamily politics of child abuse is to recognize that love and intimacy do not remove conflicts of interest, and that good parenting involves neither denial of the self (the female model) nor insistence on subordination (the male model).

Child abuse most needs a political analysis when the two levels of politics intersect – that is, when extrafamilial social change and social conflict affect intrafamily relations. The stresses of parenting are intensified by impoverishment and racism and isolation. Children are influenced by cultural patterns which offer autonomy and values alien to their parents, and the latter may fight to hold their children to more traditional norms of family life.

Taking Child Abuse Seriously takes child abuse politically. Following from Nigel Parton's earlier book, *The Politics of Child Abuse* (1985), it results from the now two-year-old discussions of a group of practising social workers and social-work academics. It shows the results of the group's continuing interaction and mutual influence, of hands-on experience, and of close attention to the conservative politics which are constructing the meanings of child abuse in contemporary Britain. The book is also an intervention into the politics of child abuse, an attempt to construct its meanings in a more democratic direction.

The approximately 110-year history of child abuse as a social problem is precisely a history of such struggles over its meanings. Nor were these struggles simply two-sided, between conservative and liberal orientations. Originally 'discovered' throughout the capitalist industrial world in the 1870s, 'cruelty to children', as the problem was then so moralistically called, was defined as a crime of the poor, the depraved, the drunken – and, in the US, of the racially inferior. At the same time a feminist influence, albeit representing a privileged sector of women and thus accepting these class and racial perspectives, was defining the problem so as to criticize male violence, to urge gentler forms of child discipline, and to promote greater public responsibility for child welfare. Late nineteenth-century Societies for Prevention of Cruelty to Children amassed great power to remove children from their parents. Within a few decades child protectors began to emphasize child neglect as well as abuse, the former encompassing a vast area in which parents failed to live up to standards of child-raising set by dominant groups; many parents were by definition guilty of neglect because of their poverty. The emphasis on neglect did not however produce any greater consensus about solutions, proposals for which ranged from punishment to 'reform' of mothers to social welfare programmes.

One can see this historical contestation over the meanings of child abuse particularly vividly in the case of sexual abuse. In the late-nineteenth century, largely due to feminist influence, intrafamily sexual abuse, mainly father-daughter incest, was highly visible. Men were blamed but they were identified, of course, as poor, depraved, inferior men. In the US in the early twentieth century sexual abuse cases were reinterpreted in two ways: first, victims were blamed, girls even as young as eight and nine labelled sex delinquents; second, child protective agencies focused more on sex abuse by strangers, disguising the fact that children are most likely to be molested by male members of their immediate household. In the last few decades feminist influence has again brought sexual abuse into the open. But in the US, where the 'pro-family' Moral Majority movements have had more influence, we are seeing today a repetition of this redefinition of sexual abuse, removing scrutiny from families and fathers in particular and reemphasizing the dangers of abuse by strangers, such as teachers.[2] (Statistically this is quite false: sexual abuse of children and women is much more likely to be perpetrated by relatives or husbands/lovers than by strangers.) Moreover, in US research and educational programmes, sexual abuse is often depicted in gender-neutral terms, the fact that it is overwhelmingly a male crime suppressed.

It should be clear, then, that it is inaccurate to treat child abuse as an individual problem, as a constant, or as a self-evident, easily recognizable wrong. *Most* cases of child abuse – indeed, the vast majority of cases – are not of the most extreme, sensational type that leads to deaths or severe injury and intense publicity. Most are ambiguous, either because it is difficult to get substantiating evidence or because the behaviour itself is open to various interpretations. There is no escaping the role of different political perspectives even in defining the problem let alone in creating solutions. This is not a problem that can, therefore, be left to professionals and to technical, supposedly objective expertise. This is a problem that must be debated publicly and must enter into democratic opinion about basic social policy.

For this reason I hope that *Taking Child Abuse Seriously* will not be considered a book only for 'experts' in the field. It is a book that should be widely read and reviewed, and should make it possible for a wide array of groups, including victims and perpetrators of child abuse, to develop and articulate their views on child abuse and its solutions.

Notes

1 In the introduction to my *Heroes of Their Own Lives: The History and Politics of Family Violence 1880–1960* (NY: Penguin, 1988 and London: Virago, 1989) I take a sample real child abuse case and suggest how differently it would have been treated in five different historical periods since the 'discovery' of child abuse in the 1870s.
2 See my 'The politics of child sexual abuse: notes from American history', in *Feminist Review*'s special issue 'Family Secrets: Child Sexual Abuse', No. 28, spring 1988, pp. 56–64.

Introduction

Child abuse is now firmly on current agendas – moral, legal, medical, political, professional, and indeed personal. So at first glance it may seem odd to many that we are urging that child abuse 'be taken seriously'. After all, since the death of Maria Colwell in 1973, there have been thirty-five public inquiries and subsequent reports into individual cases in Britain, as well as the recent Cleveland crisis of 1987 over the diagnosis/misdiagnosis of child sexual abuse. Popular opinion has swung from accusations of inadequate vigilance, particularly by social workers, to accusations of excessive vigilance, particularly by paediatricians. Something little short of a crisis in confidence and legitimacy in the domains of public policy and professional practice has developed in relation to child protection.

All this would appear to suggest that an enormous interest exists in child abuse, and indeed that child abuse is now taken seriously enough for it to be considered *the* social problem of our time. In adopting our title, we do not suggest or imply that all previous attempts to conceptualize policy and practice in relation to child protection should be negated or cynically undermined. Rather, we have come together as a collective under the working conviction that 'taking child abuse seriously' means appreciating the complexity of child abuse – in its perpetration, in professional practice, in policy development, and in its analysis through social theory.

Taking child abuse seriously means, for us, attempting to produce a text and an approach that is fundamentally critical, and that actively works at breaking down conventional academic and practical divisions, including divisions of labour. Often, it seems to us, texts on child abuse fragment the complexity of the issues by concentrating primarily on practice, or policy, or theory – so undermining the 'seriousness' of the whole. We believe that the magnitude of this difficult task of making sense of child abuse must itself be taken seriously. Our aim has been to produce a serious, critical approach to the protection of children which reflects the complexity of the task involved.

This critical approach has informed the production of this book. The Violence against Children Study Group was formed early in 1987 as a collective means of discussion, reflection, and writing on the important issue of child abuse. All of the Group live or work in close proximity; all but two have been practising social workers; all have taught social workers or have researched into social work practice; and six of the fourteen members are at the time of writing in paid social work practice. Thus the interrelation of social theory, social policy, social work, and personal practice has been necessary and inevitable, rather than an abstract goal. Furthermore, the process of producing this book has been a collaborative venture, with each chapter authored by one or more members, and subject to revisions following collective comment and discussions; similarly, the process of editing has been shared between us. This series of sometimes elaborate procedures has been an appropriate way of linking 'practitioners' and 'academics' (in some cases, the same people!) and increasing the interplay of differing practical, intellectual, disciplinary, and political positions, and indeed our own differing ethnic, gender, familial, and sexual identities and biographies. Above all, our theorizing has developed from and alongside practice. The practice of producing this book is part of the practice and theory that informs the ideas and arguments in this book: they are not distinct worlds, as is usually the case with academic social science and social theory.

Our writing and our collective discussions have taken place within a highly fluid historical context. Thus at the heart of this text is the assumption that practice on and theory about child abuse occur and have to be understood and developed in relation to broad social and political change. It was largely with that in mind that the text, *The Politics of Child Abuse* (Parton, 1985a), was produced as an attempt to take account of the growth of concern about child abuse in the previous fifteen years. The changing historical context which has brought us together has, in turn, forced us to constantly and reflexively monitor each other's work and our own writing and views. A profound sense of change and uncertainty animates our work and, we hope, our text. We regard this uncertainty, or rather our confession of it, not as a weakness, but as a necessary force for moving on. We have not sought to provide easy answers; that said, we do of course hope that the *range* of analyses that follow will contribute to the continuing reappraisal of child protection issues that marks this current period in history.

This particular phase in the historical development of the public issue of child abuse is marked by an unusually rapid pace of change. Since the publication of the inquiry report into the death of Jasmine Beckford (London Borough of Brent,

1985) in December 1985, the national telephone network Child Line and the closely associated BBC television series Childwatch were launched in 1986. These developments have heightened public interest and have also promoted survey research into the incidence of abuse. The Cleveland controversy erupted in 1987 over the relatively sudden increase in the rate of diagnoses of child sexual abuse by paediatricians and social workers. Child sexual abuse, a subject that had rarely caught public attention, quickly came to be the concern of newspaper headline writers, MPs, ministers of government, and many other public figures, usually male. In December 1987 two further important inquiry reports were published, on the deaths of Kimberley Carlile (London Borough of Greenwich, 1987) and Tyra Henry (London Borough of Lambeth, 1987). Public events reached some kind of official watershed in July 1988. First there was the publication of the report of the inquiry into the Cleveland controversy, chaired by Lord Justice Butler-Sloss (Secretary of State for Social Services, 1988). Then no fewer than seven governmental guidelines and circulars were issued, primarily, though not exclusively, on child sexual abuse. These were designed for social workers (DHSS, 1988d, 1988c), doctors (DHSS, 1988b), senior nurses, health visitors and midwives (DHSS, 1988a), those in the education service (DES, 1988) and Home Office services (Home Office, 1988), and stressed inter-agency cooperation (Social Services Inspectorate, 1988).

This recent history of child abuse is not, however, a simple chronology of events, or a simple inventory of where the dead hand of abuse/abusers happens to fall next. It is a story that has been fed by a diversity of political and theoretical approaches, and that in turn can be usefully understood and examined through that diversity of political and theoretical approaches. To put this another way, there is a dialectic between practice and policy and the theories brought to bear on them.

A number of core critical issues figure strongly and fundamentally in both the current development of practice and policy around child abuse, and the current development of social theory that may inform those practices and policies. These *simultaneous* core issues include *the very nature of abuse, violence, sexual violence, and sexuality*, and the increasing concern with the problematic relationship of child sexual abuse and 'other' forms of abuse. Such debates inevitably feed into the core issue of *incidence*, whether assessed on official statistics or the reports of respondents, usually as adults, and therefore retrospective. The increasing number of research studies of incidence, media-based surveys (like those conducted by Childwatch), and extrapolations from child abuse registers and agency samples show that both child abuse and child sexual abuse are not unusual, and are at higher levels than often and previously supposed. However, different studies inevitably use different definitions of abuse, so that detailed comparison of their 'results' demands careful scrutiny of the assumptions and methods employed (Birchall, 1989; also see Milner and Blyth, 1988). Perhaps most importantly, the search for 'incidence' is itself a social and political exercise. It occurs at certain historical times, and for identifiable and sometimes contradictory reasons, such as the prioritization of agency problems at a time of scarce resources and the development of feminist practice as a response to men's violence.

Other persistent core issues include the changing form of the state, state power, and state regulation; the impact and interrelation of gender, 'race', ethnicity, class, and age; the pervasive power of political movements and forms of knowledge, such as feminism and psychoanalysis; the demand for ethnic- and gender-sensitive practices (in both practice and theory); the continuing relation of practice, policy, and theory. Also we are keen to spell out the implications of these debates and arguments for everyday practice for those working professionally with child abuse – how to provide a response to individuals that does not pathologize; how to remain sympathetic to the victim/survivor/client, and sympathetic to the professional/state agent. In writing this book, it has been important, and increasingly so, to make our commitment against abuse and violence to children and young people explicit, and not shrouded in abstractions.

These are the core concerns throughout this book. In Chapter 1 **Nigel Parton** focuses on the assumptions, and indeed shortcomings, of the original *Politics of Child Abuse* (Parton, 1985a). In particular, he considers issues of gender relations and of sexual abuse, and the danger of not taking seriously the significance of abuse *for the child.* He goes on to specify some of the questions and tensions that need to be addressed in both practice and theory, and hence introduces some of the issues developed further in subsequent chapters. One of these major themes, the changing relationship of state forms and households, is the subject of Chapter 2 by **Nick Frost.** This initially discusses some theoretical issues before looking at the specific way the state–household relationship has developed in contemporary Britain, especially in terms of child protection. It is argued that child protection practice is a key indicator in analysing state–household relations.

The next two chapters are concerned with the importance of gender relations in child abuse. Writing from a feminist perspective, **Christine Parton** highlights in Chapter 3 some of the major gender issues neglected by the majority of research and writing on child abuse. She examines differences between men's and women's abuse, and their links with the social construction of both male-dominated sexuality and motherhood. She draws on feminist theories of child abuse from diverse conceptual frameworks, yet central to all is the belief that child abuse is rooted in the power relations between women and children and men at both personal and structural levels. In Chapter 4 **Jeff Hearn** further develops a pro-feminist analysis of child abuse by asking the question, 'What happens if we look at child abuse as men's violence?' He follows this theme in terms of policy, social theory, and practice, concluding with practical steps that men social workers can take in coming out against violence, in both child abuse cases and preventive work.

The next six chapters take state practice and professional practice as their prime topic. **Mike Horne** in Chapter 5 attends to recent child abuse cases. He discusses the way in which questions about the nature and role of social work have been brought into sharp focus following the publication of recent inquiry reports. This chapter examines what the 'essential' nature of social work is, and relates this specifically to child abuse work. **Yvonne Channer** and **Nigel Parton** in Chapter 6 focus on debates about the 'racial' and ethnic dimensions of practice around child abuse. In particular, they note the central importance of assessment skills for members of the caring professions, and the need to ask whether appropriate models are being used when clients of differing ethnicity are being assessed. Their examination of recent child abuse cases in black British communities illuminates the current professional scene and identifies areas of bad practice.

In Chapter 7 **Harry Ferguson** argues that there has been a lack of attention to historical perspectives in dominant approaches to practice. He shows that the origins of contemporary problems, possibilities, and ideologies in practices, policies, and knowledges can be more adequately understood by taking them to their modern roots in the 1880–1914 period. He offers a corrective to those accounts of practice that suggest that contemporary 'problems' are simply a product of a post-war or 1970s' malaise. Chapter 8 by **Barrie Clark**, **Wendy Parkin** and **Martin Richards** relates some of the core issues of the book to ongoing practice issues in family centre work, the ideology of 'dangerousness', tensions and complexities of child abuse cases, and the impact of organizational constraints. This chapter draws on both research material and current and past social work cases. In Chapter 9 **Helen Masson** and **Patrick O'Byrne** discuss the application of family systems ideas to problems of physical and sexual child abuse. They consider not only whether such ideas are potentially useful in these problem areas but also whether such ideas are actually used in social work practice today. The resources required to make use of them and the implications of this for practitioners employed, for instance, in hard-pressed social services departments are highlighted. Further organizational problems are identified by **Eric Blyth** and **Judith Milner** in Chapter 10. They focus on the need for multidisciplinary work in child abuse, and consider the difficulties that may exist for agencies coming together. This chapter also looks positively at how problems of poor collaboration can be overcome, what effective partnership means, and how it can be recognized.

Together these chapters address the complex problem of child abuse, and work on and against it in personal, political, professional, and theoretical dimensions. We do not seek false integrations or simple solutions, but we hope that through confronting the difficulties, uncertainties, and ambiguities, more adequate practices and theories become possible.

*　　　　　*　　　　　*

We would like to thank Liz Tunaley and Clive Tunaley for all their efficient and speedy help with the preparation of the final manuscript.

1 Taking child abuse seriously

NIGEL PARTON

Introduction

This chapter has three interrelated objectives. First, I reflect on how my own thinking about child abuse and what to do about it has developed, modified, and been found terribly wanting in recent years. It is an explicit attempt to rethink some of the ideas and arguments put forward in *The Politics of Child Abuse* (Parton, 1985a). Secondly, I shall briefly summarize some of the main developments in theory, policy, and practice that have emerged in relation to child abuse in recent years. The period since 1985 has witnessed considerable interest in and consequently very public debate about the issue in Britain. This chapter will attempt a critical analysis of these developments and suggest how they might be best understood. Finally, I shall outline three elements that need developing in theory, policy, and practice – namely the significance of power, structural abuse, and the rights of children.

The politics of 'The Politics of Child Abuse'

A major aim in writing *The Politics of Child Abuse* was to provide a counterbalance to what I saw as an excessive preoccupation with individual pathology in most literature, research, and policy concerned with child abuse. It tried to open up the possibility of a more explicitly critical analysis of the problem, and in the process feed into discussions that attempted a more radical and creative approach in terms of theory and practice.

The central argument was that debates about the nature of child abuse and what to do about it are at root not technical and professional but political. Essentially, they are about how we should bring up children and in particular the most appropriate relationships that can be developed between the state and the

family. This political nature of child abuse was illustrated in two
ways. First, it was argued that the way child abuse was recognized as a social problem in the mid-1970s was neither natural
nor self-evident. It could only be understood by analysing the
political processes whereby it was defined, brought to public
attention, and made the subject of state intervention. I demonstrated how changes in policy and practice could be traced
to the highest level of political activity. Both Sir Keith Joseph,
then Secretary of State for Social Services, and some senior
civil servants played active campaigning roles in bringing the
issue to public attention, particularly via the decision to establish the public inquiry into the case of Maria Colwell (DHSS,
1974). I argued that it was this inquiry that proved crucial
in establishing the issue as a major social problem and that
mobilized public, professional, political, and media interest.

Similarly a number of pressure groups, in the guise of the
National Society for the Prevention of Cruelty to Children and
certain small but significant sections of the medical profession,
played important roles in the early 1970s (Parton, 1979). Also I
tried to demonstrate how these developments could be related
to a more general social anxiety about the decline of the family,
the growth of violence, and concerns that inadequate families
and innocent victims were being badly let down by 'woolly
do-gooders' – particularly social workers. All of which reflected
and fed into changes in the economy and the restructuring of
the state (Parton, 1981). In the process, I argued that the way
the problem was socially constructed depended on a very particular set of assumptions and explanations. The 'disease model',
with its emphasis on individual identification, prevention, and
treatment, had been dominant in influencing the way the problem was understood and what and how it was responded to.

The second major strand of the argument developed from a
critical analysis of this 'disease model'. Its underlying values and
assumptions were made explicit, together with its inadequacies
at both the empirical and conceptual levels. Child abuse was
conceptualized as a pathological phenomenon with its roots in
the personality or character of the abusing parent. Social factors
were seen only in terms of the characteristics associated with
abusive individuals or families. In effect, the model ignored
social arrangements and denied that social and economic factors
played any significant part in the problem. It failed to explore
the social context in which abuse arises. A major focus of
The Politics of Child Abuse was to draw explicit attention to
this social context in two ways. First, the link between social
inequality, poverty, and child abuse was underlined. It was
argued that the stresses, frustrations, and lack of opportunities

for bringing up children were a major factor in explaining why the incidence of abuse was so much more concentrated in the most deprived sections of society. I argued that the traditional concentration on dangerous individuals failed to consider the significance of dangerous conditions. Similarly, by focusing on the individual causes and manifestations of abuse, traditional approaches failed to recognize the abusive, but non-individualistic practices of industrial, corporate, and government agencies. Arguments about the nature, causes, and consequences of abuse had ignored abuse at the institutional and structural levels.

In developing such arguments the analysis explicitly drew upon the theoretical insights, perspectives, and concepts that had been refined in the sociology of deviance in the previous two decades. From the outset the sociology of deviance abandoned the notion of individual pathology and focused on the ways the agencies of social control stigmatized certain groups and so exacerbated the very problem they claimed to ameliorate. Originally the approach was associated with 'interactionism' and the 'labelling perspective'.

Subsequently, *Critical Criminology* (Taylor, Walton, and Young, 1973; Taylor, Walton, and Young, 1975) drew increasingly towards Marxism and proved very productive in exploring the class dimensions of crime and thereby illuminating how and why the criminal law is selectively enforced against the powerless. The primary focus of analysis became the state and the role of law. Where differences do occur in terms of anti-social behaviour in the working class, this is seen as a direct result of poverty, deprivation, and exploitation. The sociology of deviance, in both its labelling and Marxist versions, was influential in informing the analysis in *The Politics of Child Abuse*. Four main differences in approach were itemized as being of relevance in helping to move beyond the traditional approaches to child abuse.

First, the study of child abuse had been dissociated from the operation of the processes of social control – particularly the state. No adequate understanding of child abuse was possible without considering the relationship between the control processes (reactions), abusive behaviour (actions), and the form of laws, rules, and norms. The abusive behaviour could not be analysed in isolation from the way it was defined and responded to.

Secondly, there was a rejection of the traditional approach to child abuse as being 'value free'. It was shown that quite clear value positions informed it at every point. A strong moralistic paternalism was evident in much of the material.

Closely related to this was a rejection of positivism, which was seen to be spuriously 'scientific'. The application of the natural scientific method, whereby scientific laws might be identified and applied in order to eradicate the problem under investigation, was considered inappropriate in the social world where social process, history, and the differential impact of the social situation were seen as vital.

Finally, the traditional approaches were seen as excessively deterministic, absolute, and individualistic. There was a move towards an analysis that was more relative and socially situated in orientation.

While important in helping to shift the emphasis, it was clear at the time of writing that there were tensions and deficiencies in the analysis. These tensions and deficiencies have become glaringly obvious since.

The failure to recognize the child in child abuse

It was evident at the outset that *The Politics of Child Abuse* was inadequate in at least three areas: its failure to address sexual abuse; its difficulties in taking into account the dimension of gender; and its ambiguous messages for the practitioner. It has since become apparent, however, that such difficulties were not simply the failure to address the analysis to these specific areas but reflected a much more fundamental problem with the analysis itself. What were the inherent difficulties in the sociology of deviance that subsequently informed and therefore skewed the analysis developed in *The Politics of Child Abuse*?

In recent years the re-evaluation of the sociology of deviance has pointed to two major lacunae and both are crucial for developing our understanding of child abuse. There has been little analysis of the causes of the original deviance itself (the abusive behaviour or act) and a failure to focus on the impact of the deviance on the victim (the child). Roger Matthews and Jock Young (1986), in commenting on its application to crime, have written that the sociology of deviance 'became an advocate for the indefensible: the criminal became the victim, the state became the solitary focus of attention, while the real victim remained off stage'. Neither the victim nor the causes of the original deviance received serious consideration.

As we have seen, the first phase of developing a radical deviancy analysis was associated with the interactionist or labelling perspective – the work of Howard Becker (1963), Edwin Lemert (1967), and David Matza (1964, 1969) was influential. A prime aim was to understand the experience of the offender. Rather than attempt to correct the rule-breaker, the emphasis was on appreciating their situation. The approach to issues such as drugtaking, homosexuality, delinquency, and mental illness almost celebrated such behaviour as examples of the richness of human diversity combined with elements of resistance to the monolithic and oppressive social system, particularly capital and the state. The focus was often on what were assumed to be 'crimes without victims' (Schur, 1963). When it was recognized that there may be victims, the harm was minimized. In fact, the emphasis was upon the deviant/offender-as-victim, that is, the deviant was the victim of the labelling/stigmatizing/criminalization processes.

This notion of the deviant/offender as victim was even more pronounced during the 1970s when there was an explicit move towards the Marxist approach. In this phase, the focus was much more upon the state and state agencies and their impact upon deviants/offenders and non-deviants. The deviance/crime itself was seen as a non-event of little importance. Increased attention was given to showing how the construction of deviants/offenders acted to create scapegoats, which then diverted public attention from the real problems of a capitalist society – such as racism, poverty, and exploitation.

A particularly important book which reflected such thinking was that on mugging by Stuart Hall and his colleagues at the Centre for Contemporary and Cultural Studies (Hall *et al.*, 1978). This work was influential in informing parts of *The Politics of Child Abuse*.

The mugger, especially the black mugger, was perceived as the victim of structural inequalities, unemployment, and racism, which gave rise to mugging as a solution to these structural contradictions. More particularly, mugging was analysed in the way it was socially constructed by the media and certain elements of the state apparatus in order to help resolve the economic and ideological crisis facing British capitalism in the early 1970s. Through the orchestration of a moral panic, it was conceived largely in terms of its symbolic significance and represented in part the changing political climate, the growing importance of the New Right, and the collapse of the social democratic welfare consensus. The concept of moral panic was central to the analysis in connecting the arguments about what to do about a particular social problem – mugging – with these shifts in the economic, social, and political context. As a consequence, the analysis of the mugging phenomenon never seriously addressed its impact on the victim nor did it recognize the reality of mugging for certain individuals and communities.

When applied to child abuse the analysis proved suggestive in helping to analyse why the problem was recognized as a priority for state intervention in the 1970s and why the intervention took the form it did, that is, the individualized disease model. It was also helpful in analysing why the case of Maria Colwell and the activities of social workers were symbolically so powerful and subject to media, public, and political interest at the time. The danger was that, in drawing on the analysis, it underestimated the impact of child abuse on certain children.

Similarly, arguing that crime occurs primarily amongst the deprived sections of the working class reduces the discussion of causes to notions of poverty, unemployment, and structural inequalities. There is no need to have complex analyses as to the causes, for they are obvious – so that to blame the perpetrators is to blame the victims whose actions are themselves the result of being social casualties.

While the approach is helpful in demonstrating the relationship between child cruelty and neglect and wider issues of poverty and social deprivation, it has difficulty in explaining why abuse occurs in affluent and middle-class families. More significantly, however, it has a difficulty in explaining why only some children in the deprived sections of society are subject to parental cruelty and neglect. As Olive Stevenson (1986, p. 121) has commented on *The Politics of Child Abuse*, it was not able to explain 'why some very poor disadvantaged parents abuse their children and others do not . . . indeed, it is insulting to very poor people to impute to them *all* the possibility of behaving in such aberrant ways as we have seen reported recently in the press' (italics in original).

Such an analysis is found particularly wanting when we then attempt a gender analysis. Numerous commentators have now drawn attention to the fact that women are much less involved in crime than men. The labelling and Marxist approaches to crime emphasize that it is the powerless and deprived who are most at risk of both engaging in crime and also being subject to the biased responses of the state. However, there is a woeful failure to recognize and explain why powerless and deprived women are less involved in crime than powerless and deprived men. As Eileen Leonard (1982) demonstrates, the notion that there is a direct relationship between poverty and crime means that, in order to accommodate women within the analysis, one has to deny either the lower female crime rates or the existence of female poverty. Either position is clearly untenable.

When applied to child abuse such an analysis is struggling to explain why, while women carry the main responsibility for child care and spend a far greater proportion of their time with their children than men, they account for only half the known cases of child abuse (see, for example, Creighton, 1984). Similarly, it is now evident that women suffer far more disadvantage and financial hardship than men (Glendinning and Miller, 1987) so they should, according to the logic of the proposition, be responsible for perpetrating far more cruelty and neglect. The proposition is clearly redundant when applied to sexual abuse and incest in the family, where it appears that men account for at least 80 per cent of the perpetrators.

Sexual abuse and physical abuse

It was perhaps the failure to engage the issue of sexual abuse in *The Politics of Child Abuse* which ensured that the gaps and difficulties itemized above were not seriously addressed. The decision to exclude sexual abuse from the analysis was quite explicit: because there was so much ground to cover in order to establish the validity of the arguments with the wider professional, academic, and political audience, the task was too daunting to include sexual abuse as well. I also felt, and still do to some extent, that the two issues are productively discussed separately. However, in retrospect, it is likely that two other factors were more significant.

First, writing in 1983, the issue of sexual abuse had barely entered the public domain. While there was concern within professional and feminist circles, the issue rarely entered media or wider political discourse. The failure to engage the issue reflects in part, therefore, the changing public form of the debate related to child abuse during the 1980s. The second factor, however, is more damning. Put simply, sexual abuse was not included because it did not fit in with the over-all analysis! If it had been included it would either have sat awkwardly and as a consequence detracted from the logic and tightness of the argument and evidence or, if it had been seriously included, the original analysis would have had to have been so fundamentally rethought that it would have been a different analysis. By implication, sexual abuse was *avoided* and the difficulties with the general analysis not recognized.

Ironically, a major influence forcing the sociology of deviance perspective to rethink its approach has been the work of feminist writers and researchers concerned to draw attention to the crimes of violence perpetrated against women, particularly rape. Here the priority is to analyse why such issues have not been taken seriously in public policy; to demonstrate that women are suffering considerably from such violence; to argue that it desperately needs taking seriously; and to show that it reflects the powerlessness and position of women in society more generally (Clarke and Lewis, 1977;

Dobash and Dobash, 1979). Not surprisingly, therefore, radical feminists have posed major criticisms of the Marxist approach to class, which is identified as essentially white and male. In arguing that women are oppressed in a particular way, women's oppression is seen as crossing class boundaries. Thus is is not adequate to explain violence against women as arising primarily from working-class oppression. It is essentially an act committed by the dominant class of men against the oppressed class of women. Rather than seeing such violence as arising as a reaction of the oppressed to their situation, requiring a lenient response, it is seen as being committed by the oppressor (men), therefore requiring a harsh response.

If we now consider some of the differences between sexual abuse and physical abuse, one fact to bear in mind is that the way the two were brought to public attention has been somewhat different. In Britain, sexual abuse has come to public attention only relatively recently and some time after it received publicity in America. David Finkelhor (1984) suggests that it was a coalition of the women's and child protection movements that proved significant in establishing sexual abuse as a social problem in America. Unlike in the case of physical abuse, he argues that the medical profession played little part, while the women's movement was actively involved in a way it had not been previously. A similar situation undoubtedly pertained in Britain and the active involvement of the women's movement is a significant difference from the discovery of physical abuse and neglect in the early 1970s. However, it also appears that certain sections of the medical profession, particularly paediatricians in certain local areas, saw themselves at the forefront in trying to demonstrate that this was a major problem that until now had gone unrecognized and that was in desperate need of a response. This latter group often combined the more traditional medical approach to diagnosing and treating childhood illness and epidemics with insights and research on the nature, incidence, and consequences of the problem, which were in part informed by feminist perspectives. It is also the case that the media played a rather different role. The launch of the Childwatch campaign in October 1986 drew its approach from a complex mixture of traditional child protection assumptions together with practices developed in the women's movement in relation to rape crisis lines.

The feminist concern has developed from its analysis of violence to women. In particular, sexual abuse of children was seen as another form of rape (Rush, 1980) and stressed the fact that most sexual abuse is committed by men against girls (Finkelhor, 1979). Sexual abuse not only reflects the inferior position of women and girls but also reflects the power and predatory attitudes of men. Essentially the problem is located within the patriarchal social structure and male socialization. In contrast, the child protectionist position on sexual abuse reflects the traditional perspective on child abuse in general. The problem of child abuse is seen to include that of sexual abuse, and the family is seen as central to the problem. Child abuse is a product of family pathology and all members of the family must hence take responsibility for its manifestation. This includes the mother, who is seen as colluding with the man's behaviour and failing to protect her children. As far as public and political debates and responses to sexual abuse are concerned, it is this latter perspective that has dominated.

It is not by chance, then, that feminist analyses of child abuse have their roots in concerns with violence to women, rape, and subsequently sexual abuse. Nor is it by chance that *The Politics of Child Abuse* directed its attention to physical abuse and neglect. Clearly there are major pitfalls in trying to extend the analysis of the latter and simply apply it to sexual abuse. Similarly, however, there are dangers in applying feminist analyses developed in relation to sexual abuse to other manifestations of abuse.

The focus of much public, professional, and political interest in recent years has shifted from physical to sexual abuse. The BBC national poll carried out for the Childwatch programme in October 1986 concluded that over 4 million adults in Britain had suffered some form of abuse as children. From the survey it was estimated that one child in ten suffers such abuse, totalling more than 1 million children at any one time. The really startling finding which grabbed the public imagination was that half of these were sexually abused. Similarly, the NSPCC figures of June 1986 showed a 136 per cent increase in their recorded instances of sexual abuse in the previous year. The trend was confirmed by figures produced by the Association of Directors of Social Services based on questionnaires returned by 100 social services departments. The national average increase in the number of children registered as at risk in 1985–6 was 22 per cent, with the biggest increases in relation to sexual abuse (*Guardian*, 7 and 31 August 1987).

As I have suggested, feminist analyses have something significant to say about sexual abuse, and in the process can make a positive radical contribution to current professional and political concerns and priorities related to child abuse more generally. What seems to have been happening, however, is that other forms of abuse, particularly physical, emotional, and neglect, have been subsumed within explanations of and arguments about sexual abuse. For example,

Julie Burchall (1987, p. 25) argues that 'to deny that child abuse is a feminist issue as well as a human one is as silly as denying that rape is' and points out that *child abuse* 'is not so much a problem of parents abusing children as men – 90 per cent – abusing girls – two thirds' (my emphasis). Throughout, Burchall uses the term 'child abuse' when in fact she is referring to child sexual abuse. Similarly, Lahey (1984) draws explicitly on the connection between rape and patriarchy in developing a radical feminist analysis not just of sexual abuse but of child abuse more generally.

As a consequence, the priority in child abuse policy and practice is to protect children from the more extreme manifestations of male power. While the long-term goal is the need to solve the problems arising from patriarchy, in the short term it is argued that extreme forms of abuse merit an extreme response and that more punitive measures against the perpetrators (by definition men) should be introduced. Such an analysis of child abuse is partial in failing to recognize the significance of class and race and can lead, in my opinion, to reactionary recommendations for policy and practice. It is in danger of legitimizing an approach sympathetic to proposals that are directly parallel to those propounded by conservative commentators on the best way of responding to child abuse. The radical feminist analysis is in danger of replacing the gender-blindness of *The Politics of Child Abuse* with its own class-blindness. In presenting class and patriarchy as two competing frames of reference, the two appear mutually exclusive.

At the level of theory, then, anyone who wishes to develop an approach to child abuse that is sympathetic to both class analyses and feminist analyses is presented with a daunting task. Perhaps the first thing to recognize is that child abuse takes many forms and that these need to be analysed in ways that draw upon quite different explanatory concepts.

A major difference emerges when we analyse the social distribution of the incidence of physical and sexual abuse in terms of social class. While not limited to the lower classes, a close empirical association has now been established between class and physical abuse and neglect (Pelton, 1981). It is important that this insight is not lost. However, there seems to be no such association between social class and child sexual abuse. The most representative surveys of child sexual abuse have not shown any relationship between sexual abuse and the social class of the family in which the victim grew up. Summarizing American studies, David Finkelhor (1986a) suggests that child sexual abuse may be entirely different from physical abuse and neglect in this respect.

What emerges is that the issues of gender, race, and class are central for trying to explain the nature, incidence, and causes of child abuse and the way we conceptualize and respond to it. This, however, should not be surprising as discussion about child abuse is primarily about the way society is organized to rear children, particularly, in modern Britain, in relation to the private family. It is very much concerned with the relationship between social structure and parenting and the forms of adult–child relationships. For both, power is a crucial factor.

Power and powerlessness

Until recently the issue of power and powerlessness has received little attention in relation to child abuse. It is perhaps ironic that a book entitled *The Politics of Child Abuse* should have concerned itself so little with the nature of power. It is feminist analyses of sexual abuse that have explicitly put it on the agenda. However, many feminists assume the oppression of women and children to be the same – in form, cause, and manifestation. There is a failure to disaggregate women and children as groups. As Judith Ennew (1986) has commented, there are two problems at least with such an approach. The first is that it continues the association between women and children as minors in need of 'protection' from male power. This fails to recognize that the needs and interests of women and children may differ, so that the way society organizes itself to accommodate children may be qualitatively different. Secondly, and perhaps crucially, it is arrogant to assert that women 'know best' what children need.

Moreover, if women do 'develop their own power and autonomy' it does not necessarily follow that children will automatically do the same. Indeed, the reverse is more likely to be the case. It has already been demonstrated that, in law, children are often treated as chattels of their parents. Removing the domination of fathers does not liberate children from adult domination, but can replace it with a new form of oppression. When feminists lay claim to rights over their own bodies, one often has the impression that this entails absolute rights over the products of their bodies – their children (Ennew, 1986, pp. 57–8).

At present there are a variety of adult groups claiming an expertise on child abuse and protecting children – but children are rarely given a voice.

We need a clearer understanding of the significance of power in the area of child abuse, and of the impact of power relations on children's lives. Clearly, an understanding of wider power relations is crucial for understanding the way the nature of child abuse has been publicly defined, changed, and responded to and the way this social category has proved crucial for mediating changing relations between the state and the family. It was this that received some attention in *The Politics of Child Abuse*. Similarly, Donzelot (1979) places power at the centre of his analysis. Akin to Foucault (1977 and 1979), Donzelot's reconstruction of history crucially relates to 'power and knowledge'. Not only does power constitute knowledge but power is everywhere, not because it embraces everything, but because it comes from everywhere. In effect, power is seen as the life force. Such a starting point seems far too all-embracing. In being everywhere, power is in effect nowhere, and we are left with little insight as to how such an approach helps us change the world.

Within the social sciences, however, there is an enormous literature (for example, Lukes, 1978, and Wrong, 1979) related to power, which awaits serious examination for advancing our understanding and approach to child abuse. As Ken Plummer (1984, p. 50) has shown:

> If nothing else, this literature has shown power to be defined in many ways (as a capacity, relationship or process), to exist on many levels (as a psychological need, as interpersonal, as structural), to have many bases (as coercive, as utilitarian, as normative), many dimensions (as extensive, comprehensive and intensive), many uses (as a means to some end, or as an end in itself) and many forms (as force, manipulation, persuasion or authority).

At this stage one can probably only say that there is one crucial set of power relations that should inform our discussion of child abuse: that of age. However, it is also clearly very entangled with the power relations of class and gender. While race is also of significance, our understanding of this dimension is even more rudimentary. Judith Ennew (1986) has schematically incorporated these dimensions of power relations in her discussion of the sexual exploitation of children and has drawn attention to the two poles of the overall power of rich white men and the overwhelming powerlessness of poor black girls. As she has commented (1986, p. 9):

> A child's dependence and need for protection are not entirely attributable to biologically determined 'innocence' and weakness, but arise from the power relations which render him

or her liable to exploitation, and which differ according to the age, race, class and gender both of the exploited and the exploiter.

As I shall conclude, such an approach opens up a much wider debate than the concerns of the traditional child abuse literature. In suggesting that power and powerlessness may be significant mediating factors, I am not arguing for a unitary theory of child abuse; far from it. I am simply suggesting that in trying to understand how the different social, economic, and personal variables interrelate in the violent act or abusive behaviour, we may then be in a better position to try and recognize the different forms the abuse might take. Nor am I suggesting that focusing on power and powerlessness will overcome the tensions and complexities involved in both theory and practice. It may, however, prove productive in trying to develop a radical analysis of the issues at hand.

Although abuse is the act of the strong against the weak, a number of commentators have suggested that it is carried out to compensate the abuser for their perceived lack of or loss of power (Finkelhor, 1983). For many men, sexual abuse may be an attempt to compensate for their sense of powerlessness in other areas, particularly with regard to the dominant notions of masculinity in society. Similarly, physical abuse may be crucially influenced by feelings of parental impotence, so that parents resort to violence, for example, when they sense that they have lost control of their children and perhaps their own lives. However, abuse may not always be instrumental and intended to restore (compensate) power. It may also be expressive: a way of venting anger against a child who is perceived as in some way being responsible for that loss of power. It may be an attempt to regain control by using coercion (Hartman, 1987).

Changes in policy in the late 1980s

When we consider some of the developments in official thinking as represented by circulars, inquiry reports, and legislation, many of the trends identified in the late 1970s and early 1980s in *The Politics of Child Abuse* seem to have been reinforced. The radical critique of positivism coincided with an increasing scepticism about the social democratic consensus in general and the reliance on the rehabilitative ideal in crime and childcare in particular. Not only did research show that such an approach did not work, but there was a general loss of faith in claims that wide-ranging prevention and professional intervention could control and reduce problems.

It was not only the sociology of deviance that gave up on looking into the causes of deviance. Such optimistic faith was replaced by a far more pessimistic and 'realistic' approach, which was increasingly reflected in official child abuse policy.

It is noticeable that the government circulars on child abuse during the 1970s (DHSS, 1974, 1976a and 1980) and the government inquiries (DHSS, 1982) confined themselves to attempts to develop the child abuse system with particular emphasis on multi-agency and multidisciplinary work. No attempt was made to discuss possible causes or explanations of abuse. It has become even more evident since that, although prevention is seen as the best way of coping with the problem, it is a particularly narrow conception of prevention. Reform on any level is discarded and with it the notion that the reduction of child abuse can be achieved by any reference to social justice. Prevention should simply concentrate on identifying the 'high-risk' case or dangerous individual and thereby stop the event before it happens. The crucial role for the welfare professional is to try and identify and manage the 'high-risk' individual or family (Parton, 1986; Parton and Parton, 1989). Attempts to modify wider social arrangements and social conditions are ruled out because they do not appear to be implicated in the problem.

The aim of policy is primarily to develop effective surveillance of families and efficient assessment procedures, in which sections of the community should be involved. Ideally, the informal controls of the family and the community should fulfil such a task but, where these have broken down, the formal inter-agency approach is required. However, the balance and emphasis of such inter-agency work varies. One of the issues contested via the Cleveland Inquiry has been the form and nature of accountability that such inter-agency work should take.

The furore in Cleveland came at something of a watershed in public policy towards the agencies dealing with child abuse. The political Right has shown an increasing impatience with the role, power, and assumptions of social workers and certain doctors, particularly paediatricians, in such cases. As a result, they have called for the police to play a more central role. Others have been more concerned to refine current arrangements and have defended health and welfare professionals, arguing that they deserve public and political support in the difficult job they do. We should not assume that, because there has been little explicit discussion of causes, certain assumptions are not held dear and underpin some of the policy and legislative developments. The tougher provisions introduced into the Criminal Justice Bill, whereby the maximum penalty for child cruelty and neglect will be increased from two

years' imprisonment to ten years, were for those 'wilfully and sys-
tematically' indulging in such behaviour. Similarly, the planned
introduction of a video-link in child abuse cases is designed not
simply to protect the children but also to make it easier to prove
cases against the perpetrators. The demise of the optimistic
rehabilitative ideal, with its search for underlying causes, has
been replaced by a pessimistic neoclassicist approach relying on
multi-agency surveillance to identify the 'high-risk' in order to
'protect' the individual child from the abusive parent. However,
the emphasis of this approach on the needs of the child may,
as I shall suggest below, provide an opportunity for advancing
a discussion of the needs and rights of all children. While I
am convinced that developments in policy and practice have
emphasized a much more conservative and pessimistic approach,
it is important we tease out areas where there may be room for
more progressive advances. In this respect the issues of structural
abuse and the rights of children seem particularly worthy of
attention.

Institutional and structural abuse

The dominant and traditional approaches to child abuse invariably fail to recognize the importance of abuse at the institutional
and structural levels. One reason for suggesting that the notions
of power and powerlessness should be given central consideration is the potential they provide of emphasizing the relationship
between abuse at the individual, institutional, and structural
levels. While David Gil has been sex-blind in some of his analyses, particularly in his earlier work (Gil, 1970), the conceptual
framework he outlines for analysing child abuse is still valuable.
He argues that child abuse should not be analysed as a discrete
phenomenon with discrete dynamics and discrete solutions,
but as something that reflects the social dynamics in which
families interact. However, while child abuse is related to socially
structured inequalities of gender, class, and race, as we have seen,
these relationships are neither straightforward nor consistent.

In answer to the question 'What is child abuse?' I am still sympathetic to the definition suggested by Gil (1975, p. 347) that child
abuse is 'inflicted gaps or deficits between circumstances of living
which would facilitate the optimum development of children, to
which they should be entitled, and to their actual circumstances,
irrespective of the sources or agents of the deficit'. Thus any act of
commission or omission by individuals, institutions, or the whole
society, together with their resultant conditions, which 'deprive

children of equal *rights* and liberties, and/or interfere with
their optimal development constitute, by definition, abusive or
neglected acts or conditions' (Gil, 1975, p. 348).

Two consequences immediately follow if we are serious about
doing something about child abuse. First, it is not sufficient to
restrict our attention to the abuse that goes on *within* families;
children also suffer as a result of the activities of other social
institutions and wider social processes. While we must avoid
the problems identified with the Marxist approaches to deviance
noted previously, it would be wrong to deny that large numbers
of children do suffer poverty, deprivation, and exploitation, and
that these constitute significant dimensions to the problem of
child abuse in society. To expect the individual practitioner to
be responsible for ameliorating such abuse is, however, naive.

Summarizing the developments in the situation for children in
the ten years since the Court Report (DHSS/DES, 1976), the recent
National Children's Bureau report (1987, p. 7) commented as
follows:

> Although in some areas of the country material conditions
> have certainly improved, for large numbers of children they
> have deteriorated in the following respects: the proportion of
> children living in poverty has increased – nearly one third of
> those in the lowest income group are families with children;
> many more children live in families deemed homeless; more
> children have unemployed parents and more face unemploy-
> ment in their own future as young adults; in our inner cities
> racism and general violence have increased, making many
> streets, parks and schools unsafe and frightening places for
> all children.

The report argues that economic constraints and, in some
areas, economic decline, have been linked to a lack of commitment to the care of children at government, local authority,
and health authority levels. The risks to children in terms of
morbidity, mortality, and other health risks closely reflect class
inequalities (Whitehead, 1987; Graham, 1988). Such examples
not only provide clear evidence of children suffering at the
institutional and structural levels, they also provide insights
into the relationship between individual behaviour and social
structure. The two are not distinct. For example, the higher
incidence of accidents amongst children in the most deprived
sections of society may be explained as due to more reckless
risk-taking behaviour and inadequate child care on the part of
parents (Blaxter, 1983). Yet the unsafe play areas, the lack of
fenced-off gardens, and the greater difficulty of supervising

children's play from high-rise housing all constrain and influence the behaviour of both the child and the parent.

The rights of children

The second major implication of adopting such an approach is that children's rights become a central concern and should inform both our analysis and approach to child abuse. While children's rights may nominally be the starting point for much of the concern about child abuse, this is rarely explicit and the implications are rarely thought through. In doing so, however, we should recognize that the issue of children's rights is itself complex and contested (See Wringe, 1981; Freeman, 1983a; Franklin, 1986; Secretary of State for Social Services, 1988; Montgomery, 1988).

The debate on children's rights has focused on the differences between the 'liberationists' and the 'protectionists' or 'paternalists'. Put crudely, the liberationists favour extending a number of rights, hitherto held exclusively by adults, to children. The process would ensure that children are able to exercise control over their environments, make decisions about what they want, and have an autonomous control over various facets of their lives. Protectionists or paternalists, on the other hand, favour restricting children's lives in some areas while compelling them to do other things, all of which are seen as being in their 'best interests'. In essence, adults define and articulate what is in the child's interests.

Almost without exception, different variants of the protectionist lobby have dominated approaches to and developments in child abuse. It is important to try and construct a policy and practice that not only listens to children, but seriously takes account of their wishes (Secretary of State for Social Services, 1988; Children's Legal Centre, 1988). Despite my concerns (voiced above) about recent developments in this area, children's wishes may have the potential for being taken more seriously. The establishment of ChildLine is perhaps the clearest example. It is crucial to structure the practice in a way that includes children in the decision-making. There may well be direct clashes in both policy and everyday practice between what adults (experts and/or parents) and children perceive as being in the child's best interests. An increased prominence given to children's rights should give much greater priority and significance to the child's views. Clearly, however, a myopic concentration on improving children's rights without recognizing the need for greater social justice and equality will prove fruitless.

Conclusion

In this chapter I have attempted to locate current theoretical and policy debates about child abuse in their political context. The issues raised in *The Politics of Child Abuse* need to be re-evaluated in the light of the now-evident demise of the social democratic welfare approach to childcare problems and the retreat from discussions about aetiology. The major problems at the centre of *The Politics of Child Abuse* were that it failed to address the issues of sexual abuse, gender, and, most indefensibly, the impact on the child. In stressing the wider dimensions of social class and criticizing the traditional disease model it was in danger of losing the individual child in the analysis. In the process it is not surprising if it struggled to relate its message to the experience and situation of the individual practitioner.

My approach here has been purposefully self-critical. It makes no attempt to reduce the problem to unicausal factors or 'contradictions'. Child abuse is a complex problem that needs to be taken seriously, not least for the children concerned. We have a responsibility to develop, at the level of theory and practice, an approach based on a socialist–feminist framework. In the process, I have demonstrated that, while feminist insights into sexual abuse strike at the core of the problems with my original analysis, different problems can emerge when such a feminist analysis is then generalized to other aspects of child abuse. It may be that such tensions and inconsistencies at the level of theory may not be resolvable. It is better to recognize them explicitly than to define them away. It seems most likely, however, that they will be resolved (or at least negotiated) at the level of practice where the practitioners are aware of the issues in their work.

In arguing that it is necessary to be sensitive to the different dimensions of child abuse and the different possible balances of causal factors, I have suggested that it may be worth giving further attention to the issues of power and powerlessness as potentially productive mediating concepts between wider social structures and social processes and the internal dynamics within families. In the process, the issues of structural abuse and children's rights should be given considerable emphasis. It is the attempt to locate individual experiences in wider social structures and the ability to address causal issues rooted in the wider society that should prove distinctive about any radical approach that takes child abuse seriously.

2 Official intervention and child protection: the relationship between state and family in contemporary Britain

NICK FROST

Introduction

The back cover of the book written by Stuart Bell, MP (1988) on events in Cleveland in 1987 boldly pronounces that 'It was the greatest child abuse crisis that Britain has ever faced. At the heart lay the fundamental question: who has ultimate power over children – the Family or the State?'

This chapter aims to examine the latter part of this statement. It will be argued that this consideration is indeed 'the fundamental question', but that its terms need refining if we are to approach an answer. Initially I wish to examine the use of the terms 'family' and 'state', and then move on to look at the nature of the 'family'–'state' relationship in contemporary Britain, relating this to the dominant political form, Thatcherism, before concluding with an analysis of child abuse that, it is argued, helps us understand the nature of the 'family'–'state' relationship.

Official interventions in the field of child care face a central problem, which in recent years has become particularly acute; this problem involves the issue of defining which forms of intervention by agencies into households can be justified and in what circumstances. The debate tends to centre on two key positions: first, a position that emphasizes the rights of parents to bring their children up in as much freedom from state interference as possible (Bell, 1988; Goldstein, Freud, and Solnit, 1979), and, secondly, a position that focuses on the rights of children to be protected against a range of ills that their carers may inflict upon them (Freeman, 1987–8). The controversies around the child abuse cases which have attracted extensive media, academic, and official attention (Cleveland, Jasmine Beckford, Kimberley Carlile, etc.) have at their core the issue of public intervention in the 'private', domestic arena.

The debate is not one that can ever reach a fixed conclusion. The terms of the debate are constantly shifting and being redefined, reflecting broader social changes. Such social changes are indicated by, for example, the variation in the use year by year of Place of Safety Orders or by the changing composition of the population of children in care – a variation that can be plotted against changing social influences on child care practice (see Parton, 1985b).

This chapter argues that the debate about welfare interventions is best understood by looking at the relationship between state forms and households. Attempts to evaluate this issue simply in terms of 'rights' or 'the best interest of the child', the dominant forms of analysis, fail to address the central point. I propose here that social responses to the protection of children can be fruitfully understood as a key definer of the nature of the relationship between state forms and households.

The nature of official interventions

When we speak of official interventions it tends to be assumed that behind these interventions we will find a monolithic state, all parts of which act in unison toward an agreed end. For my purposes here, two elements of diversity within 'the state' are important. First, state actions do not, in any straightforward way, represent the interest of any one social class or group. The form taken by states is a reflection of the social, economic, and political disputes occurring in a given society. The representation of the interests and concerns of any social class or group within state bodies is a dynamic process reflecting their success in political struggles. Secondly, the various institutional forms that make up 'the state' do not necessarily always 'pull in the same direction'. Thus we need to be careful in using 'the state' as if it was a unified set of institutions. Rose (1987, p. 71) puts it like this: 'The state is not a unified and internally coherent entity which is the *locus* of all social power, but a complex set of agencies which are involved to different extents in projects for the regulation of social and economic life whose origins, inspirations and power often come from elsewhere.'

This is evident in all spheres of political life but is probably best illustrated by the example, already referred to, of the Cleveland child sexual abuse 'crisis'. It is apparent that in Cleveland there was conflict involving doctors, social workers, the police, and the courts, all of whom were state employees or institutions. Clearly, then, it is not good enough to speak of 'the state' as if it was a unified body. In an attempt to overcome the simplistic and reductionist use of 'the state', I shall refer to 'state forms', in order to give a feel of the diverse nature of the institutions that form part of 'the state'. In summary, then, when we theorize about the nature of state interventions we must remember that 'the state' cannot be seen as representing any one social class or group and, secondly, that 'the state' itself is made up of a series of agencies that do not necessarily pull in the same direction.

Households and families

There is a comparable problem with the use of the term 'the family'. First, we are actually dealing with a plurality of family forms. In Britain in the 1980s the term 'the family' conceals within it one- and two-parent families, nuclear and extended families, families with heterosexual and homosexual parents, and so on. By using 'the family' in a bland way we disguise this complexity. Secondly, 'the family' contains within it a number of divisions and differences – between males and females, adults and children, parents and children. When we talk of 'family policy' or 'protecting the family', we have to be aware of these differences.

Thus, just as using the term 'the state' conceals diversity, so does use of 'the family'. Hence, I shall use the term households, in an attempt to convey the complexity and diversity hidden by a simplistic use of 'the family' as a concept.

The 'state'–'family' relationship

First of all we must be clear that we cannot understand the relationship between state forms and households fully if we see them simply as separate and independent social institutions; they actually exist in a complex relationship to each other. The complexity of this relationship is often missed, particularly by those theorists who have come to regard the family as a protection from the tentacles of the state (Mount, 1983). The opposite problem is also apparent on the political Left, where the family may be seen as a functionary of the state, a channel for the socialization of the next generation of compliant labour (Althusser, 1971). I hope to illustrate the complexity of this relationship, a complexity that an analysis of official responses to child abuse may help us come to terms with. Initially, however, it is necessary to spend some time looking in more detail at theoretical approaches to state forms and households.

I have already argued that state forms and households need to be understood in their relationship with each other. Whilst this dynamic interplay is crucial, it does not follow that there is necessarily a relationship of equivalence. Formally this is evidently not the case, as state forms possess powers of intervention in households that households, as such, do not possess in reverse. State forms have a whole series of powers to intervene in child care, such as those laid down in the 1969 Children and Young Persons' Act, which facilitates intervention to enforce child-rearing standards.

These interventions have often been understood on the libertarian Left as necessarily repressive and as a form of oppression. It seems to me that this analysis is based on two (mis)conceptions. First, it makes the assumption, which I have already disputed, that 'the state' is a monolithic form whose actions are necessarily seen as representative of dominant social or economic groups. Secondly, for such interventions to be seen as necessarily repressive, it follows that families must be seen as a wholly positive experience for children. As I have already proposed here, neither institution can be adequately understood in such a monolithic way; to understand either as having some sort of necessary unity is to make a serious error. What we are dealing with is actually a much more complex interplay of a range of state interventions in a variety of households, which cannot be explained in any simplistic manner. This means that Marxist–functionalist explanations that see the state as simply repressive, feminist analyses that view the state as simply patriarchal, and social democrats who see state interventions as necessarily benevolent fail to grasp the complex nature of these interventions (see Wetherley, 1988).

A difficult conclusion for those from certain Marxist and feminist schools is that the actions and practices of various state employees (social workers, doctors, police, etc.) theoretically can be, and in practice often actually are, in the interest of oppressed groups (see Gordon, 1986). But the exact form of these actions may not be in the interest of oppressed groups. Thus, whilst it can be argued that removing a child to a place of safety from an abusive situation is in 'the best interests of the child', it may be that their subsequent placement or treatment is clearly not in their interests. Such a mode of analysis can be applied to all state interventions, including state child care policies.⌋

How does this influence our analysis of official interventions in households? The key point is that such interventions are necessarily complex and cannot be understood without an appreciation of the diverse nature of both institutions. Hence if we attempt to understand, say, a cut in the real value of Child Benefit as an attack on 'the family' it is, at that level of abstraction, rather meaningless. Such an action has, in fact, a differential effect on male wage-earners, unwaged females, and children, and therefore requires a more subtle analysis.

Thus state interventions have a differential effect on various component elements of a household. This can be illustrated in Table 2.1. It should be clear from this that such interventions need careful and detailed analysis. Even if we accept that a specific state formation (e.g. Britain in the 1980s) is capitalist and patriarchal, it can still intervene in households in ways that are beneficial to, for example, working-class female children. Thus interventions that seem superficially to be acts of 'social control', as, for example, taking a Place of Safety Order on a child, cannot usefully be understood in this way. For instance, in a case of sexual abuse of a girl by her father, if a state employee intervenes he or she can actually act against the patriarchal authority of the father. This situation evidently requires a more subtle analysis of the state than simply seeing it as acting in the interest of patriarchy or indeed of the ruling class.

Table 2.1 *Differential effects of state intervention on households*

State intervention	*Effect on households*
Parental control over child's use of contraception	+ Parents − Female children
Cut in Child Benefit to increase father's tax allowance	+ Father − Mother and children
Abolition of corporal punishment in the household	+ Children − Adults

To sum up so far: there is a need to develop a theory of state interventions that is sufficiently subtle to avoid reductionist approaches to the state–household relationship; current dominant explanations do not achieve this. In order to focus this argument further and to assess whether the themes can be refined, I move on now to look at the state–household relationship in contemporary Britain.

The roots of Thatcherism

The main thrust of my argument will be that the current Conservative government has a particular approach to the state–household relationship that deserves close scrutiny. Thus, whilst attempting not to fall into the trap of assuming that state agencies are acting in unity, I argue that there is a definite political and ideological thrust in Thatcherite Britain.

I use the shorthand 'Thatcherism' to describe the nature of the current government. The use of this phrase has been criticized by some for reducing political analysis to personalities, for exaggerating the difference between recent Conservative governments and previous ones, and also as having overtones of sexism. I would deny these accusations, first by pointing out that such usage has a long history in political analysis – one only has to think of Bonapartism, Marxism, or Leninism, for example. The point is that political ideologies were established under the name of these individuals but the political ideology outlives the individual. An 'ism' is used therefore to identify what marks out a political position as specific to it. This is why the use of Thatcherism as a term is politically important; precisely because it is something profoundly different from previous forms of conservatism. If we are to develop coherent political strategies, it is important that we develop specific political analyses. Stuart Hall (1979, p. 5), quoting Lenin, defends the use of Thatcherism as a concept because it reflects 'an extremely unique political situation in which absolutely dissimilar currents, absolutely heterogeneous class interest, absolutely contrary political and social strivings have merged . . . in a strikingly "harmonious" manner'.

It is such an analysis that is needed if we are to understand what is happening in terms of the relationship between the Thatcher government and the household in contemporary Britain.

Developments in state forms under Thatcherism

The impact of Thatcherism on the form and the activity of the British state has been tremendous. Writing before the election of the first Thatcher government, the late Nicos Poulantzas (1978, pp. 203–4) described such regimes as embarking on a road that he called 'authoritarian statism', which involved the following features: 'Intensified state control over every sphere of socio-economic life combined with radical decline of the institutions of political democracy and with draconian and multiform curtail-ment of so-called "formal" liberties.' Stuart Hall has developed this definition into what he has called 'authoritarian populism', which has the features of Poulantzas' concept, together with the proposition that the actions of the government articu-late with 'popular concerns' (law and order, defence, etc.).

The Thatcher government of 1979 embarked on the course of 'authoritarian populism'. In this context we can only sum-marize the key features of Thatcherism. The Thatcherite pro-ject was to restructure state expenditure, in order to bring about increases in personal disposable income through tax cuts and the control of inflation; to limit the 'power' of the trade unions; to 'roll back' the frontiers of the state; and to promote the values of the market. (For a more detailed analysis see Hall and Jacques, 1983.) It is argued here that this is not simply another government (remember the popu-lar wisdom of the 1960s and 1970s that there was no differ-ence between the various political parties) but a 'hegemonic project'. By this is meant that the government is attempt-ing to establish a domination of British society that would spell the death knell of socialism and totally change the eco-nomic, cultural, ideological, and political life of the country.

The victory at the 1987 general election marked the third phase of Thatcherism, in which the struggle for hegemony reached a new stage. This stage is an attempt to generate a new culture and morality in Britain – this is why in the summer of 1988 a debate on 'morality' was launched. This debate has a great significance for our understanding of households and therefore, I would argue, a significance for the issue of child abuse.

The Thatcher government and family policy in contemporary Britain

At the heart of the current debates about child abuse and social welfare interventions lies a seemingly irresolvable tension. Social welfare is designed to protect the most vulnerable in our society and when it fails to do so, particularly in the case of children, welfare workers will be subject to serious scrutiny and, occasionally, hysterical criticism. The other side of the debate is that welfare interventions will also be criticized for being unwarranted intervention in the family, the unjustified removal of children again being a particular point at issue.

This dilemma reflects a profound ambivalence in Britain towards households and family policy. 'The family' has been exalted to become the symbol of all good. It is now well documented that the concept of family, or more exactly the concept of a particular form of family, has been central to the design of all major British social policies (Dale and Foster, 1986). An indicator of this is the way that the single homeless largely fall through the net of state welfare. A family-centred and family-based service, such as social service departments, has little to offer them. Therefore, it is left to the church and the voluntary sector to service these 'non-family' people. 'The family' is elevated in two ways: first, as the best way to live, in an ideological and moral form; and, secondly, in a concrete way as the basis of social policy.

Within these perspectives there is a further problem. First, because 'the family' is ideologically and materially privileged, the rhetoric of Thatcherism wishes to do all in its power to support 'the family', to help it, and to ensure that it flourishes. However, this very process of support undermines the ideology of family. Ferdinand Mount, for example, argues that the very appeal of family life is its 'privacy', its 'autonomy', its 'independence'. This is the central issue in the relationship between households and states: how can the privileged relationship exist simultaneously with an autonomous family? This is the very dilemma that is reflected in the contradictory concerns expressed at the beginning of this section (see Donzelot, 1979).

This issue is reflected in all social policy interventions. All recent British governments have attempted to claim the family as their own. Let us look at the concrete example of Thatcher government policies between 1979 and 1988. The Tories were keen to present themselves as 'the party of the family'. In the Thatcherite vision, the frontiers of the state should be rolled back so that 'the family' could thrive. In February 1983, the *Guardian* published a series of secret state papers concerning the Family Policy Group within the Cabinet. These meetings, held using Ferdinand Mount as an adviser, made it clear that the idea of family was central to government policy. All policies were to be assessed in terms of their impact on families. A clear parallel was drawn between the national political scene and the households – it was argued that lessons learnt in the family setting could be applied to the country as a whole. The primary example was in the conception of the national economy as being essentially the same as the family budget. These themes were spelt out explicitly in a speech by Margaret Thatcher to the Conservative Women's Conference in May 1988: 'I cannot help reflecting that it has taken a Government headed by a housewife with experience of running a family to balance the books for the first time for 20 years – with a little left over for a rainy day.'

The lesson was clear: the family was the 'building block' on which society was based and principles of family life could be applied to broader social factors. This argument flowed in another direction however – social policy also had to be aware of the impact it had on the family. The leaked documents referred to paid attention to such matters as children's pocket money. There was a clear conception of an interplay between state policy and households.

The tempo of the debate over the family, or perhaps I should say the rhetoric around the family, was heightened, seemingly as part of conscious strategy, in the spring of 1988 when Margaret Thatcher made two major speeches on the theme of morality. The speeches were mainly an attempt to claim the moral highground for Thatcherism, as part of its third stage. The very fact that the issue was raised so explicitly reinforces my earlier point about Thatcherism as a hegemonic project and needs to be understood as such. Thus the strategy is not simply about passing legislation (the major approach of post-war social democratic governments) but about changing fundamental aspects of British society.

The attempt to build a new morality based on the entrepreneurial ethos is clear; there is nothing wrong with producing wealth, the argument goes, so long as the wealth is used compassionately. Thus, soon after the budget tax cuts of 1988, which gave enormous increases in disposable income to the wealthy, a number of government ministers made speeches encouraging the rich to give more generously to charity. There is a quite explicit shift from state-funded services paid for from taxation to a twentieth-century version of philanthropy – a significant return to Victorian values. In the terms of our current discussion, what is significant about the morality debate is the centrality of the family. Thatcher has stated that 'the basic ties of family . . . are at the heart of our society and are the nursery of civic virtue' (speech to the General Assembly of the Church of Scotland, 21 May 1988). This was pursued as follows: 'The family is the building block of society. It is a nursery, a school, a hospital, a leisure centre, a place of refuge and a place of rest. It encompasses the whole of society. It fashions our beliefs. It is the preparation for the rest of our life. And women run it.'

Here presumably is an excellent reason for the run-down of the public sector. For if the family is all these things then why waste money on nurseries, schools, and leisure centres? There is also a clearly defined role for women. It is obvious that the role of women is seen as being primarily within the family; this is a major thrust of all Thatcherite social and economic policy. Further, as Fitzgerald (1983) has argued, as the market substitutes for the state in major areas, a stronger role for 'the family' develops. If government is pulling back from the concept of a 'cradle to the grave' welfare state, then this broadens the range of functions to be carried out by 'the family'. Families need to be 'free' to decide how to spend an increased disposable income as they wish to. This is fundamental to Thatcherism.

But the argument has an interesting twist in the tail. For not all families are to be so praised and seen as the main source of good in our society. Single-parent families are seen as a cause of poor results in school, vandalism, football hooliganism, to name just a few social problems, and pose a threat to the 'health of society'. This has been a major theme in government speeches (see Fitzgerald, 1983), the most notorious of which was made by Rhodes Boyson who, when a junior minister, referred to elective single parents as 'evil'. Whilst not a specific object of attack in the recent morality speeches, it can be safely assumed from Section 28 of the Local Government Act, 1988, that 'pretended' families headed by gays or lesbians are also undesirable. It is also clear that the morality debate is clearly tied in with the promotion of British Christian values. Thus there is a 'strong practical case for ensuring that children at school are given adequate instruction in the part which the Judaic-Christian tradition has played in moulding our laws, manners and institutions . . . The truths of the Judaic-Christian tradition are infinitely precious, not only as I believe they are true, but also because they provide the moral impulse that *only* can lead to peace . . .' (Thatcher, op. cit.).

This passage and the recurrent theme of national chauvinism and cultural superiority also, by implication, exclude a whole new set of households and individuals from the high moral ground – these are mainly those of the eastern religions and, presumably, agnostic and atheistic households. We could also fairly assume that the families of the unemployed should be excluded from praise, for Mrs Thatcher favourably quotes St Paul as saying, 'If a man shall not work he shall not eat'.

The point is that the rhetoric in support of 'the family' is by now rather qualified, once we have excluded single parents, gays and lesbians, the unemployed, and non-Christians. What is actually being extolled then is not 'the family' as such but, very clearly, a particular model of the family not a million miles away from the White Anglo-Saxon Protestant (WASP), or near derivative, family.

The focus on the WASP family thereby excludes, or marginalizes, entire social groups. It is argued here that the bulk of those excluded form an identifiable social group, which I shall call an underclass. Many of those in this group are identified in the 'morality' debate as not conforming with the dominant model of the family – the single-parent family, the unemployed, and the black and other ethnic minority groups. It is amongst this underclass that are found the bulk of the clients of social workers and the majority of those with children on the abuse registers.

I suggest that this group is not an 'unintended consequence' of Thatcherite social and economic policy, but a group that has been constructed as a condition upon which Thatcherism could flourish. Thus this group is marginalized economically: it becomes a source of cheap and flexible labour and, perhaps more importantly, its members raise children who will take part in 'training' schemes and thus come to regard wages previously seen as poverty wages as fair rewards. They are a new group of workers obliged to work for low wages in 'deregulated' conditions for the new entrepreneurial class. They are also marginalized ideologically: the bare bones of this argument are found in the sections of Thatcher's speech to be found above. They are 'alien' or single parent or unemployed and, therefore, not really part of the mainstream of the 'post-socialist' society. They are the sort of people who are stuck in the 'dependency' culture, who really ought to pull their socks up, or perhaps 'get on their bikes'. They also become marginalized politically, since they are often disillusioned and cannot identify with organized labour, or organized capital, as representing their interests. The introduction of the community charge will accelerate this process by encouraging such people to keep their names off any official registers. They will then disappear as 'citizens' and thus complete their own marginalization. These marginalized people are not a 'natural' or pre-existing group, but have been constructed in their particular form and are currently being reproduced by Thatcherism.

Here then we begin to get to the core of the issue. The policy of freeing up 'the family' also exposes some households and encourages them to fail. The reduction of benefits, the freezing of Child Benefit, the closure of the local day nursery, simultaneously act to increase the disposable income of some families and place intolerable burdens on others. Many of these families are then identified as failing in their child rearing and are subject to state interventions in order to protect their children. Thus, whilst state services are being rolled back, for some in the marginalized families strong interventions are needed. It is for this reason that child abuse is not a peripheral issue; the surveillance and disciplining of families is central to an understanding of all family policies, which themselves are at the heart of the Thatcherite and other political strategies. Child abuse itself becomes politically defined. I shall return to this theme later.

The creation of an underclass

The election of the Thatcher government in May 1979, as I have argued, was a watershed in British politics. This event can be seen as the end of the Keynesian consensus of the post-war period. The consensus centred most crucially around a commitment to full employment and to the welfare state. The end of the consensus was manifested in a growth in recorded unemployment that reached a peak of over 3 million registered unemployed. The impact of this on income distribution, inequality, and poverty has been argued in detail in many places (see Bull and Wilding, 1983). In this context the following illustrations will suffice. In 1976, the lowest fifth of households received a disposable income of 7 per cent of the total national disposable income, in comparison to 38.1 per cent received by the highest fifth. By 1985 these figures had changed to 6.5 per cent and 40.6 per cent, respectively. In 1979, 480,000 families were dependent on Supplementary Benefit, a figure that increased to 1,140,000 in 1986. Perinatal mortality rates in 1985 for the professional classes were 7.3 per 1,000 live births compared to 12.8 amongst the unskilled (National Children's Home, 1988).

However, whilst reams of figures can be quoted to illustrate that an underclass has been created, the phenomenon is not simply an 'empirical' one. Ben Pimlott puts it like this: 'The issue is not mainly to do with material wealth. What is clear is that cruelty to children is connected to stress and social isolation in which poverty can play an important part' (*Sunday Times*, 3 July 1988). In other words, there are quantitative and qualitative issues to consider here. The process of creating an underclass involves marginalization in economic, political and ideological forms; a point illustrated by the campaign against 'scroungers' that helped bring the Conservatives to power. Whilst this issue is at core an economic one, concerning people's relationship to production, such an analysis is not sufficient. The 'scroungers' issue raised the spectre of an 'enemy within', which has been a constant theme of Thatcherism – the enemy being variously identified as, for example, 'scroungers', 'strikers', 'single-parent families', 'football hooligans', 'peace convoys', or 'Greenham women'. The labelling of groups in this way acts as a symbol of who the majority identify as 'us' and who as 'them'; it facilitates an identification between 'the people' and the government. In this way, then, the economic inequality is but one feature of marginalization.

Child abuse and the underclass

Whilst it is not my intention to argue that poverty is in any straightforward way a 'cause' of child abuse and neglect,[1] I would argue that:

- those without material wealth are more exposed to social work and other interventions, as they are more dependent on public provision and therefore less able to keep their problems 'private';
- those who form the underclass in our society are more exposed to life events that may trigger stress situations in which children may then be subjected to abuse and/or neglect;
- as the supportive 'welfare' elements of the state are rolled back, and households are asked to become increasingly independent, the families of the underclass become more likely to be defined as 'failing' as they do not have the material resources to 'succeed';
- as the underclass are seen as 'outside' of mainstream society, so their child rearing can be judged as outside the 'norm'.

There is empirical evidence that does illustrate a link between material deprivation and child abuse and neglect (Pelton, 1978). This evidence is summarized by Becker and MacPherson (1986), who draw together the following studies:

(1) the NSPCC research that showed that the number of mothers who had children on abuse registers and who were unemployed increased from 70.7 per cent in 1977 to 81.8 per cent in 1982, whilst the corresponding figures for fathers increased from 35.0 per cent to 58.2 per cent;
(2) a Strathclyde study in 1980 which found a strong positive correlation between the registration of children and five selected indicators of poverty;

(3)   an Association of Municipal Associations survey, which confirmed an increase in abuse registrations alongside an increase in unemployment. The survey, however, concluded by calling for further research to establish the nature of any such link.

Becker and MacPherson (1986, p. 53) conclude: 'Whilst the causal link association between poverty and abuse or neglect requires detailed research, there is both quantitative and qualitative evidence to suggest that there is indeed some link.'

Whilst such research would no doubt be useful, empirical research is of limited value. The point is not that 'poor people abuse and neglect their children' but more that we need to understand the social processes by which people are identified as abusive and neglectful parents, processes that coexist alongside structural reasons for 'failure'. As I have argued above, marginalized groups cannot simply be identified economically. Political and ideological processes are also at work that reinforce this marginalization. Thatcherism has elevated 'the family' so that it is capable of becoming an active consumer of services rather than the clients of the social democratic state. The problem is that to achieve this ideal families must have economic resources at their disposal. Because Thatcherism has had to marginalize certain social groups, equally it has doomed certain families to failure. This is the contradiction at the heart of Thatcherism: the government, which has made a virtue of rolling back state support and coterminously boosting the independence of 'the family', has also presided over the largest number of Place of Safety Orders ever taken, surely the crudest and most direct form of state intervention in the family (DHSS, 1988c). This is another reason why we should not speak of a 'family policy'; the same policy that has freed some families has exposed other families to poverty, despair, and authoritarian official interventions.

This drift toward authoritarianism is compounded by the resource crisis in social services departments. Whilst child protection has been prioritized by many such departments and has been able to attract new resources, it is increasingly the case that child abuse cases are not allocated a social worker (Doran and Young, 1987). Thus the 'service' element of child protection disappears and all that is left is the fact that a child is registered, that is, the 'surveillance' element. Equally the supportive and preventive parts of social work are inadequately resourced so that social work interventions are focused on assessment and possible removal (see Parton and Parton, 1989, and Chapter 8 in this volume).

The emphasis on 'working together' (DHSS, 1988d) in official publications is also informative in this context. The DHSS response to child abuse has centred, almost exclusively, on the coordination of professional practices. One could be forgiven for reading the DHSS circulars and reports on child abuse as arguing that 'lack of coordination' is the *cause* of child abuse. As Parton (1985a) has pointed out, no attention is paid to the question of the conditions that give rise to child abuse.

In a divided society we cannot understand child protection work as being simply about the protection of children. Child protection practice in an environment of inequality and marginalization becomes a process of judging and disciplining households defined as outside the mainstream (see Chapter 7 in this volume). They are the 'lame ducks' created by the extension of the free market and the 'rolling back' of the welfare state. This is why child abuse and neglect are not peripheral concerns if we are to understand how state forms and households relate. Official interventions around child abuse, by disqualifying the families of the marginalized, effectively define the successful families who can continue their quest for freedom and autonomy.

Progressive child protection?

I have so far argued that when we talk of interventions in 'the family' we need to be wary because, in the arena of child protection, we are actually talking about intervention in certain politically identified households. On the other side of the equation we also have to be wary about how we understand official interventions. Whilst we have defined a very definite and concrete direction in the construction of state policy toward child protection, we also have to be aware that we are not dealing with a single unified 'state'. The diversity of state interventions can be illustrated despite the very strong policy direction within Thatcherism. First, at national level the government is capable of producing policy directions that do develop a partnership approach between households and official bodies. Thus the White Paper *The Law on Child Care and Family Services* (HMSO, 1987) states that 'services to families in need of help should be arranged in a voluntary partnership with the parents' (p. 2). The White Paper calls for a complaints system for children in care and makes other suggestions that the liberal or even the socialist would find unobjectionable. Hence, whilst elements of Thatcher's 'family policy' are no doubt oppressive, there are elements that cannot be so defined. Secondly, we must remember that social services are organized and delivered locally with a (diminishing) degree of local political accountability. Thus, whilst a definable national trend may exist, we cannot assume that such a trend will be found in each locality. Many local authorities are struggling to organize child care services that are supportive and helpful to children and households under stress.

It is in this sense that my analysis points out the space for progressive practice to develop. In existing legislative frameworks and within the various welfare apparatus, we can find the opportunity for forms of practice that empower the underclass and assist them in their daily struggle to survive.

Conclusion

In this chapter I have attempted to argue that official responses to child abuse are an indicator of the nature of the complex relationship between households and forms of official intervention. In order to reach this point a considerable reworking of the statement referred to at the start of this chapter (Bell, 1988) has been undertaken. I went on further to argue that the nature of these interventions is best understood by 'deconstructing' both 'the state' and 'the family', thus moving towards a specific analysis of specific interventions. The final part of the chapter argues that in contemporary Britain child protection interventions reflect the fact that we are living in an increasingly divided society in which child protection can act as an intervention chiefly within a specific, socially constructed group. Whilst this can be seen as a clear direction in government policy, it remains the case that, precisely because the state is not monolithic, clear opportunities exist to develop forms of welfare practice that resist the dominant direction and that may help put us back on path to a society that really does accept collective responsibility for our children.

Note

1. This section of the analysis applies to child abuse and neglect and not to sexual abuse. As is argued elsewhere in this volume, sexual abuse seems to have no specific correlation to social class.

3 Women, gender oppression and child abuse

CHRISTINE PARTON

Feminism and men's violence

Modern Western feminism has produced a substantial body of social theory about men's violence to women and children as well as pioneering new methods of working with its survivors. This praxis has offered a powerful challenge to dominant socio-logical and psychological explanations of men's violence as well as to the inadequate responses generated by social policy. These explanations and responses invariably focus on the 'deviant family', the 'pathological' male, or the 'colluding mother', and fail to take into account the central importance of sex, gender, and power.

Feminist analyses of men's violence are marked by diverse positions and conceptual frameworks, yet central to all is the belief that male violence is rooted in the unequal power relationships between men and women at both a personal and structural level, that is, in the patriarchal nature of society. Men's violence takes many forms: physical, verbal, and emotional abuse, sexual harassment, rape, incest, exploitation, prostitution, and so on. Feminist theory has developed analyses both of these specific types of violence as well as working towards a general theory of men's violence. In this latter perspective, men use violence against women and children, along with other forms of controls such as ideological and economic control, to enforce and maintain their dominance. That child abuse is also, at one level, part of men's violence is argued by Jeff Hearn in Chapter 4. This perspective enables us not only to conceptualize a wide range of violent, exploitative, and oppressive acts as child abuse, but also to draw upon another theoretical framework – social theories of men's violence. Thus our focus is shifted from asking why it is that a particular *family, parent,* or *social group* abuses its children on to the questions of where men's violence comes from and why society does so little to prevent it. Jeff Hearn considers two important factors: first, that the development of masculinity encourages aggression as well as involving violence to boys and young men; secondly, that fathers, in private and public, have the power to dominate children and young people.

A feminist perspective

This chapter is complementary to Hearn's perspective, for it seeks to explore some of the issues surrounding male power, masculinity, and violence in relation to specific forms of child abuse. It will also examine other gender-related issues that are raised and informed by a feminist perspective. It has three sections, which have developed out of my own interests and experiences as a feminist, a social worker, and a mother who is concerned with improving the quality of both mothers' and children's experiences of child care. The first section draws upon feminist analyses of the gender division of labour and examines their relevance to an understanding of child abuse. Feminist work has drawn attention to the failure of mainstream child abuse literature, policy, and practice to acknowledge and analyse the high level of men's abuse of children. This will be a major focus in Jeff Hearn's chapter. My central concern here, however, is women's power in the private sphere of motherhood, for women also exercise control over children and can abuse them too, an area feminist theory is only recently coming to grips with (see Washburne, 1983; Gordon, 1986). The fact of women's abuse in part reflects their role as the primary parent, the lack of support for parenting/mothering, and a whole range of issues around women's inequality in the home and outside it. The second section explores feminist contributions to the study of child sexual abuse. These contributions illustrate the links between child sexual abuse and other forms of men's sexual violence and men's domination. The third and concluding section will consider the views of two feminist writers on child abuse, which can be characterized as based on a radical feminist and a socialist feminist perspective. The strengths and weaknesses of these two divergent viewpoints illustrate the need for a synthesis between radical and socialist feminism and for feminism to address the issues of race and children's rights.

Gender division of labour, motherhood and child abuse

The differences between men's and women's abuse and whether boys and girls are abused differently is by and large ignored by much of the research on child abuse. Yet current statistics (see

Table 3.1   *Who abuses?*

	Physical injury	Emotional abuse	Sexual abuse
Biological mother	32%	50% +	1%
Biological father	31%	31%	31%
Father substitute (step and cohabitee)	18%	4%	26%
Other (brother, sister, mother's boyfriend, neighbours, etc.)	6%	7%	35%

Source: Creighton, 1987.

Table 3.1) show three gender differences. First, that the vast majority of child sexual abuse is committed by men and that girls are abused in greater numbers than boys (Baker and Duncan, 1986, report figures of 18 and 12 per cent respectively, although sexual abuse of boys appears to be greatly under-reported – Finkelhor, 1984). Second, the responsibility for physical abuse is approximately equally distributed between men and women, though when controlled for whom the child lives with the proportion of the total amount of physical abuse committed by men is 60–61 per cent (Creighton, 1987). If it was possible to control for who spends the most time with the child, this level of men's abuse would be higher, given that their participation in child care is so low. Despite some evidence of growing involvement by men in child care (Lewis and O'Brien, 1987), it is mothers, not fathers, who are primarily responsible for child care in the UK. As Cohen (1988, p. 22) comments:

> It is predominantly mothers who take time out of the labour market to care for pre-school children, who reduce their hours of work to provide for children out of school hours and during school holidays, and who are more likely than fathers to take time off work when the child is ill.

Third, women predominate in cases of emotional abuse (Creighton, 1987) and neglect (Greenland, 1987).

Several feminist writers have demonstrated that the literature is preoccupied with the mother's direct or indirect responsibility for child abuse (Lahey, 1984; Breines and Gordon, 1983; Martin, 1983). The majority of studies either focus on mothers or fail to distinguish the abusing parent by gender. Frequently the term 'abusing parent' is in fact a euphemism for 'abusing mother' as it is they who are held ultimately responsible for their children's welfare. If not directly culpable, they are too often seen as actively or passively colluding when abuse occurs.

Practice based upon a family systems model, for example, views child abuse as involving a triangular relationship between victim, abuser, and the partner who fails to protect (Dale *et al.*, 1986). While insisting that the abuser accepts responsibility, this approach expects the partner to do so as well. Unless such an analysis takes into account the gender inequalities in power, both in the marital relationship and in access to social and economic resources, it ignores the fact that the ability to protect a child is not equal for men and women.

In Jones' (1987, p. 102) typology of abusing parents, such women are described as Type 9 – 'Failure to protect':

> These are almost always women whose failure to protect a child from violent men is significant enough to be a major contributory factor. They tend to have repeated relationships with such men. These women often had a violent childhood and aggressive fathers, have low self esteem and may suffer assaults by their cohabitees. Despite this, they preserve their relationships with such men, at the expense of their children, even though they may be very frightened of them.

The crucial question must be *why* some women fail to protect their children from violent boyfriends or cohabitees or even – like the mothers involved in all the recent major inquiries into fatal child abuse incidents (Mrs Carlile, Beverly Lorrington, and Claudette Henry) – go to great lengths to protect their men from investigations of non-accidental injury (see London Borough of Brent, 1985; London Borough of Lambeth; 1987; London Borough of Greenwich, 1987).

For feminists, the reasons why some women fail to protect their children lie partly in their position of relative powerlessness within the family and the wider society. The psychological, social, and economic pressures upon a woman to maintain her relationship with an abusive man are enormous. The idea that battered women enjoy violence is nevertheless an invidious and persuasive one. The inquiry into the death of Kimberley Carlile (London Borough of Greenwich, 1987, p. 111), for example, saw Mrs Carlile as 'fatally attracted to violent cohabitees'. Such a view detracts not only from the issue of men's violence but from the constellation of forces upon a woman to stay. Many women do choose to sever a relationship with an abusive father but the costs are great – the stigma, poverty, and loneliness of lone parenthood, the threat of further violence from an ex-partner, and so on.

As feminists, we have to acknowledge that women do play a crucial role in protecting their children and we need to work towards giving women and children the power and resources to protect themselves. In Kimberley Carlile's case, Wirral social services department's concern about the children ended when the violent cohabitee, David Carlile, was no longer part of the family. Preventive work or support for a young single mother of four small children was not given, though (in retrospect) Mrs Carlile was unable to cope and the children were neglected.

The emergence of societal explanations of child abuse that emphasize the role of stress stemming from social inequality and the cultural acceptability of violence shifts the location of causes from the individual family or parent on to the social structure itself (Gil, 1970; Gelles, 1972). However, as argued in Chapter 1, while class divisions are analysed, gender is a frequently neglected dimension, as is race. Yet the use of violence in parenting and stress are closely related to the gender system. The different pattern of men's and women's abuse is related to their traditional gender roles as parents – mothers as the primary carer and nurturer and men as the disciplinarian and breadwinner. These roles have to be analysed within the context of unequal power structures within the family. Furthermore, conditions such as poverty, bad housing, and isolation all impinge more directly upon women, especially those who head households alone. Women's poverty is further compounded by racial disadvantage and disability (Glendenning and Millar, 1987).

Not all the research ignores gender. Straus (1979) concludes from a general population survey that although 17 per cent of women battered children, against 10 per cent of men, this reflected, first, women's greater time at risk due to their primary role in child care, and, second, that this time spent in child care was not necessarily the result of free and voluntary choice. Strong spousal and social expectations forced mothers to assume overwhelming responsibility, which produced frustration for the mothers. Moreover, there were similar pressures about children's behaviour, which led to a high level of anxiety and guilt if a child did not perform well enough. He found that, contrary to expectations, women who worked outside the home were *less* abusive than full-time mothers and had the *same* level of abuse as the men in the study, although carrying a double burden of domestic and paid labour. These findings suggest that the gender division of labour is a significant factor in child abuse. It is the experience of motherhood to which I now wish to turn.

Feminists distinguish between two meanings of motherhood. One relates to the relationship of a woman to her child and the other to the institution of motherhood, the particular child-rearing pattern in a society or social groups. Motherhood at a personal level produces deep and powerful emotions, both joyful and painful (Rich, 1977). These are affected by many factors: the child's and the mother's personalities, social circumstances, and

the way motherhood is constructed in our society. For the majority of women in Britain, especially with pre-school children,
this means exclusive responsibility for their children's needs
all of the time, frequently in relative isolation from supportive
family and community networks. This manner of organizing
child care is presented as the ideal one, best suiting the child's
emotional, physical and social needs (Kellmer-Pringle, 1977
and 1979). It is, however, specific to contemporary Western
industrial society and has been compared unfavourably with
non-industrial societies where, although responsibility for child
care remains a female one, it is integrated with vital reproductive
and productive tasks (Bernard, 1974).

The separation of family life from production associated
with the rise of capitalism resulted, though this was not an
inevitable outcome, in home and care of the family being
the proper place and position for women. Despite the greater
participation of married women in paid employment in the
post-war period, child care and housework remain largely wom-
en's work. This responsibility is a wide-ranging one involving
women in many aspects of health work – cleaning, providing
a balanced diet, utilizing health services, home nursing, and
so on (Graham, 1984). The assumption behind social policy
provisions is that women will carry out these vital tasks of
family health work, with supportive services such as day care or
domiciliary help being provided only when there is no woman
carer or she fails to carry out her role (Wilson, 1977). The
current restructuring of the welfare state, with its emphasis on
familial responsibility – that is, women's responsibility – and
cut-backs, will expand the expectations and burdens of women's
roles in the family. Within child abuse policy and practice
a trend is emerging that emphasizes parental responsibility,
decisive intervention, and assessment of parental dangerousness,
and unless this takes into account the gender divisions in
parenting this means emphasizing *maternal* responsibility and
privatized care by the mother within the family. Day care is
increasingly seen as a therapeutic service, to train and support
only those mothers with parenting problems, rather than a
service in its own right. The aim is to return mothers to
'independent' functioning. For example, one single mother
receiving social work intervention from the NSPCC (Dale *et
al.*, 1986, p. 152) is viewed as competent when she no longer
needs daily support at the Family Centre, yet she still 'experienced the wide range of difficulties which many young mothers
with two demanding children are liable to encounter. There
were times when she was extremely tired, times when she
became irritable and depressed, and times when her relationships

with Jeremy became more stressful'. This is viewed as a 'normal mother with normal problems'. This concept of coping pervades our ideas of motherhood, rendering women's labour invisible and denying them a voice to demand more resources. As Graham (1984, pp. 153–4) comments: 'Maintaining health is most in evidence when it is not done, when clothes and faces are left unwashed, rooms and hair are untidy, and children are ill-disciplined and noisy. When a mother works successfully to maintain the standards of dress, decor and decorum her labour is at its most invisible'.

Coping also involves culpability: when a mother neglects or abuses her children it is seen as an individual failing rather than related to the conditions in which mothering takes place. Yet the pressures upon women to cope with the role of mother are powerful, both from society and from within themselves, for to admit to cracks beneath the surface is to negate one's self-identity. In Ong's study (1986) of women attending a centre, suspected of either abusing or 'allowing' partners to abuse their children, she found that they all presented themselves according to their image of a normal mother – that is, 'concerned, sacrificing, coping' – and saw the incident of child abuse as an isolated event unrelated to the pattern of their lives. It was either an unaccountable event because they were depressed or a one-off incident beyond their responsibility. Such interpretations, Ong suggests, are not deliberately misleading or untrue; they may in part be a defensive reaction to scrutiny by the authorities, but they also reflect the women's own perception of their lives as individual, separate from society as a whole. Therefore their abuse is their personal problem rather than linked to the conditions in which they live.

These conditions were overwhelmingly adverse: poverty, isolation, unshared child care, and stressful, sometimes violent, marital relationships. Extensive evidence exists linking the personal problems many women experience with the maternal role; for example, women's poorer mental health is related to the isolation of modern motherhood (Brown and Harris, 1978). That widespread anger or violence is found among 'normal' (that is, non-abusing) mothers must also lead us to question the institution of motherhood itself. Frude and Goss's (1980) postal survey of mothers revealed that 96 per cent had days when 'everything got on top of them', 57 per cent admitted to hitting their child (aged between 18 months and 4 years) really hard at least once, and 40 per cent feared this getting out of control. Similar findings of high levels of anger towards small babies were reported by Graham (1980), who concluded that they were associated with the constraints of modern motherhood. A mother's ability to cope with a baby's persistent crying was undermined by chronic tiredness, the enormous sense of responsibility and uncertainty, and the lack of material, practical, and emotional support.

Studies of women's experience of motherhood reveal the interplay of economic and ideological influences. In our society it is assumed that all women want to 'become mothers', yet this belief in free choice is belied by the influences of our pro-natalist culture – the lack of adequate contraception or fulfilling, well-paid alternative options for women. In contemporary Britain, where youth unemployment is high, becoming a mother offers some young women their only avenue to independent adult status.

The reality of mothering is frequently very different from the romantic ideal of feminine fulfilment. While total responsibility for their children's care does bring enormous satisfaction to many women, it does not for a significant minority. Boulton's study (1983) offers one of the fullest analyses of motherhood. She examined two dimensions of mothering, distinguishing between the feelings mothers have about their day-to-day involvement with their children – the rewards and frustrations that child care involves – and the broader meaning of purpose attached to motherhood. Nearly a third of her sample neither enjoyed the daily aspects of child care nor gained much sense of meaning or purpose from their children. A further 30 per cent found only one aspect of motherhood rewarding. The negative features of motherhood identified were the irksome, tiring, and repetitive nature of child care and domestic work (two tasks that frequently conflicted with each other), the social isolation, the loss of financial independence, and a feeling of total responsibility for child care. Experiences of motherhood also show a class pattern. In Boulton's sample more working-class mothers enjoyed child care than the middle-class respondents (56 per cent and 40 per cent respectively), while 88 per cent of working-class women found their children rewarding companions as against only 25 per cent of middle-class women. However, more middle-class women than working-class women found a sense of purpose in the mothering role (two-thirds as against one-half of working-class women).

Economic factors clearly played a part. The middle-class mothers, apart from having a more pleasant environment in which to care for their children, had greater access to other satisfying alternatives such as paid work or social activities. The pressures of poverty, inadequate housing, and unshared parenting increase the amount of labour involved in child care and domestic work. For example, keeping a toddler amused or safely occupied in a high-rise flat is much harder than in a suburban semi, as is shopping around for bargains to make ends meet. Isolation in the home is a major factor in women's violence towards their children (Ong, 1986) and is more likely to be experienced by those women who have the least control over where they live and are unable to develop or maintain their links with supportive friends or family through lack of money, a car, or babysitters. The material conditions of motherhood thus interact with assumptions about gender roles. Greenland's study (1987), which shows that 60 per cent of those responsible for cases of neglect coming to the attention of the child welfare agencies were women, and 40 per cent were single mothers, says something about the conditions of motherhood in general and of single motherhood in particular.

The implications for policy and practice of such questions about the very nature of parenting are thus wide-ranging and relate to issues of class, race, and gender inequalities more generally. The marginal position of women, especially black or working-class women, in the labour market and the lack of child care facilities affect their ability to contribute to the family resources necessary to meet their child care responsibilities. Yet a woman's earnings are frequently crucial in lifting a family out of poverty and increasing her sense of self-esteem (Glendenning and Millar, 1987). Women's weak economic position also reinforces their position as the main carer, dependent upon a male partner. Paradoxically, the dominant assumption of women's responsibility for their children's welfare assumes a degree of autonomy and control over their lifestyle that many do not have (Graham, 1984).

Professionals working with child abuse must, therefore, move beyond seeing it as an individual problem. As Ong (1986, p. 166) comments, 'We have to analyse the wider context and confront the issue of violence of the institution of motherhood.'

A feminist social work practice, based on this understanding of mothers as people who are oppressed and who struggle against adverse conditions, is possible. Ong (1986) argues that, if women were encouraged to share their experience of mothering, to analyse the pressure they face, and to recognize their common features, they could begin to break out of the cycle of individual guilt and failure. However, attempts to de-individualize child abuse face limitations and contradictions. The protection of children has to be the principal priority for those working in welfare agencies, and the dilemma posed by the need to balance the interests of the parents, such as their personal development, and the interests of the child, such as his or her emotional and physical safety, cannot easily be resolved in present-day social work practice. Professionals who are directly responsible for a child's welfare have little room or time to experiment or take risks; nor does the woman, who is under pressure to prove she is a good mother. Nevertheless, feminist work with women does provide us with some avenues to stimulate solidarity and shared insights (Hale, 1983; Ong, 1986).

Improving women's self-esteem and encouraging them to take control of their lives and relationships must also run alongside initiatives to improve the material conditions of motherhood, such as better child care facilities, housing, public transport, and financial support. These involve much wider social policy issues, in general a depressing scenario at present. Yet many groups within the women's movement are emerging at the grassroots level to tackle some of these issues (see, for example, Dale and Foster, 1986, Chapters 8 and 9) and within statutory agencies (Brook and Davis, 1985; Boushel and Noakes, 1988). Lahey (1984) also urges that children's rights – to representation, to protection from abuse, and to adequate care – be given full legal expression. The invisibility and powerlessness of children must, she argues, be brought to an end, through greater public health surveillance, tighter abuse reporting laws, and enforcement procedures. However, if such proposals are not to penalize single and impoverished women further, widespread changes in society's institutional arrangements for the care and protection of children are also required.

Child sexual abuse

I argued in the previous section that women's abuse of children is an abuse of their power as mothers, but an abuse related to the material and ideological pressures on mothers. Yet child sexual abuse, which is also an abuse of power and is now recognized as widespread, is rarely committed by women, despite their greater access to children, nor is it correlated with social deprivation. Child sexual abuse, however, involves another dimension to other forms of abuse. It is not just a violent act or an abuse of power, but also an abuse of *sex* or *sexual* power. This shifts the terms of the debate into the area of sexuality and men's sexual violence.

Over the last fifteen years or so there has been a great deal of feminist research and analysis of men's sexual violence. This debate has increasingly widened the definition of sexual violence from that of a deviant and primarily violent act, i.e. rape and explicit acts of sexual abuse, to include other forms of sexual behaviour that women experience as coercive or non-consensual. Sexual violence is most commonly viewed as involving physical assault, restraint, or the use of force, but feminist research has revealed a wide range of experiences ranging from rape, sexual assault, and child sexual abuse at the one extreme, through obscene phone calls, sexual harassment, and domestic violence, to flashing, coercive sex, and pressure to have sex at the other end of the continuum (Kelly, 1987; C. A. Mackinnon, 1982). The concept of a continuum of sexual violence draws attention to the links between the extreme forms of sexual violence such as rape, incest, and sexual assault and more common, everyday male behaviour. Research into sexual harassment, for example, which was initially defined within the context of paid work and authority relationships, has revealed that it occurs across a wide range of settings and relationships and covers a wide variety of behaviour – from the leers and sneers of innuendo to overt demand and physical abuse. It is used by men, whether co-workers, superiors, subordinates, or fellow school-children, to keep girls and women in 'their place', i.e. deferential.

Feminist perspectives on sexual violence have thus increasingly moved on from analysing different forms of sexual violence, such as rape, incest, sexual harassment, prostitution, pornography, as discrete phenomena to viewing them as part of the more general process of subordinating women and women's sexuality. This had led to a critique of heterosexuality itself (which is male dominated and defined) and its role in creating and maintaining men's dominance (Edwards, 1987). Child sexual abuse must also therefore be viewed within the context of men's sexual violence and the subordination of women and children.

The extent of child sexual abuse is difficult to establish, with estimates varying according to the definition and research methodology used. However, taking into account American and British research findings, a 10 per cent prevalence rate for child sexual abuse involving physical contact by family members and close relatives is a likely, though conservative, estimate (La Fontaine, 1988).

The recent 'discovery' of child sexual abuse within the family as a serious problem needs some explanation, for such figures and evidence have been available for a long time. A review of five surveys conducted between the 1940s and the present day found a *consistent* rate of 20–25 per cent of adult women who had had a childhood sexual encounter with an adult male (Herman with Hirschman, 1981). Between 4 and 12 per cent reported a sexual experience with a relative. The experience of survivors of child sexual abuse, who are only recently beginning to speak out (through the women's movement, self-help groups, and organizations like *Childline*), reveals the disbelief and inaction that has pervaded many child welfare and legal services.

Society's failure to act lies partly within the very causes of
child sexual abuse – male power and masculinity – which have
produced male-biased theories and policies of intervention.
The legal definition of incest, for example, does not cover
abuse by a stepfather, adoptive father, or other adults. Nor
does it cover the whole range of sexual assault, exhibitionism,
touching, fondling, and forcing a child to touch the adult's
genitals, all of which can be just as damaging as vaginal sex
(Hamblin and Bowen, 1981). These come under the crime of
indecent assault, which is now increasingly recognized as serious
as incest, but there still remains in some lay and professional
circles a belief that such behaviour is less harmful than incest.

Feminist explanations of child abuse have challenged many of
the existing orthodox theories, arguing that they minimize the
problem and detract from the issue of *men*'s abuse and *why* it
happens. In an examination of some common theories of 'expert'
writers and therapists, Sarah Nelson (1987) identifies several
myths. First, there is a myth that it never happened: the child is
making it up or fantasizing. Freudian psychoanalysis is generally
blamed for giving theoretical scientific credibility to this view.
Freud argued, for example, that patients' disclosure of sexual
abuse were fantasy stemming from the daughter's sexual desire
for her father (the Electra complex). While other psychoanalysts
do accept the reality of child sexual abuse and have contributed
to our understanding of the trauma of incest and the ambivalence an abused child feels, psychoanalytic theorizing about
child sexual abuse exists within a patriarchal ideology. The
man's abuse is seen as an individual problem – anxiety about
sexual adequacy, fear of castration, rage against his mother. It
takes for granted a particular construction of male–female relationships and masculine sexuality (Macleod and Saraga, 1988).

A second myth maintains that sexual abuse is an accepted
part of certain subcultures, the 'greatest cause and justification
of inaction among welfare professionals' according to Nelson
(1987). Such beliefs not only deny the subjective experience
of those experiencing abuse; they are not borne out by
research. Figures of *reported* sexual abuse of children and
some research studies do show a bias towards the lower
end of the social scale or a rural upbringing, but it is
probable that these reflect the manner of disclosure; for
example, socially disadvantaged families are more likely to
come under surveillance from welfare agencies or biased
sampling. Results from general population surveys suggest that
child sexual abuse, unlike physical abuse and neglect, is evenly
distributed by region and occupational class. The only research
available on cultural or ethnic subgroups is American and shows

no association between sexual abuse and ethnic origin, except that abusing fathers are *less* likely to be black (La Fontaine, 1988).

The third myth, that children invite or enjoy sex, which is associated with libertarian ideas about sexuality, was a prominent view in the approach to child abuse during the 1970s. The belief that current laws on children's sexual activity were repressive to children led to a reluctance to intervene. Children were seen as able to participate willingly in sexual activity with an adult. Furthermore, the separation from a loved and loving father and the emotional reactions of welfare agencies were seen as causing greater trauma than the abuse itself.

Nelson argues that such 'child collusion or victim blame theories' interpret childish affection or sexuality in *adult* sexual terms. Children do have strong needs for physical and emotional reassurance from their parents, but this does not mean they are ready or able to participate in a sexual relationship defined in adult terms.

> I am not sure how old I was when it happened. I might have been younger than eight. My mother was out working in the evenings and I can remember my father coming down to my room and taking me back to their bedroom, into their big double bed, and my father rubbing his penis up and down my vagina. He'd talk to me and say things like 'Does that feel nice?' I would not reply but lie there looking at the ceiling with the most terrified, confused, nauseous feeling you can imagine. The light was always off and I never saw his penis or ever looked into his eyes. There was just this outline of the man, this big man, my father, doing this unknown, secretive act to me. I was told I wasn't to tell anyone, that it was something between him and me. Then he would send me back to my bedroom. (Katherine, in *Broadsheet*, a New Zealand feminist magazine; quoted in Hamblin and Bowen, 1981)

Several points emerge from accounts such as this: active initiation by the father, the use of force or authority, the girl's ignorance and confusion about sex, her shame, fear, and pain. Some children do, however, find that such a relationship brings rewards as well as painful feelings. This ambivalence, or even hostility to mother and warmth to the abusive father, has also led to a reluctance to intervene, and a belief that incest reflects or is part of a caring relationship. Such a view fails to question the nature of male–female relationships within the family, between man and wife, father and daughter or son. There is an assumption that it is a man's prerogative to expect sexual or domestic services. As two writers comment (Herman and Hirschman, quoted by Nelson, 1987, p. 54):

> Customarily, a mother and wife in our society is one who nurtures and takes care of children and husband. If the mother is unable to fulfil her ordinary functions it is apparently assumed some other female must be found to do it. The eldest daughter is a frequent choice ... This view of the father's prerogative to be served not only is shared by the fathers and daughters in these families, but is also encouraged by societal attitudes.

One of the few consistent findings of research that supports this notion that child sexual abuse is related to men's dominance in the family is that offenders are frequently 'family tyrants', who rule their families with a rod of iron, expecting their wives and daughters to perform the traditional subservient female role. While the majority of men do not sexually abuse, gender stereotypes and gender inequality nevertheless create the conditions in which sexual abuse can occur (Herman with Hirschman, 1981). The apparently paradoxical pattern has also been identified that men who are ineffectual and powerless either within or outside their families are more likely to abuse their daughters. This still, however, reflects society's assumptions about masculinity and male sexuality. Part of being male is to be dominant and have sexual power over women, thus some men turn to weaker members of the female sex, that is, girls, and boys as well.

Yet the majority of non-feminist and popular literature in effect absolves the male abuser of responsibility. The man is seen as a deviant, a product of a disturbed family history, or part of a dysfunctional family where forces such as a child's provocative behaviour or marital, sexual, and relationship difficulties push the man towards incestuous behaviour. The Report of the Inquiry into Child Abuse in Cleveland 1987, for example, sees the perpetrator, predominantly male, as ranging from the pathological personality with bizarre sexual behaviour at the one extreme to the 'widowed father with the adolescent daughter who had begun to assume maternal responsibilities and household duties' at the other extreme. In the latter type, sexual abuse arises (Secretary of State for Social Services, 1988, p. 8) 'from a normal father/daughter relationship in an isolated family, [when] a bereaved husband may sometimes, not with any great pathology in certain cases, slide ... into a sexual relationship'. In between are the fathers with a very strong sex drive, abnormal but not 'overtly pathological'.

In other words, male sexuality, whether normal or abnormal, is viewed as rampant. Men are not expected to control their sexual urges; women – daughters and mothers – are. Quoting Professor Sir Martin Roth, a psychiatrist, the report goes on to argue that 'in many cases mothers play a role in the genesis of the sexual abuse of their daughters'. Unfortunately, mothers may be physically, emotionally, or mentally ill-equipped for this task or may even encourage or tolerate the abuse. 'In many cases the mothers elect the eldest or one of the oldest daughters to the role of child mother . . . [this] is allowed to slide into a sexual relationship with her father. This is tolerated with little or no protest' (Secretary of State for Social Services, 1988, p. 8).

While the report acknowledges the dilemma a mother is faced with in the conflict between her child and her partner, upon whom she is economically and emotionally dependent, the overall message is that it is not so much male sexuality that is the problem but a dysfunctional family in which the mother is not discharging her traditional function adequately. As feminist analyses point out, however, the roots of child sexual abuse lie not so much in deviant family and sexual values but in *normal* ones (Macleod and Saraga, 1987). According to one influential text (Ciba Foundation, 1984, p.9):

When a mother withdraws from her family, her children and husband may turn to one another for support, practical assistance or comfort, and the foundations of an incestuous relationship are laid. In other cases a man deprived of his conjugal rights may turn to the nearest available source of gratification – a dependent child.

This acceptance of traditional gender and sex roles – that is, that a man must have sex and has a right to expect domestic and sexual services, and that a woman is responsible for her child's safety – fails to acknowledge the role of power, gender, and sexuality in child sexual abuse. For child sexual abuse has its roots in male power and a male-dominated sexuality.

As Rick Snowden found in counselling groups of male offenders, they were just 'ordinary men who, like him, had grown up expecting to dominate women and children and that there was nothing to keep us from using their . . . bodies for our pleasure and anger . . . incest offenders are men who simply have the power to take what they want and who take it' (quoted in Nelson, 1987, p. 87).

The sexual abuse of girls also includes a wide range of other behaviours, some commonly experienced both within the family *and* outside it. In Liz Kelly's research (1987) on women's experiences of sexual violence, this included rape, sexual assault, sexual harassment, flashing, coercive sex, and pressurized sex. Using a definition of abuse that covered situations where the women she studied felt they did not freely choose to have sex or sexual experiences, Kelly was able to include many threatening and distressing incidents normally excluded from child sexual abuse. Recent research in Britain and the United States is also demonstrating the high level of sexual harassment and sexual assault by adolescent and even younger boys, suggesting rates of abuse much higher than current prevalence rates (Ageton, 1983; Mahoney, 1984). The sexual abuse of boys outside the family, a significant proportion of sexual abuse cases, is also an under-researched and under-reported area. The current focus of media and professional attention is, however, on the family – the disturbed family or the perverted stepfather. That girls and young women are frequently touched up, jeered at, coerced into sex, or raped by boys and young men as well as by adult men at school, at leisure, everywhere and anywhere, calls for a far wider perspective.

The sexual abuse of girls and boys can, therefore, be viewed as part of the general phenomenon of sexual violence and male sexuality. A major concern of feminists has been to expose the extent to which sexuality has been defined by men and is experienced by women as coercive and objectifying. The 'normal' male is expected to take the initiative, choose a smaller, younger partner, prefer positions in which he is in control. Men use their sexuality aggressively against women; flashing, for example, one of the commonest forms of sexual harassment, is mainly used to intimidate, humiliate, and frighten women. The explicit violence to women in hard core pornography both reflects and reinforces this aspect of male sexuality. Men are socialized to see their sexuality as uncontrollable and to separate sex from loving emotion. This encourages them to objectify their partners, rather than see them as human beings with their own sexual and emotional needs. The selection of children, especially girls, as sexual partners and the apparent oblivious attitude to the physical and emotional pain inflicted can thus be viewed as an extension of 'normal' male sexuality (Coveney *et al.*, 1984).

The analysis of child sexual abuse as being a product of the construction of male sexuality and unequal power relationships between men and women, adults and children, poses enormous problems for statutory agencies and individual workers. A feminist-based practice is, however, being developed within the statutory sector as well as outside it. Feminist practice has developed from the initiatives of the women's movement on rape and domestic violence. Groups such as Rape Crisis Centres, Women's Aid and Incest Survivors Groups offer an alternative service based on the experience and knowledge built up from working with women and children who have been assaulted (see, for example, Nelson, 1987; Bell and Macleod, 1988; Bogle, 1988). Within the statutory and voluntary sector, work in child sexual abuse involves three levels – prevention, protection, and rehabilitation – which need to take into account the issues raised by a feminist analysis.

Preventive programmes such as Michelle Elliott's 'Kidscape', which teach children to be more assertive, are of value but it is not enough just to teach children to say no. In the long term we have to take on board the problem of masculine sexuality and power right across the whole continuum of sexual violence. The development of strategies within schools to deal with child sexual abuse, therefore, needs to acknowledge its links with sexual harassment and other forms of sexual violence. As O'Hara (1988) suggests, they cannot exist in isolation from the total school environment. A commitment to protecting pupils from general bullying, racial as well as sexual harassment, and assault is required. Sex education in schools is also important. However, much of the sex education currently taught has been criticized by feminists for neglecting *female* sexuality and thus failing to challenge men's and boy's dominance in sexual relationships. Work with girls and young women needs to help them understand their own bodies and sexual feelings and to distinguish between relationships based on sexual exploitation and those based on equality and mutual consent (Meulenbelt, 1981; Myles *et al.*, 1985). As O'Hara (1988, p.160) comments, 'The kind of sex education which can most effectively challenge sexual abuse takes the potential for a positive, autonomous, female sexuality as its starting point.' Similarly, sex education with boys and young men must take an anti-sexist stance.

It is perhaps the issues involved in protection work, in the identification of sexual abuse, and in subsequent intervention that have currently received most attention in the media and statutory agencies, especially in the aftermath of Cleveland. There has been an expansion in training courses and literature and a growth of specialist units and specialist workers in both the statutory and voluntary sector concerned with this area of work. Some of the dilemmas and controversies surrounding these developments are discussed elsewhere in this book; here my focus is on suggestions for a feminist social work practice.

The dilemmas and anxiety surrounding protection and intervention are great. If the offender cannot be prevented from having access, the immediate safety of the child is frequently only assured by his or her removal from the family, thus creating a further punishment for the child. The mother's role in protecting the child, usually if the offender is not placed in custody, is crucial. While some mothers do believe their children and support them, some are unable to do so. Feminist practice begins by restoring the mother–child bond, recognizing the extreme stress the mother is under:

> In addition to coping with father's pressure and threats, she is compelled to shoulder the responsibility for her family alone, something she does not want to do, or feel capable of doing, and she is sacrificing whatever financial or emotional security existed in her marriage for the sake of a daughter who has often seemed more of a rival than a child. However hard she tries to avoid blaming her daughter, there may be times when she quite simply hates her. (Herman with Hirschman, 1981, p. 145)

Both the mother and the child therefore require intensive support, practical, material, financial, and emotional, while the child's process of recovery will need long-term therapeutic work.

Such a practice must also incorporate an understanding of racism and different cultural patterns to avoid the imposition of white middle-class heterosexual norms of good child care, as well as an awareness of the impact of statutory intervention upon a black family living in a racist society (Macleod and Saraga, 1988). Islington social services department have developed policy and practice guidelines that attempt to recognize these issues around race and culture and to try and prevent the child's removal from home, utilizing non-abusing family networks to ensure their protection (Boushel and Noakes, 1988).

Some feminist-oriented programmes concentrate on the restoration of the mother–child relationship and treatment ends once they are able to protect themselves. Yet as Herman and Hirschman (1981, p.149) argue, 'There is no way of getting rid of the fathers . . . excluding them from the family does not put an end to their abusiveness as new victims do not seem to be in short supply'. However dealt with by the criminal justice system, there is an urgent need for an offender to receive effective treatment; yet this is currently rarely available. The question of readmitting him into the family is a highly emotive issue. Should a child be abused a second time by being deprived of a father or should a man who has abdicated and abused his position of parental trust and duties ever be allowed to return? Herman with Hirschman (1981) suggest that in any case fathers should not be readmitted into their families until three conditions have been met. First, they should be under the supervision of the court as long as the daughter remains at home. Second, they should be actively involved in an appropriate treatment programme. Third, they should have accepted complete responsibility for the sexual abuse and made this clear to *all* the family. Significant changes in the pattern of family relationships have also to take place, towards a strong mother–daughter relationship and a shift in power from father to mother. In the long term, fathers must learn to become more submissive and nurturant, and mothers more dominant. 'When men no longer rule their families, they may learn for the first time what it means to belong to one' (Herman with Hirschman, 1981, p. 218).

Conclusion – outstanding issues for developing a feminist theory and practice

In this chapter men's sexual abuse of children has been linked to men's domination and the masculinization of sexuality. The fact of women's abuse has also been linked to their oppression and to their unequal position in the gender division of reproductive and productive labour.

Feminists differ in their analysis of the structural causes of women's oppression. Radical feminists argue that the main cause of women's and children's oppression is patriarchy, a 'sexual system of power in which the male possesses superior power and economic privilege' (Eisenstein, 1979, p. 17). Their analysis of how patriarchy, through the institutions of motherhood and heterosexuality, controls and constrains women's fertility, reproductive labour, and sexuality has exposed the reality of sexual and physical violence, alienation, and drudgery behind the ideology of motherhood and femininity. Lahey (1984, pp. 173–4) attempts to apply this perspective to child abuse and links all forms of child abuse to patriarchy:

> Assault, and battery of children, appears to serve patriarchy as an outlet for the desire to dominate, to overpower, to put inferiors in their place as well as an outlet for frustration and aggression socially fostered by overwhelming expectation. Neglect is [due] to the deprivation suffered by mothers rendering them unable to fulfil their traditional role. Incest and sexual exploitation of children demonstrate the availability of children to satisfy male sexual needs.

Contemporary legal and liberal reforms have thus failed to solve the problem of child abuse because women and children remain powerless, and male values such as autonomy, power, revenge, domination, and masculine thinking pervade. Women's values of continuity, nurturance, and contextualized and relativistic decision-making processes are thus denied. Children do not have the same rights to human dignity and protection as adult males; they are treated as chattels, to be controlled and taught to conform. Thus it is *patriarchy*, whether feudal, liberal, or socialist, that is the cause of child abuse.

One of the strengths of radical feminism is its explanation of *men*'s sexual and physical violence, but Lahey's view that women turn to abuse only when terrorized, impoverished, or overburdened by men is only a partial explanation. It has been argued earlier in this chapter that the conditions of contemporary motherhood are exacerbated by patriarchal gender relations as well as those of class and race. Power structures are also divided along the lines of age; that women, too, are capable of domination, revenge, and abuse is demonstrated in Gordon's (1986) historical research. Women negotiate with, participate in, as well as struggle against male domination. 'We need a more complex view of patriarchy which can take into account both women's and children's oppression' (Gordon, 1986).

Lahey's concept of patriarchy is ahistorical as well as classless. This concept of a universal patriarchy has been criticized by socialist feminists. As Gordon in her study of the growth of the child-saving movement in the USA at the turn of the century demonstrates, patriarchy is not a fixed and immutable, independent, autonomous force. Capitalist class and cultural relations interact with patriarchy to shape the conditions of child rearing. Gordon argues that the conditions of industrial capitalism in the 1870s both created a new sensitivity to the treatment of children and probably worsened children's lot. Conditions of labour and the restructuring of the patriarchal family under industrial capitalism, she suggests, may well have caused poverty and stress to bear more heavily on children. Women's dependence upon the arbitrary authority of their husbands was actually increased by the new wage labour system and urban life. When fathers deserted or failed to support their families (a frequent occurrence), the resulting destitution of mothers caused many of the recorded cases of child neglect. Paternal authority over children was weakened and many of the physical assaults on children (by women as well as by men) were the result not just of children's insubordination but of *inadequate* parental authority. The child protection agencies in the USA attempted to reinforce this authority by developing a new parent–child bond based on WASP child-rearing norms and a new male supremacy. These often clashed with those of the immigrant culture and indeed fears of being swamped by a culture with conflicting values fuelled the child-saving movement.

Such a perspective suggests the way forward to develop a socialist feminist analysis of child abuse that recognizes the development of patriarchal productive *and* reproductive relations under capitalism, and the psychological production of gender as the underlying determinants of women's, children's and indeed men's oppression. Such an analysis of men's sexual violence to women is now emerging (Messerschmidt, 1986) and offers the possibility of a synthesis of the radical feminist understanding of patriarchy, of men's control of women's reproduction and sexuality, and the development of gender identity, with a class analysis. Feminist analyses of race have yet to fully account for the complex dynamics of race, gender, and class inequality, for neither race nor class is a mere extension of patriarchal domination nor can their disadvantages be understood simply as cumulative. The liberation of many white women from child care and domestic labour, for example, is frequently based on the exploitation of black and white working-class women. Nevertheless, the fact that the experience of all women and children as well as racial exploitation can be tied to class relations suggests that socialist feminism can provide the best starting point for an analysis of race (Anderson, 1983).

A final inadequacy in feminist theory is its neglect of children's rights and power. With the exception of a few radical feminists such as Firestone (1970), who called for the abolition of the status of childhood, or Lahey's demand for children to have greater legal rights, there has been a tendency to assume that children's rights are coterminous with women's. Feminist analyses of child sexual abuse see the empowering of *mothers* as one of the most important contributions to preventing the sexual exploitation of children. The strengthening of mothers is also seen as vital in tackling the issue of women's violence to children, for it is their own subordination and the gender division of labour under capitalist relations that forms the context of contemporary child rearing. However, the fact that the problem of child abuse emerges from the powerlessness of women *and* children does not mean we can assume women's superiority over men in their ability to nurture and protect; feminists must also extend their concept of democracy and power to children. As Kitzinger argues (1988, p. 83):

4 'Child abuse' and men's violence

JEFF HEARN

I have previously argued, sometimes tenaciously, that an important challenge facing men is for us to become more involved in the care of children (for example, Hearn, 1983). I have seen and still see men's avoidance of both care of and work for children – childwork – as one of the major roots of men's oppression of women, and indirectly of men ourselves, within patriarchy. In this chapter I shall try to look at some of the problems of pursuing this line of argument, particularly in relation to child abuse. While increasing the involvement of men in childwork might seem one way of reducing the quantity of such work done by women, that alone fails to deal fully with the complexities of gender and power in the domain of child care.

This is so for three main reasons. First, to speak of childwork primarily in terms of quantity – a supposedly finite quantity of (good enough?) work and care – may be to neglect the importance of structural relations between women and men in such institutions as fatherhood, marriage, the professions, state laws, and so on. Childwork in any society does not exist just as some fixed or given amount of social activity, to be distributed and redistributed to different locations and agents; instead, it exists in and is partly formed by structural relations, especially between women and men. Secondly, and more directly, childwork is, like all reproductive work and people work, fundamentally qualitative in character (Hearn, 1987): 'it's not (just) what you do, it's the way that you do it.' Thirdly, and most immediately, there is the specific problem of men's physical and sexual abuse of children. To put this last point more bluntly, any increase in men's involvement with children and their care has to be weighed against the potential increase in men's abuse of and violence to children. While men's physical and sexual abuse of children certainly has a long history, there is the possibility that the recent upsurge in recognition of this abuse may partly follow from some men's greater access to children and more active engagement in the private sphere than a generation ago.

Even so, child abuse is still generally seen as an exceptional problem – one that is worthy of the status of scandal, in perpetration, professional negligence, misdiagnosis, or interference into the personal privacy of adults. In a variety of discourses, of the media, of clinical medicine, of law, as well as in the politics of 'dangerousness', child abuse is seen as necessarily individual, localized, and particular; indeed it is reified. Uproar at the 'scandal', discussions of the 'clinical case', and inquiries into the 'legal case' fit easily together and alongside explanations of 'misconduct' of professionals and/or adult 'client' that derive from administrative, inter-professional, or inter-organizational error. Individual pathology of the worker and/or the abuser may be seen to be realized through procedural misjudgments in particular cases. A focus on individual pathology, such as 'dangerousness', even latent dangerousness, and a focus on organizational pathology are not just easily reconciled, but assist in diverting attention from broader questions, such as *why* such violence occurs. This is clearly seen in the way that recent reports on the child murders of Kimberley Carlile (London Borough of Greenwich, 1987) and Tyra Henry (London Borough of Lambeth, 1987) have emphasized the *mistakes* of professionals not the *reasons for the perpetration of violence* in the first place. When reasons are given or implied, they are usually located in individual not social constructions. Even the wide-ranging *Report of the Inquiry into Child Abuse in Cleveland* (Secretary of State for Social Services, 1988) is primarily concerned with administrative and professional interventions and arrangements after abuse has occurred or is suspected rather than with the causes of child abuse.

These observations give a first lead towards a broader perspective, namely that child abuse, or children abuse, or better still the abuse of *young people*, is a matter of violence. Here I focus on one major perspective on that violence – that is, male violence, or more accurately, men's violence. The term 'men's violence' is preferred to that of 'male violence' as it clearly and unambiguously refers to the violence of men, actual and potential. The term 'male violence', although widely used, adds some ambiguity, as it may suggest that this violence is based in or defined by biology – an issue that is a complex debate in itself.

This chapter is concerned with the practical and theoretical implications of seeing 'child abuse' as a matter of *men's violence to babies, children, and young people*. It begins with an outline of some of the questions that follow from this focus on men and men's violence. The next three sections form the central body of the chapter and consider, first, the relevance of theories of men's violence for an understanding of child abuse; second, the association of child sexual abuse and men's violence; and third, the way this perspective highlights the importance of other forms of men's violence, not usually labelled 'child abuse'. The last three sections are concerned with action: first, the practical and professional implications of this analysis; second, the political imperative for men to come out against violence, in its many forms; and, finally, the need for attention to the problem of normal masculinity.

The focus on men and men's violence

It is strange to note that child abuse is often discussed without direct reference to violence, and less still to men's violence, just as 'football hooliganism' or 'police brutality' is commonly discussed with reference to *deviance* rather than to men's violence. To talk of child abuse is to talk in terms of child abus*ers*, young people abusers, men's violence to young people, violent men's violence to young people. Many major texts on child abuse, and even specifically on child sexual abuse, fail to explore questions of men as perpetrators and of men's power in any depth. A typical example is MacFarlane, Waterman *et al.*'s (1986) recently published *Sexual Abuse of Young Children*. This is a mine of relevant information on the social, psychological, developmental, medical, and other aspects of child sexual abuse, and notes that '[t]he large majority of sexual perpetrators appear to be male' (p. 9); but beyond that, and a short discussion of father psychodynamics and the father's place in the 'incestuous family' (sic), it fails to explore men and masculinity.

And yet some might say that the construction of 'child abuse' as men's violence is unwarranted, because some figures indicate that men and women are involved in physical abuse and neglect in approximately equal numbers (Creighton, 1987). There are at least three problems with this view (also see Chapter 3 in this volume). First, this contrast between women and men does not hold for sexual abuse, where heterosexual men are overwhelmingly the main perpetrators. A second set of questions surrounds the fact that present levels of men's violence are enacted despite the fact that men spend far less time with children, are relatively rarely the 'primary carer', and are more rarely still the sole 'primary carer'. A third set of issues surrounds the ways in which the official identifications and prosecutions of 'child abuse' are inseparable from questions of gender, and so are themselves gendered (Hearn, 1988; Kelly, 1988).

To recognize the association of 'child abuse' and men's violence immediately directs attention to a series of questions that
are not usually to the fore. Some of these questions have already
been well explored in feminist analyses, such as the relevance of
the gender division of labour, the separation and interrelation of
the public and private domains, differential forms of violence to
girls and boys, the undervaluing of women and of children each
by association with the other, lack of day care provision, and so
on. However, by focusing specifically on men and men's violence in 'child abuse', a number of further issues are highlighted:
the place of violence within 'normal' forms of masculinity, the
enduring significance of the power of the father, the relationship between men in private (for example, fathers) and men
in public (for example, police, lawyers, medics), and so on.

For example, the development of an ideology of 'dangerousness' (Parton and Parton, 1989) and 'dangerous families',
whereby a clear demarcation is made between the 'dangerous'
and 'non-dangerous', draws on and feeds into many other bifur-
cations, including ethnic, class, and gender divisions. In the gender case, the 'dangerousness' of the 'neglecting mother'/'whore'
may be contrasted with the 'purity' of the 'good mother'/'an-
gel' (cf. Chodorow and Contratto, 1982); the 'dangerousness'
of 'other men' – as 'monsters', 'villains', 'animals' – may be
contrasted with the 'purity' of 'us' – as 'ordinary persons'; the
'dangerousness' of 'rough' working-class men can be opposed
to the 'respectability' of other men; or the 'dangerousness' of
(certain) objectified black men can be opposed to the 'safety'
of (most) subjectified white men (see Chapter 6 in this volume).
The bifurcation of danger/non-danger in men parallels men's
assumed 'two natures', the animal and the social, discussed by
Mary O'Brien (1981) and others. These are the ingredients
(or symptoms) of some classic cases of men's projection and
externalization of our own violence. Indeed there is a developing
space here for bringing together a number of critical theories,
such as theories of alienation, object relations theory, and
the feminist and post-structuralist critiques of binary oppo-
sitions in language and elsewhere. The dangerousness thesis,
in focusing on the dangerous minority, is directly antagonistic
to radical feminist and similar perspectives on the entrenched
and structural nature, even universality, of men's violence.

Such a critical view of 'dangerousness' needs to be understood
alongside the social composition of those who perpetrate the
concept of 'dangerousness'. The first thing is that the official experts of 'dangerousness' happen to be virtually all men
– Louis Blom-Cooper (chair of the Jasmine Beckford and
Kimberley Carlile inquiries), Cyril Greenland (the influential

expert witness at the Beckford inquiry), Peter Dale and the other three authors of the Rochdale NSPCC team publication *Dangerous Families* (Dale *et al.*, 1986), the DHSS Inspectorate (Social Services Inspectorate, 1986). Professional interventions in and around 'child abuse' are structured in terms of gender. Usually this involves on the one hand predominantly female social work, nursing, and educational staffs, and on the other more powerful and predominantly male police, legal, and medical staffs, and senior social work, nursing, and educational managements. Is it purely chance that the key figures at the centre of the Cleveland controversy are two women, paediatrician Dr Marietta Higgs and social worker Mrs Sue Richardson? They in turn are surrounded by willing male advice-givers – other medics, the police, politics, law, and government – an impressive and overlapping collection of male bastions (Hearn, 1982). The analogy of the 'witchhunt' of women workers used recently by a male-dominated press, politics, and professions seems particularly appropriate (Levidov, 1987; Nava, 1988). A similarly gendered pattern was observable in the inquiries into the deaths of Maria Colwell and Jasmine Beckford, with women social workers on the ground seen as failing to prevent men's violence to girls, so receiving the blame of male experts, not on the ground. In this context, the health minister's appointment of the (now Lord) Mrs Justice Butler-Sloss, sister of the then Lord Chancellor, Lord Havers, to head the Cleveland inquiry is all the more interesting.

More subtle, yet definite, ideological movements have occurred in recent years around the professional treatment of abusers or potential abusers. Prescriptions in the early 1970s for a 'nurturing model', with the goal of 'a transference of mothering', as advocated by the Denver House NSPCC Special Unit in London (see Baher *et al.*, 1976), have been superseded in the late 1970s by prescriptions for a 'responsibility model', as advocated by the Rochdale NSPCC Child Protection Team. This latter approach can be characterized as an attempt to work to the goal of 'a transference of fathering', whereby adults, usually parents, are provided not with direct nurture *by* social workers but with the *context* to take responsibility for their own actions, change those actions if possible, and suffer the consequences if not. The family context set by the individual, distanced father of private patriarchy is replaced by a context set by distanced social workers, police, and other state workers of public patriarchy. Child abuse cases bring responses from a succession of social services departments and other state and para-state organizations which, structurally if not individually, may be seen as new forms of patriarchal family.

The professional concept of 'dangerousness', the threat of the 'transference of fathering', and the child protection strategy in child abuse fit easily within the developing form of *public* patriarchy, in which the rights and duties of individual fathers under private patriarchy are appropriated by the state as the collective father (Burstyn, 1983). The historical development of public patriarchy is a profoundly contradictory political process: it represents a structural means of both increasing men's power over and oppression of women and children, *and* decreasing certain men's power, especially in private. This includes the overriding of the power of the private father by the state and para-state agencies, and the establishment of potential means of controlling men's private violence, in incest, rape, and domestic violence. In this historical process, 'children' become (potential) subjects, yet are spoken for, even denied a voice by more powerful professionals (Hearn, 1988). Some men 'police' not only women and young people, but also other men (see Chapter 7 in this volume). Accordingly the concept of 'dangerousness', set within the context of public patriarchy, especially state power, is itself profoundly contradictory. The discourse of 'dangerousness' may be a means of increasing some men's power and decreasing that of other men. It may be developed from what are usually opposed positions, just as certain sections of both the New Right and radical feminism in the United States and elsewhere have used (patriarchal) law to oppose pornography.

Theories of men's violence

This focus on men and men's violence moves us to the question of how theories of men's violence might help to understand and explain men's 'child abuse'. Some theories have attempted to explain men's violence in terms of biology, innate physical and/or psychological aggression. This is a happy hunting ground for sociobiology, functionalism, and psychological essentialism, and as such is open to criticism for neglecting questions of power, cultural and historical relativity, and morality. While there are difficulties in drawing exact parallels between violence to women and violence to young people (Schechter, 1982), general theoretical work on men's violence can assist the explanation of men's violence within 'child abuse'. In his survey of practical and theoretical responses to 'wife abuse', Gondolf (1985) identifies, drawing on the work of Gelles (1983) and Bagarozzi and Giddings (1983), three major theoretical explanations: 'psychoanalytic themes [that] focus on stress, anxiety and anger instilled during child rearing . . . ; social learning theories

[that] consider the abuse to be an outgrowth of learned patterns of aggressive communication to which both husband and wife contribute . . . ; sociopolitical theories [that] hold the patriarchal power plays of men oppressing women to be at the heart of wife abuse'. For writers such as Brownmiller (1975) and Dworkin (1982) men's violence, especially in the forms of rape and pornography respectively, lies at the very heart of patriarchy and its perpetration. While such universalist arguments, whether couched in sociological or social terms, are the subject of great debate, radical feminist ideas of this kind represent the most profound and solid challenge to men and our (that is men's) power/violence. They go far beyond the insights of psychoanalytic and learning theory. Individual acts of men's violence, including assaults, rape, incest, murder, and so on, are instances and evidence of men's structural power as a class over women.

All of these various theories are of interest in trying to understand men's violence to young people. Not only do they suggest several different levels of explanation of men's violence, focusing on individual men's upbringing, on the 'family system', on men ourselves, but they also vary in their position vis-à-vis patriarchy. They may be critical of patriarchy, or directly or indirectly supportive of patriarchy. Furthermore, while different kinds of explanations are distinct, they are not always mutually exclusive.

Let us consider the sociopolitical critiques and the psychoanalytic theories and then their interrelationship, a little more closely. According to anti-patriarchal critiques, men's violence is a general means of maintaining and reinforcing power that is available to men. Carlson (1979), in her discussion of violence to women, says:

> Part of [the] tradition [of the family home] has the husband and father as absolute ruler. Out of generosity he may give some of his power away. He may help with the dishes or help with the kids. But it is understood he doesn't have to do it; it is 'helping': it is a gift. His work is to maintain his version of a proper family. His wife and children must be trained to his standards of decorum. If he feels the need to use physical force to maintain the version, he has had considerable social support.

In this context, men's violence to young people is a development of dominant–submissive power relations that exist in 'normal' family life. These power relations include the tension and stress, the psychological violence, that comes in the anticipation of the arrival home of the 'absent' father, with its own tension, stress, and potential violence. Men may resort to violence when men's power and privilege are challenged, and other strategies have failed. Such violent actions may be available as part of men's repertoire at all times but are most used at times of particular threat, such as the physical and emotional demands of babies and young children, or the resistance to authority of teenagers. Furthermore, men's violence to young people may itself develop in association with feelings of threat when women do not do what men expect, in terms of child care, housework, paid work, sexuality, and so on. Frustration and anger at possible or potential loss of power in one sphere may be acted upon in another sphere or relationship, where there may be less resistance.

This structural perspective on the 'normality' of men's violence within masculinity and men's domestic power within patriarchy is not necessarily at odds with psychoanalytic accounts of men's violence. The fact that there are violent men is not the product of psychological traits – all men can be violent. However, it is certain men who do violence to young people, and it is possible that these men, like other men, can be assessed and understood psychodynamically. This still leaves the question of the place of violence, both in general and to young people, within the psychodynamics of men who are not currently physically violent, and within what is seen as 'normal masculinity', a point developed further at the end of this chapter.

That said, psychoanalytic theories, both feminist and non-feminist, have connected men's 'overmothering' (and 'under-fathering') as infants and boys with the development of excessive dependence on their mothers, and subsequently other women. One argument is that a process of 'more emphatic' individuation of boys takes place, initially from the mother and later from others. This entails the defensive establishment of ego boundaries as an overlay on fundamental emotional insecurity (for example, Chodorow, 1978). In turn, these defences may develop to become forms of compensatory hypermasculinity, forms of violence when women cannot or do not satisfy men's dependency needs, and misogyny itself. Although such accounts are couched largely in terms of the connections between the initial mother–son relationship and the subsequent husband–wife relationship, these arguments may be extended to men's violence to young people. For example, men's overdependence on sisters as boys might be transferred to hostility to daughters or to other girls. Alternatively, men's compensatory hypermasculinity may be enacted by fathers upon sons, especially when fathers experience again the pain of their own boyhood, through the restimulation of living with sons who are not hypermasculine.

More simply, and this is where sociopolitical and psychoanalytic explanations can meet, men may lash out when threatened in terms of material power and/or rigid ego boundaries.

While certain types of psychoanalytic thinking, such as strict Freudianism, can be antipathetic to sociopolitical critiques of patriarchy, psychoanalysis is not, of itself, for or against patriarchy. Indeed, feminist and anti-patriarchal psychoanalytic thinking has emphasized the way in which patriarchy is reproduced at the psychodynamic as well as the social level. The practical and political implications of seeing men's violence as both psychodynamic and social in character are returned to at the end of this chapter.

Child sexual abuse as men's violence

In addition to the theoretical positions outlined above, it is necessary and important to confront the issue of men's sexual abuse of young people specifically in terms of men's violence. The relation of physical and sexual abuse is clearly complex. While some actual cases of men's physical abuse may not appear to be sexual in nature and some actual cases of men's sexual abuse may not appear to be violent in nature, in reality the connections are numerous. Whereas physical abuse is not necessarily sexual abuse, sexual abuse, other than psychological sexual abuse, is also physical abuse. Exhibitionism and flashing invade the young person's physical and visual space, and thus are also physical abuse. Men's sexual abuse is both part of the broad practice of physical abuse, and a special and specific practice with its own extra complications of power. Thus all of the general arguments of the previous section on the explanation of men's violence can be applied to men's sexual abuse, but there are also some additional ways in which the explanation of men's sexual abuse may be seen in terms of men's violence.

First, sexual abuse may involve or occur in association with explicit physical violence that may appear to some people as non-sexual in nature.

Secondly, physical abuse itself, which may appear to some people as non-sexual in nature, may be sexual in the eyes and minds of the man/men. Indeed, one major problem is the way in which violence has often taken on sexual meaning for men. Dominance, including violence, has become eroticized for most men and some women (Mackinnon, 1983; also see Macleod and Saraga, 1988). I refer here not just to what is usually labelled 'sexual violence', but to the more general association of violence and sexuality for men. Indeed, Liz Kelly has argued for the use of the general term 'sexual violence' 'to cover all forms of abuse, coercion and force that women experience from men' (1987, p. 59). According to Andrea Dworkin (1987), sexual intercourse may be understood as the cumulative reduction and annihilation of women – the practice of men wishing to kill women (also see Cameron and Fraser, 1987).

Thirdly, sexual abuse is itself violence. This is most obviously so in (father–daughter) rape; it applies both in the use of overt force – assault, slapping, beating, pushing, and bodily invasion – and in the more subtle use of caress within an empowered (that is, acting within power relations) and abusing relationship. Caress can be just as much a form of violence as more overt force: it can be a means of manipulation; an unwanted intrusion; a sign of power; an additional encroachment on and domination of parts of the body, most obviously genitals, that are, in this society at least, associated with personal/sexual privacy and extra-personal/sexual power.

To see caress as possible violence may sound 'unfair' to some (men). I do not think so. Although there are occasionally some fine lines between ambiguities around different forms of touch, comfort, caress, cuddle, hugging, interference, and sexual abuse, I think we men usually know when we are or could be selflessly loving, taking advantage, or exerting power in touch. Such culturally specific 'knowledge' of particular men is likely, however, to neglect the full weight of power relations between men, women, and young people, especially in the family. For this reason, I think it is unlikely, and probably impossible, for men to touch young people in a completely non-dominant, and thus potentially non-abusing way, unless the whole relationship is itself without dominance. To put this another way, men living and acting within dominating, hierarchical relationships with young people may touch them with what is felt to be 'selflessness' and 'love', yet at the same time some touching may be (received as) an exertion of power, even as abuse. This applies as much to men's relationships with boys as to those with girls. Indeed, while girls are more likely than boys to be sexually violated by men, it is becoming clear that men's sexual violation of boys is far higher than previously supposed (Waterman, Lusk, 1986). This last point is in line with recent research on the high level of men's sexual violence to each other as adults. Men's sexual violence to other men, especially in the (relative) absence of women (Wooden and Parker, 1982), may be understood as a transfer of 'family relationships' from girls and women to men, or as part of general forms of violence between men. Both processes of dominance may be characteristic of patriarchy.

This brings us on to the significance of the ideology of family 'love' within the complex relationship of men's sexual abuse and men's violence. 'Within the family ... rape is possible and other violence is not uncommon, alongside references to "love", attempts to acquire "affection", and in contradiction with searches for intimacy' (Hearn, 1987, p. 91). In this arena, men's power, men's violence, and men's sexuality are all in intimate connection, most clearly so in father–daughter rape (or man–young woman rape). What is at issue here is the way men's power/violence/sexuality persists in a form whereby the Other, be it Woman, Child, Young Person, Girl, Boy, even the Non-Sexual Object or Non-Sexual Situation, as in the Organizational (Hearn and Parkin, 1987), can be reappropriated as material for sexual domination. This process of power involves the mystification of love, particularly paternal 'love', the assumption of 'desire' for others, including young people, as 'primordial' (Mackinnon, 1982), as well as real feelings of reciprocity and mutuality.

From 'child abuse' to men's violence to young people

Debates on the possible *causes* of men's violence are an important and necessary part of the continuing struggle to end men's violence. Although these debates usually attempt to encompass psychological and emotional violence, as well as directly physical, interpersonal violence, they tend to focus on the hit or the blow within the domestic setting as their paradigm case for attention and analysis. Such direct, physical violence is tragic and painful enough, but it is by no means the whole story in considering men's violence to young people. There are several reasons for this.

First, and paradoxically, you do not have to be directly violent to be violent. Actions performed following violence may be construed as violently intimidating or may be responded to as such to avoid further violence.

Secondly, living in a society and culture where men's violence is naturalized and normalized means that the threat and the fear of men's potential violence may be real to young people, even when a particular man has not been violent or patently does not appear violent at the time. To put this a slightly different way, some of the main measures of power and strength in this society are still *size, strength, bodily facility*, and *age*, so that the mere sight of a large, strong, muscular man be perceived as (potentially) violent. Even Father Christmas, the great benefactor in the sky, is not a man whom the very young would feel safe about playing up (and is indeed in some cultures quite a malevolent figure).

Thirdly, men's violence can be indirect but just as lethal: A may be told by B to hit C. After all, there is the past violence that produced the violence in present-day men (like the violence that produced the first property). This is a disturbing insight, for it means that much general, 'normal' 'child rearing' can be understood as indirectly contributing to subsequent violence. Boys may be encouraged to hit other boys, even if they are not hit themselves. In order to make 'boys', it is usual to make clear that violence is part of the social worlds of boys and men; in order to make 'girls', it is usual to make it clear that they are not part of those worlds. Thus, in addition to direct violence, the imposition of expectations that boys will be violent and girls will be non-violent is a form of violence to those young people. To socially create 'masculinity' in 'boys' and 'femininity' in 'girls' frequently involves doing violence to that person in terms of the coercive overriding of them in almost every way – toys, tastes, clothes, language, moods. At what point does the removal of all the options, other than becoming a 'masculine' 'boy' or a 'feminine' 'girl' become (or cease to become) violence? In the Netherlands, 'family socialisation processes typified by extreme, sexist views which, in turn, constrain a female child's life experience and opportunities' are becoming recognized as cognitive abuse (Findlay, 1987–8, p. 380).

Fourthly, a major form of men's violence to young people that is not usually counted as violence is the wholesale removal of the body from one place to another, without consent. The forcible placing of the bodies of young people, in the name of manners, morals, and social order – in the home, bedroom, homes, care, school, classes, chairs – is so normal and widespread that it disrupts dominant conceptions of violence to young people.

A final point that is closely related to several of those above is that of the violence that may exist within structured social relations. Whether particular actions are violent or non-violent, they occur within social relations, that may themselves be violent or historically have depended on violence for their development. For example, the social relations of paternity, of domestic economy, and of state formation are historically meaningless without a consideration of violence. Men may not be violent to young people but may still act within social relations based on violence.

What these complications do is to reconstruct the problem of 'child abuse'. The question is not so much what are the wider social causes that account for 'child abuse' as currently defined, but how does the perspective of men's violence on 'child abuse' broaden the understanding of the abuse of children to actions, situations, and structures that are usually defined as not abusive. Let us now look a little more closely at some specific examples of this broadened view of child abuse and men's violence to young people.

To begin with a difficult question – is abortion an example of men's violence to young people? Well, if it is enforced or performed by men without the full consent of the woman, it is primarily violence to women, but also to the (potential) baby whose consent must be part of the woman's. Likewise, experimentation in the field of reproductive and genetic engineering where eggs and foetuses are removed, worked on, cut up, without full consent is violence to women, and also to (potential) babies (Arditti *et al.*, 1984; Corea *et al.*, 1985).

More difficult still is the question of the link between men's violence in heterosexual intercourse and 'child abuse'. The revolutionary feminist claim that male heterosexual 'penetration' is an assault on women may be contested, but it does raise the possibility of seeing such intercourse as simultaneously violence to women and abuse of the potential child. This position is reinforced in rape and more generally where intercourse takes place in the context of men's violence. The connections with 'child abuse' are three-fold: first, there is the nature of violence at intercourse, most obviously in rape; second, there is the association of that violence with the production of (potential) babies, and the impact upon their development, at least *by way of the body and experience of the woman* and perhaps in their own right; third, there is the experience of the child born and eventually of the adult. These points may seem somewhat metaphysical – but they are surely as material as our own brains and bodies. To some people it may be of no interest how they were conceived; to others, conception in rape, violent circumstances, or heterosexual intercourse is of utmost importance, and may incorporate experiences and senses of abuse and violence for many years after.

In addition, violence to pregnant women is violence to both woman and the (potential) baby. According to Martin (1977, p. 14) a quarter of all victims of domestic violence are pregnant women. Thus women who are pregnant are far more likely to suffer violence than women who are not. Cases of assault on pregnant women may lead to charges of child destruction under the 1929 Infant Life Protection Act (*Guardian*, 22 September 1987; Kane, 1987).

The history of men's violence at and around birth is horrific indeed (Shorter, 1982). Continuing the arguments above, this is violence to both women and babies. While many of the most grotesque practices are now discontinued in this society, the unwarranted use of surgery, instruments, induction, drugs, and other technologies can all be forms of coercive, and thus violent, control of the body, even though they may also save lives on certain occasions. The strength of controversy around 'natural' childbirth and attempts by Wendy Savage and others to increase women's control of their own bodies, including their babies, is well known, and speaks to some men's determination to retain control in this sphere.

After birth there are a number of sites where men's violence may impact upon young people in ways that usually might not be considered 'child abuse'. These include the home, the employment market, the school, sport, and the battlefield. It has already been noted how fatherhood as a social institution and a social relation has a history of violence. The social and historical meaning of fatherhood includes the treatment of children as possessions, appropriated from the mother: human property as human theft! What this means is that even a man who is a 'nice' father carries with him the possibility of becoming a 'nasty' or violent one. This is especially important for those men who themselves had violent fathers. Although the strict discipline of the Victorian father may have been superseded, paternal authority is still routinely oppressive in the placing and arrangement of young people in time and space, if necessarily forcibly, for example at bedtimes. This takes many forms. The routine avoidance, denigration, insulting, ignoring, and putting down of young people by fathers, which is seen as a legitimate part of being a father, accumulates to 'child abuse'. In an age of relatively high separation and divorce, the direct and indirect exertion of paternal authority in the regulation of care, custody, and access to young people may constitute new forms of 'child abuse'. Some of the most oppressive forms of access and custody have developed as a result of mothers being deemed unfit on the grounds of their lesbianism (Harne, 1984; Rights of Women, 1984). Enforcement of paternal access, as well as a variety of disruptive informal tactics, can be extremely abusive to young people. Indeed, while the 1984 Matrimonial and Family Proceedings laws reduce men's economic responsibilities after divorce, the Family Reform Act, 1987, extends the 'rights' of the father outside marriage. One of the most extreme consequences of paternal *authority* for young people, especially girls, is incest.

While father–daughter sexual intercourse itself may be relatively rare, it is not unusual for children to live in a pornographic environment, where images of Page Three and pornographic videos are freely available. In many corner shops and front rooms, this is normality. As Katherine Whitehorn (1987) recently remarked: 'Certainly the society that screens "Pretty Baby" oughtn't to be astonished that girls further and further down the age range seem fair game.' Child prostitution and the use of children in the making of pornography (Ennew, 1986) are less usual forms of men's violence to young people that certainly should be included more centrally within the 'child abuse' arena. These involve both sexual exploitation and the exploitation of labour.

Other exploited labour by young people, which may or may not be underwritten by violence, includes that done as paid employees, as unpaid carers, as participants in criminal activities, such as drug trafficking. More broadly, child labour, like labour in general that is socially necessary, is generally exploited and set within exploitative relations.

It has already been noted how much of men's violence to young people is indirect and that this applies in different ways to boys and girls. The indirect facilitation of boys' violence and indirect restriction of girls' violence take place both in the home and in the public domain, through the arrays of socializing influences, including parents, peers, television, school and so on. 'Normal' patterns of male socialization, whereby boys are brought up to be violent to other boys, are in effect an indirect form of 'child abuse'. This may take place in the home or on the street, but it also persists in more institutionalized forms in a variety of violent and contact sports. The question of 'sports injuries', especially in boxing and rugby (itself often another euphemism for men's or boys' violence), is receiving much increased attention, and is now the subject of debate and controversy between official educational and sporting bodies.

Teacher authority in schools is the routine means in the public domain of arranging, allocating, and placing the bodies of young people in classes, lines, spaces. Until August 1987 this 'educational' authority was reinforced in Britain by the *legal* use of corporal punishment. Britain was the last European country to abolish this legal use of violence in state schools (Hearn, 1985). However, even in July 1987, Judge Hodern in the Knightsbridge Crown Court dismissed a charge against the headmaster of Friern Barnet Grammar School, a North London private school, of causing actual bodily harm. He had beaten a 13-year-old young man for not getting 55 per cent in his exams. Judge Hodern pronounced: 'If one has the misfortune to be caned, one expects to be hit rather hard. That's the point of it' ('Reasonable punishment?', 1987).

This survey of men's violence to young people has already been wide-ranging, but seen in the world context the problem takes on vast new dimensions. The Minority Rights Group report on Children (Boyden and Hudson, 1985) analyses the maltreatment of children in terms of not only 'child abuse and neglect' and 'sexual exploitation', but also 'collective maltreatment: poverty' and 'collective maltreatment: politics'. The basic issue of economic poverty accounts for infant mortality rates that are ten to twenty times higher in the poorer as against the richer societies (UNICEF, 1987). The UN Declaration of the Rights of the Child includes 'the right to adequate nutrition and medical care'. Absence of these may often lead to relatively slow abuse of disease, ill-health, and death; it is often in these same societies that cheap child labour is extensively used. And while there are difficulties of cultural relativism in the detailed analyses of this labour, the massiveness of the problem remains. For example, the International Labour Organization (Blanchard, 1983) estimates that 52 million under the age of 15 are 'economically active'; Bouhdiba (1982) estimates a figure of 152 million for the 10–14 age group alone, taking particular account of the importance of domestic service, in his report to the United Nations. In particular, there is the full range of 'child exploitation': in dangerous work, in bonded labour, in unpaid service and slavery, in child prostitution and pornography, in the selling and trafficking of babies and young people. Such inequalities, neglects, and violent effects are typically underwritten by men's power and men's violence, locally, in families and communities, nationally, in state militaries, and internationally, in world patriarchal and capitalist relations.

Economic poverty is not simply a result of a lack of production or productive efficiency. It arises from expenditure on arms and the international interplay of the patriarchal military systems and the patriarchal capitalist systems, both of which may be institutional forms of racism. Thus the links between poverty, international politics, and international relations of violence are intense. The involvement of young people, usually as survivors and victims, less often as perpetrators, in political conflicts and political violence, in militarism, war, and terrorism, is widespread and tragic. Young people receive the violence of warfare, massacre, arrest, political imprisonment, torture, and execution. Despite the international law prohibiting active participation in combat under the age of 15, young people have become members of state or counter-state armed forces in Ulster, Azania/South Africa, Lebanon, Kampuchea, Honduras, Nicaragua, Peru, Iran, and elsewhere, in recent years (Grounds, 1987). They have also been used in military intelligence and allegedly as mine detectors (*International Children's Rights Monitor*, 1984). Increasingly wars involve civilian deaths and injuries (80–90 per cent of the total in the Vietnam War) (Boyden and Hudson, 1985, p. 5), and young people are particularly vulnerable during such dangerous times. The state of young people, including their abuse, is heavily dependent on the power of adults, and men's violence to and possession of them.

Further implications: the practical and the professional

There is so much abuse of young people – as violence, threatened and potential violence, and routine ageism – that it is not something that can be 'solved' by professional interventions and professional intervenors. It is a problem of this patriarchal society. Furthermore, what can be done by professional interventions is itself limited by the form and interrelation of agency setting (see Chapter 10 in this volume), and the total resources devoted to this work in state and other agencies.

In fact, having surveyed and reconstructed the problem of child abuse in terms of the violence of men, it is tempting to try and spell out the implications of this analysis for professional interventions, such as social work, with 'male family members'. Posing the question in that way, however, misses a major point. It is not possible to discuss the subject of intervention with men as if that intervention is itself being performed by non-gendered intervenors. The issue of the appropriate form of intervention *with men* as fathers, brothers, lodgers, and so on, is not distinct from the issue of the appropriate form of intervention *by men*, for example, as social workers. To give an extended example, in the commonplace situation of scarce social work resources, a mixed-gender team of social workers may develop a policy of giving priority to the needs of the recipients of violence, in this context the young people. Within such a policy, I certainly see no reason why women social workers should be obliged to divert their resources of time and energy from young people to men as perpetrators of violence, unless that is in the interests of the young person and/or women. In this sense, a decision for a young person permanently to live separately from a violent father may well mean that fewer resources are devoted to work with the man than would be the case if they remained together.

Above all, men should be very cautious in prescribing what women should do in their interventions with violent men – this applies to men managers' supervision of women social workers; men social workers with women social workers; and men social workers with mother, wife, and other female family members. Indeed, in considering the practical implications of this analysis of the pervasiveness of men's violence to young people, a major structural factor facilitating and constraining the action of men workers is the gender division of labour in welfare agencies. The realities and possibilities for men social workers and other intervenors will be very different depending on whether they work in a single-gender all-men agency, in an agency with only one or a few women workers, with a more even gender division of labour between women and men, or with a predominance of women workers. In this way, agency policies that stipulate that sexual abuse cases should involve two workers, of whom *at least* one should be a woman (Hadley, 1987), are positive ways of linking practice with clients and the structural gender divisions of the agency. Furthermore, divisions of hierarchy, authority, and responsibility by gender may also have their own indirect effects on sexual harassment and other power relations. These and other divisions impinge on the gendered construction of 'agency work'.

For men to work effectively against the abuse of young people, and indeed against men's violence more generally, involves more than just developing the 'correct' professional practices with 'clients'. It also involves working against sexism in the agency, including the structure and style of organization, which is often based on putting down and other patterns of psychological violence. It involves assisting in the process of increasing women's power there, and promoting agency aid to women's refuges and similar projects. To lose power in this way – for example, to reduce the number of men in management (Hanmer and Statham, 1988) – is typically difficult and emotionally demanding for men. This is one good reason for men who are concerned to work against sexism in agencies to join or help form a men's group for themselves, either within or outside the agency.

Within social work and similar agencies two main sets of day-to-day activity have an impact on the abuse of young people: interventions in 'child abuse cases'; and preventive and other forms of social work interventions. Both of these may involve men as social workers or men as 'clients', and as such they present dual opportunities and challenges for men. These distinctions occur within the context of the gendered nature of both agency work and client work. While it is possible in the short term that individual men social workers may complete effective client work against violence even within patriarchal agencies, in the longer term this is clearly not enough, and may even lead to the men's further domination of state and other welfare agencies. Other problems include the difficulties of making strict separations between the 'people work' of men social workers and the activity (or work) of men clients; and between men social workers' professional practice and private or familial practice.

With these qualifications in mind, I shall briefly consider men's involvement as social workers in, first, social work other than child abuse cases and, second, specific child abuse cases. All forms of social work intervention that involve working with men or boys provide opportunities for working against sexism and against men's violence, and thus men's potential violence to young people. Social work, like other forms of people work, like youth work and educational work, can be in part preventive work in relation to the abuse of young people, and to sexism more generally. While such preventive work may include marital work, intermediate treatment, assessment centre work, residential work, and so on, the general issues around sexism change little. Men social workers may work with men clients towards the prevention of future or potential violence to young people in a number of ways, which include:

- *recognizing their involvement as men* rather than just as 'worker' and 'client';
- *recognizing their mutual involvement* in the process, which necessitates work on the part of both participants rather than just the 'client', and a reciprocal, not one-way, process of helping;
- *recognizing the need for change in masculinity* in general – in what is seen as 'normal' masculinity, as well as in what is seen as the 'abnormal' or 'aberrant';
- explicitly *working on sexism with men who are in favour of sexism*;
- *working with sympathetic teachers, youth workers, and others* against sexism in schools, youth work, and elsewhere;
- *working on the relationship of sexism and other oppressions*, such as ageism, classism, racism;
- *raising the priority given to day care* and other social services provisions that are likely to enhance women's opportunities;
- *working on their own sexism*, including their practice 'outside work';
- *joining a men's anti-sexist group* or similar initiative either within or outside the agency.

In working with men in specific child abuse cases, all the above points are relevant to practice, but there are some additional possibilities for men social workers (see Wild, 1988). As already noted, the potential for different forms of intervention varies according to the gender structure of the agency in all its facets, including its relationship to the state and state laws, its gender divisions of labour and authority, and its gendered discourses and practices. Furthermore, working with child abuse cases raises many major dilemmas: what priority, if any, should be given to work with men perpetrators, or is that merely diverting resources from work with survivors? What is to be done with men who do not take responsibility for their violence (Herman and Hirschman, 1981), or with men who do and for whom custody is the prime alternative? Should the preferences of the survivors of the family dictate the time and energy devoted to the man perpetrator, or should work be done with the man if only to try to prevent further violence in the future, perhaps in a new family? How are any ambivalences and uncertainties of the survivors, especially towards the man, to be satisfactorily assisted or resolved? It is hard to see how all these and other possibilities are resolvable by a fixed set of agency procedures or policies for all contingencies. That said, positive work may be done by men social workers in ways that include:

- *developing co-work with women workers so that the facility, if not the necessity, exists for men to work with men family members,* and women with women (see Holdsworth, 1987);
- *developing groups for men and/or boys with different kinds of involvement* in child abuse cases, for example, as abusers, abused, or brothers of the abused (see Leith and Handforth, 1988; Leith, 1988);
- *contextualizing, and where necessary resisting, patriarchal authority of other more powerful professionals,* especially medics, police, and lawyers – this may apply where violence is either being ignored or being asserted without warrant, in case conference and similar situations;
- *supporting other workers, women and men,* doing work on child abuse;
- *being clear with men* at different legal stages of abuse cases on their position, legal and otherwise;
- *working on the relationship between men's violence and other oppressions,* such as ageism, classism, racism and sexism;
- *working on their own violence,* including their practice 'outside work';

- *making a priority of ending men's future violence*, alongside working for the best interests of the child;
- *being clearly against violence*.

This division between child abuse cases and other cases is itself open to criticism. As previously discussed, social work and other professional interventions tend to focus on certain kinds of 'child abuse' and not on others. Other kinds of violent acts may be known of but not so fully explored or opposed. Recognition of such actual or potential 'normal violences' might open up ways of assisting women who are not actively seeking to leave such violent men. In working against men's violence it is necessary to recognize short-term strategies that assist in the *avoidance* of violence and situations of potential violence, medium-term strategies that *work against* violence in men and violent, dominant relationships and long-term ones that *challenge* those social institutions and attitudes that produce and reproduce violence (EMERGE, 1986).

The political: coming out against men's violence

In short, we men need to come out against violence, in all its guises, including our own. We need to ask ourselves how we can best reduce and abolish men's violence; we need to listen to women and young people on this. While there are organizations of doctors, psychoanalysts, and social workers against the nuclear threat, I know of no organization of men social workers, or others involved in child abuse intervention, publicly committed to opposing men's violence. In the United States, the National Organization for Changing Men (the national men's pro-feminist alliance) has a task group on 'Ending Male Violence'. For men social workers to create a similar organization around the question of child abuse would be radical indeed. In addition to changing men's practice as social workers and other professional intervenors, we need to change ourselves, to work on our own violence, as a way towards reducing and stopping it. The avenues to this are many, and include the creation of men's anti-sexist groups in social work offices and amongst men social workers and others. In such arenas a safe space can be created to both oppose violence and admit feelings and acts of violence of our own. In this way, working against violence is a central part of working against sexism and against patriarchy, and indeed of developing a pro-feminist commitment among men (Tolman *et al.*, 1986).

The modern women's movement, and the creation of women's refuges, in the case of the United Kingdom particularly by Women's Aid, have done much to bring the question of men's violence to public attention. One indirect result of that has been the growth of men's anti-violence projects. This has been especially so in the United States (e.g. RAVEN and EMERGE), but also now increasingly in Britain (e.g. MOVE – Men Overcoming Violence; Mason, 1986), Germany (e.g. Männer Gegen Männer Gewalt), and elsewhere. These projects typically combine men counselling violent and potentially violent men, with educational and public campaign work against violence. Men who have been violent who join as counsellees may go on to become counsellors. Social workers and professional counsellors have been involved relatively rarely.

A similar kind of approach could be developed by and for men to deal with men's violence to young people. This would involve men who have been violent or fear they may become so, as well as men counsellors, social workers, and others, coming together with the explicit aim of working against such violence. The principles that the existing men's anti-violence projects work on include a commitment against violence, opposing men's controlling attitudes and behaviour, increasing men's responsibility for their actions, and increasing men's self-esteem. The development of men's groups working against violence to young people would be a radically different approach to current alternatives, and perhaps an adjunct to both therapeutic work and legal proceedings. One of the things social workers can do is facilitate such groups, possibly within, though probably outside, agency frameworks, at the same time working on *their own* actual or potential or felt violence. This would be a major change from the limitations of social workers' 'balance' and 'neutrality' (Maynard, 1985).

The problem of normal masculinity

Finally, it is necessary to recognize that part of abolishing men's violence to young people is the transformation of our relationship to each other, including the violence that we do to each other and to ourselves (Hearn, 1987, pp. 97–98). This is not just a matter of violent acts but also, as Kaufman (1987) has explained, concerns 'the very structure of the masculine ego'. He continues (p. 22):

> The formation of an ego on an edifice of surplus repression and surplus aggression is the building of a precarious

structure of internalized violence. The continual conscious and unconscious blocking and denial of passivity and all the emotions and feelings men associate with passivity – fear, pain, sadness, embarrassment – is a denial of part of what we are. The constant psychological and behavioral vigilance against passivity and its derivations is a perpetual act of violence against oneself.

Rather similarly, Frosh (1987b) suggests a contradictory association, within dominant forms of 'masculine sexuality', of the denial, yet sexualization, of the emotions in the case of child sexual abuse. Macleod and Saraga (1988) develop this perspective in terms of the sexualization of rage, particularly rage towards men, the father, and the self, displaced on to and acted out against women and children (p. 42). While these insights are fundamentally psychoanalytic, the construction of men's denials, sexualizations, and rage is also socially structured in nature.

The state of 'normal masculinity' is a personal and a political problem, and one that lies at the base of much child abuse. This persists in the objectification of and hostility towards women that is part of that 'normal masculinity' (Thompson and Pleck, 1987); in the 'normal family values' from which father–daughter incest is derived (Nelson, 1982); in the 'normal' male sexuality, characterized by power, aggression, penis orientation, the separation of sex from loving emotion, objectification, fetishism, and uncontrollability (Coveney *et al.*, 1984, pp. 14–17); and indeed in the entrenched homophobia that most men carry, sometimes proudly. Homophobic relations between men and boys in families may mean that ' . . . violence against other men [in this context, from fathers to sons] is one of the chief ways through which patriarchal society simultaneously expresses and discharges the attraction of men to other men' (Kaufman, 1987, p. 21). Fathers' beating of boys may be in part a 'homoerotic pummelling' over a homosexual subtext (Wood, 1987); fathers' beating of girls may be in part a 'heteroerotic penetration' over a heterosexual subtext. Both exist in the confusion and blurring of sexuality and violence of 'normal masculinity'.

Coming out against our violence is necessarily both a personal process and a structural process; it is equally a matter for practice and theory.

5 Is it social work?

MICHAEL HORNE

The context

This chapter comprises an examination of social work with particular reference to child protection. It asks: what is the nature of the social work role and task?

This question has always been (and probably always will be) the subject of much debate and argument, but it has been brought into sharp focus since the publication in 1985 of the report into the death of Jasmine Beckford. This report (London Borough of Brent, 1985) was the result of the thirty-fifth child abuse inquiry to be held since 1970. Closely following this came two more child abuse inquiry reports into the deaths of Tyra Henry (London Borough of Lambeth, 1987) and Kimberley Carlile (London Borough of Greenwich, 1987). In all these reports the respective social services departments and social workers involved were criticized for not doing enough to protect the children in question.

In 1988, the *Report of the Inquiry into Child Abuse in Cleveland* (Secretary of State for Social Services, 1988) was published; this was an inquiry not into an 'under-reaction' on the part of the child protection services in an individual case, but into an 'over-reaction', for which all the professionals involved were criticized.

This underlying dilemma of social work is well illustrated by the quote below from Mr Justice Hollis:

> The Social Services, of course, always have a thankless task. If they are over-cautious and take children away from their families they are pilloried for doing so. If they do not take such action and do not take a child away from its family, and something terrible happens to the child, then likewise they are pilloried; so it is a very difficult position they find themselves in. (Mr Justice Hollis, quoted in the Cleveland Report, Secretary of State for Social Services, 1988, p. 85)

This chapter will examine the nature of this 'difficult position'.

Whilst the examination below is not in itself intended to be a detailed or comprehensive analysis of recent reports, it draws significantly on the Jasmine Beckford Report and also refers to the Cleveland Report. More than any other report since that into the death of Maria Colwell in 1974 (Secretary of State for Social Services, 1974), the Jasmine Beckford Report stands out for the range of comments and criticisms of social work that it makes, both specifically with respect to child protection and on social work practice in general. Also, the report has had a considerable effect and influence on the policy and practice of child protection social work, not the least in Cleveland. Many of the issues and questions raised in the report are of central interest and concern to any examination of the nature of contemporary social work practice.

The Cleveland Report is obviously very different from previous inquiry reports, being prompted by a contrasting sequence of events. However it too makes a number of comments on what social work is, and should be, which are particularly relevant to an examination of social work, especially when looked at in the context of the Jasmine Beckford Report. Reference to the Jasmine Beckford Report (and to a lesser extent to the Tyra Henry and Kimberley Carlile Reports) is made in a number of places in the Cleveland Report, and in subsequent comments on the report. All of these references indicate the importance of the report in terms of child protection social work, policy, and practice in Cleveland and elsewhere.

For example, referring to 1987, the Cleveland Report states that:

> The public climate had changed ... Proceedings associated with the deaths of Jasmine Beckford, Tyra Henry, and Kimberley Carlile led to public criticism of social workers for failing to act promptly and positively to secure the protection of children. These events had the effect in Cleveland of creating a renewed sense of determination to ensure that if serious risks to children were seen, effective steps would be taken to intervene ... They [social workers] had been reminded by the Beckford report of the importance which social workers should attach to their child protection responsibilities. Social workers and their managers were anxious not to have been seen to fail the children involved by leaving them in situations of risk. (Secretary of State for Social Services, 1988, p. 84)

'Post-Cleveland' comments also point to the importance of the Beckford Report:

I would never have believed this could have happened in Cleveland. We went into Beckford in a lot of detail and set up systems to prevent it happening here. (Mike Bishop, Cleveland Social Services Director in *Social Work Today*, 7 July 1988, p. 12)

I think the climate created by Louis Blom-Cooper's reports [Jasmine Beckford and Kimberley Carlile] and the publicity which surrounded them played a significant part in the events which took place in Cleveland. (John Chant, Social Services Assessor on the Cleveland Inquiry panel in *Social Work Today*, 7 July 1988, p.16)

Events in Cleveland obviously relate specifically to sexual abuse of children, which in many ways is increasingly being recognized as being different from (non-sexual) physical abuse, in terms of both its nature and the issues that it raises (see Chapter 1 in this volume, which discusses some of these issues). However, for the purpose of examining the nature of social work practice against the backcloth of the Jasmine Beckford and Cleveland reports, I will refer to child abuse 'generically' (which includes physical, sexual, and emotional abuse and neglect). This is not to deny the validity of distinguishing between different forms of abuse, but in the context of this discussion I shall be focusing more explicitly on the essential nature of the social work response to child abuse and child protection – the role of the social worker in general.

Certainly, as can be seen in the quotes above, and as is evidenced in recent inquiry reports (especially Jasmine Beckford and Cleveland), the main points of comment on, and criticism of, social work relate to and question what the social work role is or should be. To what extent can the social worker legitimately intervene in the family and in what ways?

Given the importance of the Jasmine Beckford Report, I shall start by briefly examining some of its key comments and criticisms. Following this, I shall offer a description of the nature of social work and relate it specifically to child protection social work and events in Cleveland.

'Beckford' – the questions

Throughout, the report makes it clear that social work can be understood only in relation to its statutory responsibilities – in terms of its statutory charter. 'We are strongly of the view that social work can in fact be defined *only* in terms of the functions required of its practitioners by their employing agency operating within a statutory framework' (London Borough of Brent, 1985, p. 12; original emphasis). Again, on page 152, the report states that: 'We are conscious that social workers do not always take kindly to legal intervention in the practice of social work ... but the law provides the basic framework in which social services must operate.'

As Nigel Parton has commented: 'Rather than the law being simply an important area of knowledge that social workers should be familiar with – along with other areas of knowledge – it is seen as fundamental and providing the social charter for contemporary social work' (Parton, 1986, p. 513).

Within this legal framework, the report describes social work as having a dual mandate, which imposes on social workers a responsibility for both social care and social control – the control part of the mandate being formalized by social work's statutory responsibilities. 'We have been at pains to point out at every twist and turn of this unhappy story, that social workers ... displayed a total lack of understanding of, and indeed lack of commitment to the statutory ingredient in the dual mandate' (London Borough of Brent, 1985, p.206). Related to this, the report also criticizes social workers (specifically with regard to the Jasmine Beckford case as well as generally) for their failure to exercise 'authority' – specifically by not using the powers conferred by the Care Orders on Jasmine and Louise Beckford, which provokes an attack on the whole profession for its 'negation of any authoritarian role in the enforcement of Care Orders' (London Borough of Brent, 1985, p. 294).

A major theme of the report, which is evident from the comments and quotes above, is that social workers fail to understand their statutory responsibilities, and because of this they fail to appreciate their role and functions as social workers. With respect to Jasmine, the report states that, 'Jasmine thus became the victim of persistent disfunctioning social work while the law demanded, above all, her protection' (London Borough of Brent, 1985, p. 127).

The Jasmine Beckford Report's conception of social work and of the role and function of social workers obviously raises many important questions, perhaps the most fundamental of which is, does the report accurately or sufficiently describe the nature of social work practice, or is there more to it; is it a more complex enterprise than simply executing the relevant legislation? (The Cleveland Report offers an interesting and important perspective on this question, which I will come to later.)

Dingwall, Eekelaar, and Murray (1983, p. 148) have argued that the reality of the role of social work is much more complex than is acknowledged in the Jasmine Beckford Report.

> Doctors, health visitors and social workers are not law enforcement officers permanently and selectively attuned to discovering breaches of statute. They are better characterised as problem solving agents for whom the law exists as one possible resource for dealing with social troubles.

Parton (1986) and Corby (1987b) have also commented with respect to the report that, particularly in the area of child care, the law itself is somewhat ambiguous and open to varying interpretations and applications, so it does not provide the social worker with a clear-cut 'mandate' for intervention as characterized within the report.

However, before going on to examine these issues in more detail, there is another aspect of the Jasmine Beckford report that is highly pertinent to an examination of the nature and role of social work and that, in a sense, is the 'flipside' of the criticisms of social work's lack of understanding of its statutory responsibilities.

The report's emphasis on the law is primarily concerned with social workers' attitudes towards and their professional relationships with their clients, particularly regarding their work with children and families. The report criticizes social workers for allowing themselves (partly through a lack of adequate supervision) to become 'emotionally involved' and thereby lose objectivity and to adopt an attitude infused with what the report refers to as the 'rule of optimism'.

Basically the 'rule of optimism' means that 'the most favourable interpretation is always put upon the behaviour of the parents and that anything that may question this is discounted or redefined' (Parton, 1986, p. 516). The 'rule of optimism' was seen by the report to be evident throughout the case of Jasmine Beckford in that the social workers involved 'always' put the most favourable interpretation on events, particularly with regard to the parents of Jasmine. Consequently the social worker was 'fobbed off with implausible excuses on almost every occasion of her visiting the house about the whereabouts of Jasmine' (London Borough of Brent, 1985, p. 85). In the same vein, 'as soon as the social workers thought they saw the first signs of improved conduct on the part of Morris Beckford and Beverley Lorrington, an overwhelming optimism took hold' (London Borough of Brent, 1985, p. 127).

The report also extends this criticism beyond the Jasmine Beckford case, arguing that the rule of optimism and a failure to focus on the child is not uncommon in social work.

> We fear that their attitude in regarding the parents of children in care as the clients, rather than the children in their own right, may be widespread among social workers ... We have listened to a number of social workers and expert witnesses, and in each case have detected this attitude which is the negation of any authoritarian role in the enforcement of Care Orders (London Borough of Brent, 1985, p. 294).

While this description of the Jasmine Beckford Report is brief and selective, it does indicate the general focus of its comments, criticisms, and pronouncements, both specific to the case in question and in a general sense.

Below I will show that the report fails to understand and take account of the full nature and process of the social work task – that it misunderstands and misrepresents the nature of the relationship between social workers and their clients. This is true of the complexities of child protection work in particular, and of social work in general.

Whilst I will argue (as the report does) that contemporary social work exists within a framework of law and what social workers do is determined by agency function (see Howe, 1979, 1986; Davies, 1981; and Horne, 1987), how social workers operate within this framework of law/agency function is not understood by the report. The special nature of the relationship between social worker and client, which identifies social work as a distinct activity in its own right, makes it more than law enforcement, which, too simplistically, the report appears to be suggesting is all that social work is, or should be. Social work is essentially more complex than the report recognizes.

So what, then, is the 'essential' nature of social work? What is special to the nature of the relationship between social worker and client that the Jasmine Beckford Report ignores?

What is social work?

This question is usually asked to try to identify what is, or is not, 'good professional practice' in the context of the relationship between the social worker and client. However, framed in such a way the question is fundamentally flawed, as it ignores the important relationship between the social worker and 'society'. Particularly in the context of contemporary social work, the vast majority of which takes place under the auspices of local authority social services departments, it is essential to consider and understand this relationship between social worker and society in order to understand the nature of the relationship between the social worker and the client.

> Never simply is it a matter between a social worker and the client . . . what social workers do, and who they do it with are socially determined matters. Social work might, therefore, be seen as an activity carried out under social auspices. (Howe, 1979, p. 33)

David Howe argues that the 'social' in social work is best understood in the context of it referring to the socially sanctioned nature of social work. Society sanctions certain of its members (social workers) to take an interest in and intervene in the behaviour and conditions of certain other of its members. This interest and intervention may take place because of a request from other individuals or perhaps because of statutory demands, for example, child care law with respect to suspected or actual child abuse.

Relating very closely to this description of social work is the concept of agency function (referred to in the Jasmine Beckford Report), which originated in the writings of the functionalist school of social work. This concept attempts to describe the nature of the relationship between the individual (client), social worker, and society.

Agency function represents and focuses what it is that social workers are expected to do, and to/with whom they do it. Within this framework their tasks may be clearly defined by statutory responsibilities (for example, child care work) or be more generally defined by or through societal norms and expectations about how and to what extent certain groups, for example elderly or disabled people, should be cared for.

> Social work ceases to be such when it fails to reflect the norms of the society it serves. (Fowler, 1975, p. 91)

> . . . notwithstanding the welfare practitioners' desire for professional autonomy, the welfare professions are rooted in the values of a wider society . . . (Nokes, 1967, p. 111)

These two quotes, which support the description of social work above, are interesting and important to the discussion here, as they clearly indicate that what social workers do, and who they do it with, are determined by the 'norms of the society' in which they work, and that these are inextricably linked to the 'values of wider society'. However, as will become clear below, this does not mean that these norms and values are necessarily straightforwardly translated into social work practice. With regard to working with families and child protection, they may actually be in conflict when they are translated into agency function and the expected roles and tasks of the social worker.

Having briefly established the framework within which social work exists, which describes the nature of the social worker's relationship with society, it is now possible to examine more closely the nature of the relationship between the social worker and the individual (client). Basically, this relationship revolves around what I will argue is the essential and necessary task of social work – that is, to relate to individuals as 'subjects' with 'subjective characteristics'. If social workers do not relate to individuals as 'subjects', then it is debatable whether the activity being engaged in is social work at all, or that the problem (individual) is the concern of social work.

The full significance of this statement will become clearer when I relate this argument to child protection work below. In the context of the relationship that the social worker has with the individual and with the state, Phillip (1979, p. 92) describes social work as 'straddling a split' between the subjective states of the individual and their ascribed objective statuses. The subjective states of the individual may be characterized by, for example, an individual's needs, suffering, pain, and emotions (love, hate); and their objective statuses may be characterized by, for example, old age, disability, mental illness, crime, and child at risk, abused child, child abuser.

The objective status of an individual results from social processes within society that identify areas of their behaviour or experience as being of social interest and concern, to which agency function responds. Within agency function, the social worker identifies, relates to, and represents (though importantly does not necessarily act as an advocate for) the subjective state(s) of the socially identified and defined individual.

How this works can be seen in the following illustration (adapted from Philp, 1979, p. 101, and also cited in Horne, 1987). If an adolescent A commits an offence and is brought before court, he will be seen (legally) through his objective status as B(a). That is, he will be seen principally as an offender and only secondly as an individual (with a family background, life experiences, needs, and so on); hence symbol (a) rather than A. If the offence is not serious, the social worker may be able to present a picture of the 'subject' (in the social enquiry report) that transforms B(a) into A(b), so that the offence is seen as secondary to the individual's subjective characteristics. If the offence is more serious, or previous offences have been committed, the adolescent may be made the subject of supervision, in which case his B status will fade, and he will again be accepted as A, if after a period of time he does not commit offence B again. The social worker may use various forms of intervention or 'therapy', which will help in presenting a 'scientific or objective picture of the process of change in a client . . . essentially these explanations serve to change the client's status from B(a) to A(b)' (Philp, 1979, p. 101).

As can be seen in this illustration, the social worker is performing a mediating role between the 'marginal'/'objectified' individual and the state.

> It [social work] negotiates on behalf of the mad, bad, and the stigmatised; between those who have been excluded from power and those who have the power to exclude . . . between the sound in body . . . and the handicapped, between the law abiding and the law breaking . . . and the sane and the borderline. (Philp, 1979, p. 97)

Similarly, Howe (1979) describes social work as operating on the perimeters of different worlds – that of the individual and that of those with the power to legislate how behaviour is to be judged.

There are, however, limitations to the extent that social work can represent the individual as a subject. 'If that [socially identified] behaviour becomes too far removed from the way things ought to be, it is dealt with as alien, threatening and in need of sharp control' (Howe, 1979, pp. 42–3). Basically, the social worker's relationship with the individual is limited; that is, society's commitment to allowing a subjective picture of the individual to emerge from within their objective status is tolerated only within socially sanctioned boundaries. The social worker cannot speak for those whose objective status totally overwhelms their subjective states/subjectivity (or potential for it to be recognized). The 'subject' will not be heard when 'the objective characteristics of the feared outweigh all of the subjective possibilities . . . social work is allocated those whose objective status is not too threatening . . . it cannot operate . . . when an individual's act has removed him from the right to be perceived as human' (Philp, 1979, p. 98). For example, where would a child abuser fit into the analysis above? I shall discuss some of the implications of this question later on.

To return to the illustration above; if the adolescent in the illustration was appearing in court for his sixth 'breaking and entering' offence, for example, and he had already been in the care of the local authority, his objective status may well be considered greater than his subjective characteristics or potential by the magistrates, and he may well be sent to detention centre or youth custody. Interestingly and disturbing here, Pitts *et al.* (1986, pp. 167–81) suggest that, if the adolescent is black, his objective status might actually be compounded in his social inquiry report through reference being made to his ethnic/cultural background in a stereotyping way, which denies his individuality (subjectivity).

Social work values and the rule of optimism

Before considering in detail how this description of social work relates specifically to child protection, it is necessary to look at the 'value' base of social work, as this informs our understanding of, and forms the basis of, the social work task of creating subjects. It also helps to explain the place of the rule of optimism in social work, which was so heavily criticized in the Jasmine Beckford Report.

Previously, I have argued that the basic social work value of respect for persons (sometimes referred to as individualization) is central to the task of creating subjects (Horne, 1987). The British Association of Social Work's 'Code of Ethics for Social Work' describes respect for persons in the following way: 'basic to the profession of social work is the recognition of the value and dignity of every human being irrespective of origin, sex, age, belief or contribution to society' (BASW, 1975). Respect for persons requires the social worker to acknowledge and relate to the 'inherent worth of man [humankind] . . . independent of his actual achievements, or behaviour' (Butrym, 1976, p. 43). In attempting to present the underlying subjective characteristics of the individual, the social worker relates to and acknowledges the experience and character of the individual. In this sense the value of respect for persons (individualization) can be seen as essential to the role of relating to individuals as subjects.

Curnock and Hardiker (1979, p. 165), in the conclusions to their research into practice theories of social work, describe the nature of the social work task with respect to assessing referrals and writing social enquiry reports as:

However typical or general a client's situation and problems seem to be, a way has to be found of finding out what they mean to that particular person. Individualization is the theoretical key which helps us to be rather more specific about the making sense process.

Here they are referring to the importance of creating the 'subject', of understanding the subjective experience of the individual, central to which is individualization/respect for persons. Importantly (and none the less so in child protection, as I shall show below), they go on to describe how, in order to make an assessment or come to any conclusions about the individual, it is necessary to individualize the presenting problem in relation to the client's life situation, such as 'strengths and stresses in his personal or social circumstances' (Curnock and Hardiker, 1979, p. 165). This tends to suggest that the focus on protecting the child should not exclude consideration of the context in which the abuse takes place, by relating to and considering the abuser/family as a 'subject(s)' – not simply identifying them through their objective status as abuser/abusing family.

   To summarize the argument so far. The role of the social worker is to relate to and speak for the 'subject' (though not necessarily act as an advocate for) within their 'objective status'. She is sanctioned by society, through her employing agency, to speak for the individual as a subject, and for someone who can return to or achieve subjective status. However, the extent to which this task is possible is limited by society, its norms, how it defines a problem and its expectations of the social services agency. It is also a part of the social worker's role to represent these norms and expectations. Hence the social worker's role includes aspects of both care and control. Social work's basic value, 'respect for persons', is of central importance because it is necessary to the creation of the subject. 'Without values [respect for persons], there can be no subject, without the subject there can be no social work' (Horne, 1987).

The rule of optimism

'Respect for persons' also helps us to understand the role of the 'rule of optimism' in social work. The 'rule' was given prominence by Dingwall, Eekelaar, and Murray (1983). They described the concept as interpreting the behaviour of parents in the most favourable way possible. The main components of the rule are two 'institutional devices' – cultural relativism and natural love.

Cultural relativism refers to the assumption that all cultures are equally valid in the way that they formulate human relationships. In this respect, a person from one culture has no grounds for claiming moral or social superiority over someone from a different culture. Natural love refers to the belief that the relationship between a parent and a child is instinctual and stems from basic human nature. That this relationship is instinctual and in what ways is obviously debatable, but for the sake of the argument here it is not crucial whether it stems from human nature or may be explained by dominant social forces and/or societal expectations.

The fact that the rule of optimism relates closely to respect for persons, and can in fact be seen as an aspect of it, becomes clear by looking briefly again at this basic social work value.

Respect for persons refers to 'the inherent worth of man [humankind]' (Butrym, 1976) – that is, a belief in the essential goodness and potential for 'good' in human nature. The existence of *'natural'* love between parent and child can be seen as a part of this basic faith in, and optimism about, humankind. This optimism is also expressed in BASW's formulation of respect for persons: 'Basic to the profession of social work is the recognition of the value and dignity of every human being irrespective of origin, status, age, belief, or contribution to society' (1975).

The inclusion of the rule of optimism in respect for persons is of significance to the argument here because it helps us to understand the legitimate 'institutionalized' place of the rule of optimism in social work practice, as well as something of society's expectations of social work. As described earlier, the Jasmine Beckford Report is very critical of this aspect of social work, seeing it as something that social workers can choose whether or not to indulge in. In this context, the report sees it as a weakness, an avoidance of executing authority or control by the individual social worker.

This, though, is to misunderstand the 'rule's' use if one accepts its close relationship to and inclusion in respect for persons, and the latter's central place in creating subjects, which in turn is central to the nature of social work practice. From a different perspective (which I shall examine more closely shortly), the Jasmine Beckford Report fails to appreciate that social workers do not arbitrarily choose to be optimistic about clients and suspected cases of child abuse (as indicated in the argument above); such an approach is also determined by the requirements of the 'liberal democratic' society in which social work is practised in Britain.

This has been a relatively brief and general overview of the nature of social work in contemporary Britain, but it does provide a basic framework within which to consider and examine more closely the social work role in child protection.

Social work and child protection

One of the key concepts emerging from the examination of social work above is that of agency function, which reflects and represents society's concerns about certain ('marginal') individuals in society, and gives social work a mandate to work with such individuals. However, as I briefly indicated above (page 93), it is not necessarily the case that this mandate and the expectations lying behind it are straightforward, or do not have an element of contradiction within them. This is the case with regard to social work with families, including those where child abuse is suspected or apparent. To examine this further, we need to look again at the relationship between social work and society, but this time focus more explicitly on the nature of society's norms and expectations, which determine agency function.

These norms and expectations are referred to in Dingwall (1986), who, drawing on the work of Donzelot (1979), argues that the social work task takes place in a space created by the liberal democratic state, in which the perceived autonomy of families should not be undermined (for example, by state intervention), except where families are clearly identified as having 'failed' in the socialization and nurturing of their children.

The complexity of the role of social work not only is rooted by society's concern for the protection of children, but also relates closely to the primary socializing role of the family, which is particularly pertinent to child care work. This creates a difficult dilemma over the extent to which social work can monitor or 'police' the family, because this task is limited by the dominant belief that what goes on in the family is essentially private.

In the context of a liberal society, the privacy of the family is taken to be indicative of what is meant by a free society. However, Freeman (1983a, p. 12) points out: 'Unfortunately, in a world of basic structural inequalities, individual freedom can be so exercised as to undermine not only the freedom of others but also their human dignity. The parent–child relationship is a microcosm of this imbalance.' In a similar vein, Bill Jordan (1976, p. 60) has argued that: 'The case against intervention in family life often rests on the freedom of more powerful members (usually husbands in relation to wives and parents in relation to children) to exercise their power without restriction.' (See also Chapter 3 in this volume.)

Within our liberal society, it is argued by Dingwall (1986, pp. 502–3) that the role of the rule of optimism compromises or limits the degree to which the protection of children is possible, because it guarantees that the monitoring and policing by social workers (and other state agents) will not be carried out in a way that fundamentally imposes on the 'privacy' of the family. Whilst the social work task is to protect the child, to consider the child's interests first, this is limited by a general but powerful acceptance that the family should remain free from state intervention. It is interesting to note briefly here that this acceptance does not appear to have been strong enough to withstand the 'state's' intervention into the sanctity of the family circumstances that arose in Cleveland.

Arising within the Cleveland Report (Secretary of State for Social Services, 1988) is the important point that parents have rights. This is not a new notion (indeed, it is a central tenet of social work that *all* individuals are treated with 'respect', which includes the basic right to non–interference), but is one that was misunderstood in the Jasmine Beckford Report and later denied to a large extent in the events in Cleveland: 'The parents should be given the same courtesy as the family of any other referred child. This applies to all aspects of the investigation into the suspicion of child abuse, and should be recognised by all professionals concerned with the family' (Secretary of State for Social Services, 1988, p. 246).

These limitations to, and aspects of contradiction in, the social work task bring into child protection work an element of 'agency failure . . . Efforts to increase effectiveness of child protection agencies impose a cost in forgone liberties' (Dingwall, 1986, p. 503). These complexities and contradictions of the social work role in child protection work are well illustrated by Brian Corby (1987b) in his research study of the daily practice of social workers with families suspected of abusing their children. The following quote from one of the social workers interviewed highlights the difficulty of the task:

> The worst thing that I found is where the child has been injured and the parents are under suspicion and actually confronting parents with the fact and trying to do it in a relatively non–judgmental way and just not trying to be too heavy about the whole thing. I found that difficult. (Corby, 1987b, p. 51)

Corby remarks that most of the social workers interviewed in the study reconciled themselves to this role, despite their unease about it. Referring to how social workers used the rule of optimism, he found that there was an initial screening of cases, particularly of those considered to be ones of moderate abuse where social workers were already involved. Some of these cases were kept out of the system of child protection practice procedures. He explains this reluctance to draw families 'into the net' as stemming from 'the requirements of our liberal democratic society to intervene into families only with great care' (Corby, 1987b, p. 58). This relates closely to the study of Dingwall *et al.* in which they found that social workers were reluctant to bring cases into the open unless they were forced to because of the involvement of other agencies.

Corby also makes the point that often child abuse (particularly when it was 'moderate abuse') within a family was considered to be only one of a range of problems that they might be experiencing, and that there was a need to respond to all of the problems, including the child abuse, rather than, as a matter of necessity, making it the priority. To do this though, he argues, social workers need to be able to exercise greater autonomy and discretion than the system allows.

The difficulties of the social work task were also evident in the monitoring of clients, most of which, he comments, was done indirectly. In the more serious cases, where statutory orders had been made, monitoring was done more explicitly and directly, although still with some reluctance. Often other agencies were used, for example schools, nurseries, health clinics, etc. Few social workers saw monitoring and surveillance as their main function and most preferred to give it a low profile. In practice, much of the work with families where abuse was suspected or proven was a combination of help and monitoring, underlying which was an avoidance of the more explicit elements of social control. Corby comments that this was 'supported to some extent by personal preference, professional ideology and societal expectations' (1987b, p. 131).

As a result he found that much intervention was unstructured and vague in its intentions. But:

> Such a form of practice should not be attributed to incompetence on the part of social workers. To a large extent they were supported in such an approach by the professional ethos of social work and liberal beliefs about freedom from interference for individuals unless there is a legal or statutory reason for denying them this. (Corby, 1987b, p.103)

It is evident from Corby's research and the preceding analysis of the limitations placed upon social workers as agents of control in a liberal democratic society that social work is a complex enterprise. On the one hand, individuals should be subjected to a minimal amount of interference from state agencies; at the same time, sufficient regard should be paid to the need to protect children. 'While child protection is the main aim of the system, the whole enterprise is made extremely complex by the competing demands that families remain free from unnecessary interference' (Corby, 1987b, p. 135).

To return briefly to the Jasmine Beckford Report, the reluctance of social workers to use authority in their work derives not from an inappropriate liberalism or lack of understanding of the authority/social control mandate vested in them, but from the basic social work task of relating to individuals as 'subjects', which has its roots in the primary social work value of 'respect for persons', which itself is an aspect of a socially sanctioned 'deep attachment to a non-authoritarian ideal of social order' (Dingwall, 1986, p. 503).

One consequence of this is that complete protection for children at risk in their own families is not possible unless society sanctions greater public/state scrutiny of the family. In the absence of this, an element of risk must inevitably exist in a large number of cases that come through the system. Whilst individual social workers may make mistakes in assessing the degree of risk in a particular case, the existence of risk cannot be construed to be indicative of bad practice. In fact it could be argued that an acceptance of risk is necessary if the rights of parent, siblings, and 'potential' victims themselves are not to be denied.

Cleveland

In the light of this argument it is interesting briefly to look at what happened in Cleveland in 1987. In a period of five months, 121 children were 'diagnosed' as being sexually abused, most of them being consequently separated from their parents – 70 per cent 'or so' by Place of Safety Orders. From the description of events in this report, and in the context of the above description of what social work is, it is questionable to what extent the social workers were engaged in 'social work' with the children and their families in Cleveland. The response of the social services to the diagnoses of sexual abuse does appear in a large number of the cases to have been based on the objective statuses ascribed to the individuals (abused, abuser, siblings, abusing family, and so on), to the extent that their subjective status/characteristics were denied. This included the children themselves. 'There is a danger that in looking to the welfare of children believed to be the victims of sexual abuse the children themselves may be overlooked. The child is a person not an *object* of concern' (Secretary of State for Social Services, 1988, p. 245; my emphasis).

Social work takes place with 'subjects' not 'objects'. If there is no space for the social worker to relate to the individual as such, then, following the argument above, the activity being engaged in is not social work. That child protection is the concern of social work is, however, strongly pointed to in the report, as indicated in the quote above. This includes 'seeing' the child in the context of his or her family.

> We would suggest that a child's needs and best interests cannot be fully considered in isolation from knowledge about and full understanding of all the circumstances relating to its parents. Their strengths and weaknesses as individuals, their functioning as a couple, their capacity as parents, and the known risks which any facet of their behaviour or attitude may have for the child concerned or any other children in the family must be taken into account. (Secretary of State for Social Services, 1988, p. 75)

This quote appears clearly to emphasize the validity of the social work relationship in child protection work, which was so severely questioned in the Jasmine Beckford Report and which perhaps was lost sight of in Cleveland in 1987.

This is not to suggest that what happened in Cleveland was solely a response to the Jasmine Beckford Report – it clearly was not. But certainly, as evidenced in the Cleveland Report quotes cited at the beginning of this chapter, 'Beckford' had a significant impact on Cleveland social services department, and to some extent their response to the diagnoses of child sexual abuse, both initially and during the 'crisis', was shaped by the Jasmine Beckford Report's criticisms and recommendations. In trying to avoid a similar tragedy possibly happening in Cleveland, social work was lost sight of.

Final thoughts

Social work is not static. Its priorities and its focus of attention change according to agency function. This in turn responds to the changing expectations of society/the state, which may be formalized through statute or emerge through 'acknowledged' or general opinion. Child protection work is no exception to this.

This is clearly evidenced by the shift in reactions, comments, and recommendations following events in Brent (re Jasmine Beckford) and later in Cleveland. It is important, though, that changes in social work practice do not lurch from one extreme to another – from obvious under-reaction to over-reaction, depending on the circumstances and findings of each new inquiry report.

Referring to the events in Cleveland, John Chant (Director of Social Services, Somerset, and the social services assessor on the Cleveland Inquiry Panel) has commented: 'One can understand why, on the basis of looking at Jasmine Beckford and Kimberley Carlile, Louis [Blom Cooper] and his colleagues came to their conclusions, but to look at two cases and seek to promote a fundamental change in emphasis of social work practice was arrogant' (*Social Work Today*, 7 July 1988, p. 6). In the same article, John Chant went on to comment that the model of 'bad cases not making good law did not seem to apply when lawyers were sought to change the basic premise of social work practice'.

Whilst social work changes to meet different demands and roles, these changes (according to the analysis here) must accommodate the basic and essential social work task of relating to individuals as subjects. Whether or not this includes the abuser/abusing family (alleged, potential, or actual) is a crucial question, which is evident from the analysis and evidence presented above, and which also indicates that it is not a question that social work as a profession has the power or authority to answer itself.

However, the above analysis does suggest that child protection work (as part of *social work*, and whilst not denying the control element of the social work role) does entail an element of risk if all individuals are to be related to as *subjects*; this cannot be avoided if the rights and best interests of the child and the rights of the family are to be respected. This leaves 'society/the state' and, individually, everyone concerned for the protection of children with a very difficult reality to face, summed up by Dingwall:

the child protection system contains an inherent bias against intervention anyway. If we wish to change that, then we must confront the social costs. If we do not consider that the costs are worth paying, then we must frankly acknowledge the

human implications that some children will die to preserve
the freedom of others. (1986, p. 531)

If the 'human implications' boldly spelt out here are too high a
price to pay, then we must ask the question: is child protection
the business of social work, and to what extent?

6 Racism, cultural relativism and child protection

YVONNE CHANNER and NIGEL PARTON

In our experience, a central issue concerning many white practitioners, particularly in inner city areas, is how to protect children and work with parents who are members of black communities. While some priority has recently been given to reducing racism and increasing the ethnically sensitive dimensions of practice within social work (Ahmed, Cheetham, and Small, 1986), it is also a fact that two of the public inquiries that have ushered in the increased public concern about child abuse during this period (London Borough of Brent, 1985; London Borough of Lambeth, 1987) have involved children from black families. We feel that many of the issues and dilemmas addressed throughout this book are most cogently illustrated in this area of practice. Thus, while our central focus will be upon the practice tensions that arise from white social workers working with children and families from black communities, in doing so we will be addressing issues of wider significance, in particular highlighting the problems associated with assessment (Department of Health, 1988). Is it possible to judge absolute standards of family care and functioning while also understanding the different approaches to rearing children within different cultures? We are centrally concerned with the problems of developing a practice that takes seriously the subjective realities of other cultural norms and values but that attempts at the same time to protect the interests of the children concerned. Our attempts to reduce racism in social work have to recognize that protecting the interests of black children may well involve intensive supervision of their parents. There is a danger that discussions of racism in social work, based on the assumption of a unitary black constituency, fail to recognize that the interests of different parties within black families may differ crucially along the dimensions of gender and age. Such tensions raise central dilemmas for day-to-day practice.

Certainly, at present, social work and its practitioners seem to be caught in a crossfire between on the one hand being accused of racist policy and practice while on the other being criticized for operating according to 'a rule of optimism' based, in part, on the assumption of 'cultural relativism'. As a result, they fail to address the central issues and become incapable of taking important decisions. As a beginning, therefore, it is important to understand the nature and content of the criticisms related to racism and cultural relativism.

Racism and child care: the tendency to rescue and assimilate

While race can be viewed from many different perspectives (Husband, 1982), this chapter proceeds on the assumption that race is a socially constructed category rather than a biologically defined concept. We also proceed on the basis that racism forms a major reality for many ethnic minorities in modern Britain. Racism refers to the construction and institutionalization of social relationships based on the assumption of the inferiority of ethnic minority groups, their customs, lifestyles, and beliefs. As a result they experience marginalization and exploitation in both the economic and social spheres. Prejudice and crude racial stereotypes reinforce and legitimate such divisions. While there is a range of ethnic minority groups, the major division is in terms of black and white. Thus, while we recognize that there are major differences – for example between the Afro-Caribbean (whose origins are in Africa or the Caribbean) and the Asian (whose origins are in the Indian subcontinent) – within the black community, we feel there are also considerable similarities in terms of their experience of British society. These similarities emerge primarily as a result of their experience of racism (Inner London Education Authority, 1983; Dominelli, 1988).

There is considerable evidence to indicate that race, in particular blackness, is a major factor in determining life chances, influencing social divisions, and creating disadvantage (Brown, 1984). Much of this arises from discrimination against members of the black community, who are assumed to be racially inferior and different (Cashmore and Troyna, 1983).

Alternative routes for black communities start in schools, where the drafting of disproportionate numbers of black children into special schools has been only slightly modified by the administrative workings of the 1981 Education Act (Tomlinson, 1982). It continues to be the case that more Afro-Caribbeans than whites and Asians are suspended from school, and they are more likely to end up in custody where they receive proportionately longer sentences than whites and Asians (Home Office Statistical Bulletin, 1986).

A similar process has operated within social work, with a higher proportion of black children in care than non-white children (Lambeth Social Services Committee, 1981; Batta and Mawby, 1981). Whilst the proportion of children in care nation-ally is 7.75 per thousand, in inner cities this rises to 22.5 per thousand, a differential that is undoubtedly related to class and social deprivation generally. A breakdown of this latter figure, however, shows that, within inner cities, 20.16 per thousand are of white parentage, 24.32 per thousand are of Afro-Caribbean parentage, and 143.24 per thousand are of mixed parentage. Interestingly, only 0.63 per thousand are of Asian parentage. These percentages do not accord with the demographic patterns, and are higher than one would expect even allowing for the fact that the vast majority of ethnic minority families live in inner city areas. Similarly, while fewer than 40 per cent of children in care nationally have been in care for over three years, the figure rises to 75 per cent among children of mixed parentage (Caines and Mignott, 1987). A study in Brent (McAdam, 1987) demonstrated that disproportionately more Afro-Caribbean children came into care and spent longer in care than children from other groups and disproportionately more were subject to the assumption of parental rights resolutions (Section 3 of the Child Care Act, 1980) – a factor that is well established as increasing parental hostility to social workers (Lowe, 1987).

Some of the worst conflicts between social services and the black community have occurred in the field of child care. They strike at the heart of the values of the black commu-nity, its position in society, and its parenting role. Likewise they put into sharp focus the attitudes of society and the ethnocentric outlook of social services (Liverpool, 1986, p. 19).

In 1983 the Association of Black Social Workers and Allied Professionals submitted evidence to the Social Services Com-mittee (HCP 360/1, 1984). The Association had conducted a survey of the views of the black community groups and found that social services were seen as enforcement agencies that wittingly and unwittingly broke up black families and aimed to take children away from their homes. It stated: 'white social workers were nosey, *wanting blacks to be like whites*, imposing their views and values on another community – the community even going so far as to say that white work-ers are encouraging a subtle form of slavery but this time only using black children' (Ely and Denney, 1987, p. 91; our emphasis).

Experience sustained by members of black communities suggests that there is deep and ingrained racism that perceives them as more threatening than whites and, accordingly, metes out harsher measures to them. It seems that the strengths of black families and communities are not recognized, and this claim is supported by whites (Heptinstall, 1986).

Such criticisms can be better understood by locating the situation briefly in historical context. During the 1960s and early 1970s, the number of black children being admitted to special schools was matched by the number of black children being received into care. This movement can best be described as religious zeal (Coombe and Little, 1986, p. 139). Ethnic monitoring procedures have only recently been developed in some social services departments, but some reasons for this 'missionary' behaviour have been suggested.

One of the earliest and most influential texts to look at these problems of the over-representation of West Indian children in care was by Katrina Fitzherbert (1967). She argues that there are several aspects of the West Indian cultural background which, when combined with 'the problems of migration', result in many children being in need of care. These aspects are: a tradition of unstable families; many 'single mothers'; Victorian child-rearing practices; the break-up of the extended family through migration; housing and economic problems for first gencration immigrants. She also argues that the desire for financial security, the priority of earning an income above the children's needs, and the lack of stigma associated with fostering, all contributed to a greater willingness to request care by West Indian parents. The net result is a pathological view of the West Indian family that makes no attempt to analyse the structural position of West Indian people in British society and fails to address the issue of racism (Denney, 1983). The main recommendation made to overcome the problem is that practitioners should be much tougher and resist requests for such children to come into care. In the process, the problem is seen to reside essentially within the West Indian family. Such stereotypes thus reinforce the power of the professional and fail to address the particular needs of the children and families involved.

The liberal, colour blind, assimilationist approach has been aggravated by misunderstandings about language. For example, the richness of Afro-Caribbean patois has not been appreciated as easily as the need to communicate with groups who speak English as a second language. Gibson and Barrow (1986) found that black pupils and their teachers assumed that they both spoke the same language and made no allowances for subtle differences. This had obvious effects on the attainment of black children in schools and it seems probable that similar misunderstandings were evident in social workers' attempts at communication with black families in child care.

Any strengths within black families, as well as the 'future' of black communities, were largely ignored, since the feelings and opinions of many white social workers about black people were often based on the assumption of white superiority and black inferiority. Even where social workers attempted to understand black families, they were usually informed by what black professionals now term disparagingly 'airport sociologists', who described Afro-Caribbean family forms without any real understanding. Increasingly it has been suggested that the disproportionate number of black children who have been and are being received into care may have less to do with the capacity of black families to care for their children than with the prejudiced perceptions and interventions of white professional carers (Dominelli, 1988).

The major set of factors contributing to an over-representation of black children in care can be associated with an approach characterized as liberal, assimilationist, and colour blind. Much policy and practice, in assuming that the 'British way of life' is best, finds fault with other cultures and assumes that the best way of overcoming such problems is to assimilate them into the mainstream culture. Such an approach, however, is left implicit and its consequences barely recognized because it proceeds on the basis of 'treating everyone the same' and fails to recognize colour as a significant dimension requiring attention. It is assumed that all children and families are the same and hence should receive the same *professional* response and be subjected to the same *objective* criteria for the purposes of assessment and intervention. Such an approach not only denies the experience of racism but ignores the positive but different elements in black family life. These issues have been increasingly highlighted within both social work and the black communities themselves, with heated criticism and argument – the issues surrounding transracial adoption being the initial focus for concern (Ely and Denney, 1987, p. 91–2; Stubbs, 1987).

As McGoldrick (McGoldrick *et al.,* 1982) pointed out, while it seems natural to look at ethnicity when working with families, this dimension has until recently been largely ignored by members of the caring professions in Britain. She states that race is a major factor, as skin colour identifies certain ethnic groups and marks them out as different. As a consequence they are not in a position to 'pass' as members of other ethnic groups might do. Black individuals have no choice about their ethnic and racial status identification and Afro-Caribbeans, particularly, have had difficulties in being seen as culturally different rather than as inferior whites. McGoldrick (McGoldrick *et al.*, 1982, p. 4) makes the point that 'human behaviour cannot be understood in isolation from the family, the cultural and racial context in which it is embedded'. The apparent avoidance of this dimension could be due to the fact that ethnicity/race touches deep unconscious feelings in people. As this can give rise to stereotyping and prejudice there is a need for these differences to be explored, thus laying to rest any myths and erroneous assumptions in relation to cultures, social conditioning, and child rearing. All these relate crucially to judgements about norms and values and how these might differ between different racial groups. Only when these are analysed and understood can agencies and individual workers practise in a sensitive and informed manner.

In recent years, many local authorities have given some consideration to anti-racist and race awareness training (Coombe and Little, 1986; Sivanandan, 1985). As a consequence, the issues of race and racial differences have been given increased prominence. While there has been much debate about the content, aims, and impact of such training on white practitioners, there can be little doubt that race and prejudice have been addressed in the 1980s in a way in which they were not in the 1960s and 1970s. A part of this awareness has focused on the wider significance and implications of institutionalized racism. As a result, some 'liberal' white workers have been faced with facts and processes about which they may feel guilty, deskilled, and powerless.

Cultural relativism and social work: the tendency to neutralize and ignore

While the issues addressed so far suggest that black families may be subject to inappropriate and heavy-handed interventions, leading to an over-representation of black children in care, recent public inquiries and research suggest the opposite may be happening in child abuse cases. The problem here becomes one of practitioners failing to identify high-risk situations and thereby failing to protect the child. Such a failure is seen to be crucially associated with a pervasive 'rule of optimism' amongst social workers, which is in part dependent on 'cultural relativism'.

In essence, the rule of optimism means that the most favourable interpretation is always put upon the behaviour of the parents and that anything that may question this is discounted or redefined (Dingwall, Eekelaar, and Murray, 1983). This tendency in practitioners is attributed to two institutional devices – cultural relativism and natural love. By cultural relativism is meant the assumption that all cultures are equally valid in formulating human relationships. Thus members of one culture have no right to criticize members of another culture by using their own standards of judgement. Natural love refers to the belief that all parents, instinctively, love their children. The implication arising from cultural relativism seems clear. White social workers will not assess a child as being at high risk in a black family, particularly if that means removing that child.

The problems inherent in this are particularly evident in the Jasmine Beckford case (London Borough of Brent, 1985), where a Swedish social worker and her American senior were working alongside a Chinese health visitor and an Asian general practitioner. One wonders how they could have explored their own notions of culture and prejudice, and it is noteworthy that they were later accused of accepting the black parents' values and norms as the basis for making judgements.

As Horne has pointed out in Chapter 5, this means that their practice was not conducive to relating to the individual as a subject. In the Jasmine Beckford Report it is argued that the net result was that the workers failed to focus on the child and failed to use the authority needed to fulfil their statutory obligations. The notion of 'cultural relativism' articulates the view that white social workers have particular problems in assessing minimum child care standards when working with families that do not conform to their own views about family life. However, rather than over-react as they may have previously done by admitting large numbers of black children to care, the implication is that they hesitate to intervene at all and hence put children from black families in real and serious danger.

Dingwall, Eekelaar, and Murray (1983, p. 66) quote the following case from their research in illustration of this point. Here, a health visitor is talking about an Asian woman:

'She has got eight children under ten, a boy, six girls, and another boy. Now she has had this second boy she has at last been allowed by her mother to have family planning. [Health visitor] likes her. Although there are a lot of children it's not a particularly deprived household. There is a lot of love and things going for the children.

Dingwall *et al.* suggest that the health visitor seems well aware that a simple statement, to the effect that the woman has eight small children, could be interpreted as a moral attack, and therefore immediately discounts this possibility by reference to cultural norms, 'A second boy . . . allowed by her mother' and also by reference to 'a lot of love'. Any possible serious concern is thereby avoided.

Another extract quoted by Dingwall, Eekelaar, and Murray (1983, pp. 83–4), from a case conference on a West Indian girl who had made allegations of sexual assault against her stepfather, demonstrates typical assumptions made by professionals when working with people from other cultures:

SSW: So you wouldn't take any action on them?

SW: I think we should just want to monitor them.

SSW: Yes, monitor them via school and the health visitor. I think we have learnt to accept a variety of family situations on the Atlee estate and to accept them . . .

SW: . . . her father was very annoyed and beat her with a strap.

SSW: With a strap?

SW: Oh, this sort of thing does happen in this community . . .

SSW: This violence is very difficult to prove and we just have to accept that it is part of West Indian culture.

What begins to emerge is that perhaps the notion of 'cultural relativism' is related to a reconstructed racism, which leads to a failure to act at all. A new set of stereotypical assumptions are brought into play which immobilize the worker. This was apparent in the Tyra Henry case (London Borough of Lambeth, 1987). The report expressed grave concerns about the social worker's assessment of the grandmother's coping skills and abilities:

> Here was a woman, recently widowed, previously traumatised by the death of a young son, recently traumatised by the maiming and the loss of a baby grandson, living on social security with five children in a grossly overcrowded flat and precious little financial or other help for her teenage daughters. It seems pertinent now to ask, could she be expected to cope as Tyra's surrogate parent and first line protector? (London Borough of Lambeth, p. 107)

In an attempt to assess this grandmother's potential contribution to the case, the report concludes that:

the assumption that Beatrice Henry would cope ... was rooted in a perception of her as a *type* rather an as an *individual* ... there is also a positive but nevertheless false stereotype in white British society of the Afro-Caribbean mother figure as endlessly resourceful, able to cope in great adversity, essentially unsinkable. (London Borough of Lambeth, 1987, p. 108; our emphasis)

Although the report does not spell it out explicitly, it suggests that the social work assessment seemed to consider a lower standard of social service support was appropriate for poor black clients compared to others; that is, that a woman like Beatrice Henry would find a way of coping no matter what. Such suggestions are littered throughout the case records and are briefly but accurately epitomized in the entry for physical appearance on the placement form – it describes Beatrice Henry as a 'plump, motherly lady' (London Borough of Lambeth, 1987, pp. 108–9).

However, the main issue here is, we would argue, the unthinking stereotyping involved in accepting notions of 'cultural relativism'. It is the failure to relate to the client as an individual, a subject rather than a typical object of that ethnic group. Typical objects do not, of course, exist – except in the muddled minds of white workers who perceive that they are treading in a minefield when they have to make assessments on parenting in black communities. In actual fact, there is *some* evidence to show that black mothers have an increased capacity to cope, certainly in terms of their children's educational achievement (Bristol Child Health and Education Study, 1986), but they still need to be treated as individuals with individual needs. When a social worker's stock in trade is supposed to be the ability to form relationships, it is tragic to consider that these relationships with black families have simply moved from one of missionary zeal to convert black to white to one in which black families' parenting performances are accepted unquestioningly as culturally different but valid. Equally problematic is trying to use predictors in assessing risk with families of different cultures.

Individualized risk indicators: the tendency to pathologize and marginalize

The approach of trying to separate out and identify 'high-risk' families as a significant way of protecting children has received serious attention and debate in recent years (Parton and Parton, 1989; Chapter 8 in this volume). Not only has it informed a number of recent public inquiries, but it has received particular attention in research, policy, and practice. It is assumed by many to be the prime way in which knowledge should be advanced and is seductive to workers immobilized and deskilled in their relationships with families from different cultures and worried about the consequences of 'getting it wrong'.

We are particularly concerned that such an approach may have serious implications for such families, especially as it fails to recognize the direct implications of wider structural factors for certain families, particularly in the most deprived sections of society. It is just these sections of society where a number of black families are located. Thus, rather than overcoming some of the biases and prejudice previously identified, such an approach may reinforce the problems we are trying to address. There is a significant racial dimension that such approaches fail to consider. We will illustrate these concerns by reference to the work of Greenland (1987) because his approach proved so influential in the public debate over the Beckford case, which provided his work with a high degree of prominence.

Greenland has itemized a simple checklist for identifying 'high-risk' families. The high-risk factors associated with vulnerable parents are:

1. Previously abused/neglected as a child
2. Age 20 years or less at birth of first child
3. Single parent/separated; partner not biological parent
4. History of abuse/neglect or deprivation
5. Socially isolated/frequent moves/poor housing
6. Poverty – unemployed/unskilled worker – inadequate education
7. Abuses alcohol/drugs
8. History of assaultive behaviour and/or suicidal attempts
9. Pregnant/post partum or chronic illness.

We will briefly indicate some of the reasons why this checklist cannot be uncritically adopted and why it needs to be set within a wider social–structural framework that acknowledges a racial dimension but does not uncritically accept 'cultural relativism'. The latter merely serves to perpetuate disadvantage.

Many black families could be rated as high risk on these indicators, particularly with reference to youthful parenthood and single parenting. However, there is a need to recognize possible culture/generation clashes and conflicting value systems between parents and younger black individuals, which often lead to young people leaving home early. Such pressures are exacerbated by the stress and anxiety of living in a racist society. In addition, stereotyped images of the British Afro-Caribbean society view them as operating a freer model of making relationships (note Fitzherbert's comments earlier). Such comments feed the stereotypical images of black communities, omitting the strength and dignity present in such families. For instance, it is not readily recognized that black girls often achieve significant examination results at around 14 years of age (Driver, 1980; Spencer, 1982). This picture of responsible black teenage girls is at odds with the stereotype of feckless, welfare motherhood. It has been suggested that young Afro-Caribbean mothers have an advanced sense of responsibility for their years (Blyth and Milner, 1987b). Phoenix (1988) explores numerous 'myths' about the Afro-Caribbean family. She highlights the failure of practitioners to contextualize many 'facts' concerning this racial group.

The so-called high-risk factors associated with previous abusive experiences and a history of neglect should be considered in the light of black children's experiences in Britain in the 1960s and 1970s. As we have outlined earlier and as the conference on 'Black and in Care' (Children's Legal Centre, 1986) indicates, white workers' perceptions of black children's needs have not been significantly challenged. Much of the neglect suffered by black children has been imposed on them by the care system itself, not least of which has been a neglect of black children's need to become aware of their own racial identity – what Maxime (1986) refers to as 'psychological negrescence'.

Certainly, Greenland's risk indicators referring to educational attainment and unemployment can be seen as the results of prejudice and stereotyping. Children in care receive a less than adequate education and the recent evidence about underachievement of black pupils in schools has been considered (Egglestone *et al.*, 1985). The research evidence concerning black underachievement in schools usually neglects to mention that black children who do well at school tend do so because of the help they receive from home. Unemployment is difficult to use as an indicator when it is well established that young black people are three times more likely to be out of work than young whites (Hewitt, 1986).

Similarly, being socially isolated may indicate nothing more than the generally unwelcome reception that black mothers experience when they venture into traditional white areas such as mother and toddler groups, coffee mornings, and so on (Ely and Denney, 1987, pp. 27–9). Hewitt (1986) found that, where black people comprise a sizeable minority, they quickly establish effective community support via churches and community associations. Workers should be aware of the need to look at the community support, or lack of it, rather than make bland assertions about social isolation, if they are not to make the same mistakes as workers in the 1960s and 1970s.

With regard to drug abuse, workers need to become more informed on the debate about Rastafarianism and the use of ganga (Coombe and Little, 1986, pp. 77–8) and how police procedures can influence this. As mentioned earlier, black youths are far more likely to be identified and prosecuted, particularly for behaviour involving drugs and assault, than are their white counterparts (Hudson, 1987, personal communication). The issue is not as simple as racial prejudice resulting in police harassment and long prison sentences for blacks. Subtle interactive processes are at work, as is indicated when one looks at the take-up rate for intermediate treatment and community service (Blyth and Milner, 1987b).

Professor Greenland's assessment of high-risk families seems to identify them as being engulfed by a 'culture of poverty' (Valentine, 1968), unwilling and/or unable to extricate themselves from the bottom rungs of society. Such an individualized checklist is in great danger of defining out the structural factors that lie behind but that are so crucial to understanding their significance in any particular situation. As Lashley (1987) argues, such a research methodology defines situations as they are apparently seen and dismally fails to probe beyond such situational observations and tease out causal factors. There is also a great danger of treating black families as if they were poor, disadvantaged white families, only more easily identified because of colour. They clearly are not, having strengths and resiliences of their own that sadly do not get the social work support they deserve. Too often, black families are either pathologized or excused on the grounds of 'cultural relativism' practice, which leans towards 'blaming the victim'. The need is, we emphasize, to individualize and subjectify them, within an understanding of structural racism, in a search to understand more fully in what ways people are different but the same.

Conclusions: towards ethnically sensitive child protection work

In this chapter we have tried to demonstrate how we have experienced some of the conflicting expectations of carrying out child protection work, particularly as they relate to white social work with black families. However, we do not feel

that these problems are associated only with work with ethnic minority families and thus are issues exclusive to race.

Such problems exist whenever a social distance, and hence
a power differential, is in evidence between worker and client
when the former is attempting to assess and judge behaviour in
the latter. For example, it is not uncommon when investigating
an allegation of overchastisement to be confronted by, 'Why me,
when everyone else in the street is the same?' One is aware that
there are wide class differences in the nature and significance of
parental disciplining of children (Newsom and Newsom, 1968;
Korsch *et al.*, 1965; Gough and Boddy, 1986).

We have argued that the attempt to judge a bottom line
of parenting behaviour that ensures the safety of children is
one that workers find anxiety provoking and is experienced
at its sharpest in the relationship between white workers and
black clients. Again, it is not unusual for white workers to be
told that 'You don't understand black families'. For example,
Liverpool (1986, p. 21) has pointed to the particular problems
of assessing the difference between normal chastisement and
physical abuse.

We would argue that developing an ethnically sensitive and
anti-racist approach is the prerequisite for all workers, whatever
their colour or culture. This is qualitatively different from
a practice based on cultural relativism, which is subject to
racist assumptions. What social workers seem to require is
an approach that gives them certain confidence and empathy
and helps them to understand the problems of their clients –
whatever the cultural difference. Such an approach is crucially
dependent upon a recognition of one's own values, stereotypes,
and prejudices and an admission of the limits of one's knowledge
and experiences. It is not good enough to assume a colour and
race blind position of 'We are the same'. Ethnically sensitive
practice encourages the worker to proceed in an open-minded
fashion, prepared to rethink many long-held and taken for
granted assumptions – a willingness to be conscious of their
own as well as their clients' ethnicity.

Culturally relative practice must be abandoned, since it leads
to simplistic, polarized, and stereotypical views of clients and
their situations and does nothing to challenge the workers' own
norms and values. Ely and Denney (1987, p. 14) suggest that those
who are:

> trying to learn about other cultures often seek to reduce them
> to a set of prescriptive (often religious) rules, by which the
> behaviour of individuals is determined and explicable. This
> leaves no room at all for choice between alternative courses

of action and whites would not dream of explaining their own behaviour in terms of such 'rules' . . . rules are more properly regarded as emphases, cultural preferences, or as an idiom of ideology with which people discuss relationships. They may well reflect the cultural ideal rather than actual behaviour, and to confuse one with the other is a very frequent mistake.

As we have seen in Chapters 3 and 4, these rules may be male rules. Devore (1988) argues that the major principle of ethnic-sensitive practice is the simultaneous attention to individuals and systemic concerns.

A Eurocentric view is quite unhelpful. For example, when Western child-rearing techniques and practices are seen through the eyes of some non-Western cultures, the conclusion is that Western parents do not love children or care for them properly. Practices such as isolating infants and small children in rooms or beds of their own at night, making them wait for readily available food until a schedule dictates that they can satisfy their hunger, or allowing them to cry without attending to their needs or desires would be at odds with many non-Western cultures.

Similarly, Westerners often point to examples of practice that appear to them abusive or neglectful – punishments such as severe beatings to impress the child with the necessary adherence to cultural rites, harsh initiation rites that include genital operations, deprivation of food and sleep, and so on. It is essential to note that the parent who 'protects' the child from a painful but culturally required initiation rite would be denying the child a place as an adult in that culture. That parent, in the eyes of cultural peers, would be abusive and neglectful for compromising the development of the child.

What is of most importance is to look critically at the social theory that informs workers' understanding of child care. It is clear that most theory is dominated by white male thinking (both the examples given above could fall into this category) and needs critical review. Fortunately, more women and black people are developing child care theory and some research findings have universal application, such as attachment theory (see Bee, 1986, for an overview). Workers developing ethnically sensitive practice can be at the forefront of this movement – for example, it took Halifax health visitors several months to convince hospital staff that the chanting routinely engaged in by Asian mothers during the birth process was not dissimilar to the breathing exercises promulgated by converts to natural childbirth methods.

Clearly, however, there are issues of particular significance when working with ethnic minority communities. Smith (1986) notes that speaking out about child abuse in the family frequently involves a conflict of loyalties and this conflict may well be more intense for individuals in a black community. The 'reporting' of such incidents may be perceived as betrayal of or disloyalty to the whole community. Members of black communities are aware of many of the stereotypical images of their communities generally held by white society, and it is fair to assume that white professionals are also affected by these images. Smith outlines some of the stereotypes held by members of the white society: that black men are naturally both physically and sexually violent; that single-parent families are predisposed to the occurrence of sexual abuse, with abuses coming in the form of multiple boyfriends; that sexual abuse is 'culturally defined' and is not seen as such in some cultures, especially primitive ones. Members of a black family in which child abuse has taken place might fear that revelation of the abuse within the black community will possibly be used to feed the racist assumptions of white people. The reporting of any 'offence' will mean bringing predominantly white authorities, such as the police and social services, into the lives of the family, a situation from which many black families are constantly protecting themselves.

It would be extreme to say that white workers can *never* work with black clients, but the acknowledgement of the issue is not always enough. The realization of the particular power imbalances that variables such as race bring into play underlines the need for more ethnically sensitive work among white workers and the need for more black professional carers. There are enough misconceptions surrounding child abuse for any family (abuser and abused) to deal with, without having to take on board the ignorance or, worse, racist ideas about black people and black family life held by supposed helpers and by professionals. Aware and conscious welfare workers who are seeking to improve their practice need to move from the counterproductive model of 'cultural relativism', which, in effect, impedes practice. The goal of ethnically sensitive practice is inaccessible and impossible without the worker allowing their practice and their values to be challenged and without time and effort being put into unlocking deep-rooted stereotypes. Undoubtedly this exercise may lead to a sense of being deskilled. Kutek (1987) outlines a number of escape routes available to workers experiencing such turmoil: 'putting on the authority hat', intimidation, or being 'nice and liberal' are just some of the tactics and strategies used to escape from a difficult event. Securing ethnically sensitive practice permits the worker

7 Rethinking child protection practices: a case for history

HARRY FERGUSON

My objective in this chapter is to situate many of the key themes in child protection practice that are taken up in this book in historical context. This practice is in reality a century old. In the 1880s, reformers and social workers developed a systematic legal and social child protection practice in response to what they regarded as a major problem of child abuse. By 1908, in the Children Act of that year, a specific child protection practice had been codified and institutionalized into the foundations of the modern welfare state, which was constructed in a period of liberal reforms (Thane, 1982).

Such historical considerations have, however, barely penetrated into the vast amount of conceptual rethinking that has gone into child protection practice since child abuse re-emerged as a major social issue two decades ago. The tendency in even the most important official texts continues to be to regard child protection, its problems and possibilities, as a product of the post-war welfare state and major developments since the work of Kempe *et al.* in the 1960s, the Maria Colwell tragedy, and so on (see, for example, London Borough of Brent, 1985, ch. I). This remains so despite the fact that some awareness of this longer history has been represented in the literature (May, 1977; Parton, 1985a; Jones 1982). But, as George Behlmer observed in his important social history of this formative period of practice, one result of the intense recent interest in child abuse has been an invalidation of the past and a foreshortening of historical perspective in which 'social scientists have tended to belittle earlier child protection work' (1982, pp. 224–5).

In this chapter I attempt a correction of this 'belittling' by presenting a case for history as essential to any proper rethinking or routine understanding of child protection practices. I do this quite literally. I take a single child abuse case from the 1890s, which details casework undertaken by the NSPCC, describe its features, and analyse it in depth.[1] I will adopt an approach that involves using the empirical evidence, not to explore what should have been done in practice, but to try and make sense of and interpret what *was* done in practice in the context of a particular time and place.

As Gordon's (1985, 1986) recent work has shown, historical case records provide exceptionally useful, if neglected, sources through which to construct a history and analysis of practice. Indeed, in the British context virtually no history of this kind exists (Fido, 1977, is an exception). Not unlike critical readings of contemporary child abuse cases (Parton, 1986), the historical case in question can be read both as a text that displays its own particular features, and for how it expresses more general aspects of social and historical processes – in this case the emergence of modern child protection policy and practice.

A case for history

The Pearson household were clients of the NSPCC intermittently between 1891 and 1898. Mr Pearson was a labourer, Mrs Pearson a houseworker. There were seven children, five of whom lived at home and whose ages ranged from 12 years to an 8-month-old baby. An older daughter (17) had left home, while another boy was in an industrial school, 'the result of neglect'. The family were well known to other agencies – police and school board officials – in the area. They were a mobile household, having, in the Inspector's words, 'lived . . . in different parts of the town, their selections always being the most degraded localities'. In 1898 when their 'case' reached a head, they lived in a three-roomed house for which they paid 3s 6d per week rent. Mr Pearson earned 20s per week, which on Rowntree's calculations (1901) would have classified them as living in extreme primary poverty.

The Pearsons had always been viewed as neglectful parents, having been 'warned over and over again'. Both had been prosecuted for neglect in 1891 and served prison sentences of two months with hard labour. In 1894 'they really deserved further prosecution, but owing to their pleadings . . . were given a further chance'.

In March 1898, in 'consequence of a message', the NSPCC Inspector visited the household to investigate a complaint of child neglect and ill-treatment. Both, he felt, were well founded. Much of the neglect was attributed to Mrs Pearson's drinking habits. A neighbour gave particularly vivid and damning evidence, saying that Mrs Pearson, whom she had often tried to help, was drinking the housekeeping money and utterly neglecting to see to home and children. The neighbour's patience ran out when some bread she threw into the street for the birds was eaten by the Pearson children, whom neighbours were constantly helping out. When confronted by both neighbour and social workers, Mr Pearson said he knew nothing of his wife's daytime habits as he was at work all day. She, meanwhile, was proving difficult to pin down at home but later revealed that she was living with her brother because 'she said her husband was a brute to her and she was afraid to go home'. Her husband had already told the Inspector that, on receipt of the complaint, 'she would be afraid he would thrash her for her neglect and drunkenness'.

This was characteristic of how thorough NSPCC Inspectors were in their enquiries. As many statements as possible were gleaned from willing neighbours, although workers were regularly frustrated in such attempts as a significant number of local people resisted cooperating. Statements of evidence from other welfare workers were also routinely gathered. Many of these practitioners appeared just as vigilant in their work as their NSPCC counterparts. A school board officer explains:

> I visited the house of [Albert Pearson] . . . on Monday March 21st at eleven o'clock, twelve o'clock and five o'clock and saw the children at each of these times in a wretched lost and distressed condition. At five o'clock they were all huddled together on the fender, before a small fire, with no one to look after them . . . This family are a dirty lot and the house generally dirty.

In terms such as these the 'neglect' was vividly portrayed. The Inspector himself 'examined all the children and found them running alive with lice on their clothes and bodies, whilst their backs are all of a rash with bites and dirt'.

As well as neglect, a major concern was for an injury to 12-year-old Amy's eye. After a good deal of investigative work it was established that Mrs Pearson had caused the injury when, in a fit of rage, she threw a basin at Amy and split her eye. Amy confirmed this herself in a statement (always handwritten by the Inspector), which indicted her mother and corrected an earlier deception: 'I told the Inspector on Monday that I fell down onto the kerbstone. My mother told me to say this. I told him on Tuesday afternoon, in front of Mr D. [school board officer], that my mother did it which is the truth.' Mrs Pearson denied causing the injury and wanted to implicate her husband. She 'accused him of kicking the girl a fortnight ago. She then called the girl a bad wicked thing and maintained she could do nothing with her'.

A doctor's medical examination and certificate confirmed the extent of the injury and the neglect and offered the 'opinion that the condition of the children and their surroundings would tend to cause them unnecessary suffering'. Amy was removed to a 'place and safety' under the provisions of the 1889 and 1894 Prevention of Cruelty to Children Acts. She was settled temporarily in an NSPCC shelter which serviced this local area. The shelter that housed Amy was closed in 1903 as a directive of national organizational policy.

The NSPCC Legal Department advised on all serious cases. The Pearson file was adjudged 'a very bad case and there must be a prosecution'. Mr Pearson was charged with neglect and Mrs Pearson with neglect and ill-treatment. As a result of the proceedings Mr Pearson was 'cautioned', while his wife was sentenced to three months' imprisonment with hard labour. This differential treatment was attributed to having less to do with Mrs Pearson's additional charge than with how the courtroom drama proceeded. Mr Pearson had set things up so that only he would appear to the summons. He then 'artfully admitted the evidence of the prosecution and added that he had the misfortune to have a bad wife'. The Inspector subsequently accompanied a police officer to arrest Mrs Pearson at home. Her view was that if she had not been misled into avoiding the court appearance, 'he would have got the punishment and she let off'.

Supervision of the case continued while Mrs Pearson was in prison. Mr Pearson had secured the help of his 17-year-old daughter to take care of the home and children in his wife's absence. Amy was returned home from care at the beginning of May, 'clean and freshly clothed. June 10th she is disgustingly filthy'. On this date Amy was again found with a badly cut head – about which the Inspector had received another complaint.

Mr Pearson was interviewed and admitted causing the injury. He explained that he had got a 'bit drunk' during a visit to the theatre and on his return Amy had burned some food, 'which vexed me and I hit her with my hand (doubling his hand in temper to illustrate)'. Additionally, concern about neglect had persisted. Legal advice again regarded it as 'a bad case, and eminently one for court proceedings'. Moreover, 'The lives the children have been leading lately seem to have been terrible in the extreme consequence of the drunken brutal conduct of the man rendering their lives more one of heroism and misery than anything else'.

Mr Pearson was prosecuted and sent to prison for five months with hard labour. As both parents were now in prison, alternative care arrangements were made for four of the children at the local workhouse. More permanent care arrangements were made for Amy as her position within the family was now regarded as untenable. On the day of the court proceedings 'her condition impressed the whole court', and the chairman of the Bench 'expressed his intention of doing something for the girl's future welfare and there and then arranged with the Court Missionary to take charge of her until other arrangements could be made'. Amy was subsequently fostered locally.

These are the main features of the Pearson case history as it is told on the file. The vividness and complexity of the case, which I have chosen fairly randomly, may seem surprising to us today, but it is typical of the period in this regard. In considering how this casework was experienced and given meaning in practice I shall now develop the many themes and issues it raises on two main levels: one concerns the more structural aspects of the case and interpretation; the other attends to the more subjective dimensions of practice. Such a distinction is, of course, schematic and has rather more meaning in theory than in practice, but it does have the virtue of ordering a more coherent discussion.

The birth of child protection practice

In order to begin to make sense of child protection practice and contextualize it in its time and space, it is necessary to explore it through a dialogue with wider social processes, which were very much larger than the lives of the participants they so influenced. The duration of the Pearson case in fact straddles and expresses the unfolding of key aspects of a major transformation that was in progress in the relations between families and the state. The dynamics of much of this were perfectly visible in their own locality, indeed even in their own home, which seems the necessary context within which to situate the investigation. Its most vivid expression was that prior to 1889 they could not expect to have been troubled by a child protection worker at all. Only two years before they were first prosecuted for neglect in 1891 the first ever specific English Prevention of Cruelty to Children Act was passed in 1889, under which they were subsequently charged.

These developments did not represent the first attempts to regulate household relations, however. Local authorities, voluntary organizations, and the church have always shown some interest in childhood well-being (Holman, 1988; Heywood, 1959). The same is true of local communities and extended familial relations, which have always played active parts in family – or should we say household – life. To suggest that there was ever a time when households were free from 'outside' regulation is to protract a 'myth of family independence' (Gordon, 1985). Indeed, as Pollock (1983) shows, for at least a hundred years *before* the passing of the specific Prevention of Cruelty to Children Acts, child cruelty was condemned, punished by the state, and regarded as socially aberrant.

Yet it remains crucial to insist upon and delineate the radical dimensions of what households like the Pearsons' began to experience from the late 1880s onwards. They felt the weight of new social practices and powers, which began to register a break at this time with traditional Victorian strategies of administering welfare, regulating households, and punishing deviations (Garland, 1985). A national crusade and organization to prevent child abuse was both an outcome and a constitutive force of such social changes. Having sown the seeds of organization in Liverpool and London in the early 1880s, by 1889 a National Society for the Prevention of Cruelty to Children was established (Behlmer, 1982). In 1898 the Pearsons' Inspector was one of a national network of 163 officers servicing 812 'centres of work', from where in the same year they investigated a total of 28,758 new cases. In 1909, by which time there were now 250 Inspectors nationwide, child cruelty had shown an alarming increase to 52,670 new cases (see NSPCC Stockton, 1911, p. 25).

In their 'districts' Inspectors answered to a local branch committee who met monthly in order to manage fund-raising and, selectively, to partake in case management. In addition, there was the Annual General Meeting, the symbolic high-point of the voluntary supporters' and reformers' calendar from which extensive local reports were produced. The NSPCC was no exception to the Victorian rule in philanthropy of attracting the support of powerful local dignitaries. In the Pearsons' locale the impressive lists of supporters represented more than simply symbolic figure-heads. They were also key personnel in the local state. The same year in which the Pearson case appears in the Annual Report both as a statistic and in the form of a vivid case-illustration of work carried out during the year, the local Mayor, who was a vice-president of the NSPCC branch, was also the local Chief magistrate. He could inform the AGM of how impressed he was with the Society's work brought before him on the Bench. He shared the podium and an executive NSPCC position with three other Justices of the Peace.

Members of this social class were not represented at all in the lists of agency clientele however. Representations of child abusers took a characteristic form: 'The general character of the complaints has been much the same as in former years; drunkenness with accompanying dirt and squalor, accounting for a large share of the neglect' (NSPCC Stockton, 1899, p. 13).

Statements such as these are indicative of how the character of child protection practice was shaped from the outset through the interplay between the locality, ethnicity, politics, class, and gender. They betray an immediate social class and political sensibility that reflects upon the enormous social, moral, and physical gulf that increasingly separated reformers and the lower orders through nineteenth-century social changes. The manner in which these developments led to the 'labouring classes' being commonly regarded by distanced upper-class groups as a 'dangerous' threatening race apart has been classically illustrated elsewhere (Stedman Jones, 1971). Philanthropic organization and ultimately social work, including child protection practice, were spawned from these kinds of social processes.

Undisguised sentiments of disgust, which local anti-cruelty reformers routinely displayed in their representations of child abuse, underlay such a distrust and ideology of 'dangerousness' in this work. But, as scholars have begun to show through closer consideration of the complex meanings of such statements, they are part of a fundamental ambivalence that Victorian reformers experienced in their tasks. They coexisted with a complex desire and fascination in relation to these 'dangerous' classes. Given that reformers and agency clientele barely knew each other, except through the cultural mediation of social workers, the committee meeting, like the courtroom drama, brought these curiosities close, but kept them equally at a safe distance (Stallybrass and White, 1986).

Gendered assumptions predominated in Victorian conceptions of the home and the sexual division of labour (Williams, 1987; Lewis, 1986). The attitude towards the consumption of alcohol by women like Mrs Pearson is one of many examples of how moral standards were constituted in practice on terms that were not equally applied to men.

The Pearsons were local people born and bred. There is little evidence that practice in the locality was premised upon distinct patterns of ethnic difference, as it was, for example, in other English towns such as York, where efforts were persistently made to assimilate large numbers of post-famine Irish settlers into a dominant indigenous culture (Finnegan, 1982). Yet, as Smith (1987) makes clear, this should not lead us to infer the absence of an ethnic dimension in social practice. A coherent code, of in this case 'Englishness', was applied as an essential aspect of ideologies of what constituted 'normal' White Anglo-Saxon Protestant family life.

In sum, the mobile, uncertain, hand-to-mouth, 'immoral' lifestyle of households like the Pearsons' represented to reformers and *perhaps* to social workers the worse excesses of 'disreputable' character. 'Neglect and starvation' was by far the most common category of child abuse. Out of a total of 165 new complaints/cases made in this locality in 1898, 113 were classified in this way. In this regard, Amy Pearson's physical injury was not statistically typical, being one of twenty-five cases classified under 'ill-treatment and assault'. Other classifications included: 'exposure' (nine cases); 'causing to beg, etc.' (six cases); 'immoral surroundings' (one case); 'abandonment' (one case); 'other wrongs' (ten cases).

This context of how households with problems like the Pearsons' were regarded and classified by reformers and their institutions is crucial to reaching an understanding of the casework strategies and child protection welfare ideologies that flowed from them. The Pearsons' prosecutions in 1898 were included in a total of 20 cases (12 per cent) 'dealt with' in this way out of the 165 new openings; 102 (62 per cent) were 'warned'; 36 (22 per cent) were 'otherwise dealt with'; and 7 cases (4 per cent) were 'not proved'.

In relation to the other dimension of legal proceedings, the power to remove children from parental custody, Amy Pearson was part of an annual trend that disturbed supporters. From a total of 413 children who had come to the Society's attention in the locality over the 12 months, it was considered that:

> There have been an unusual number of cases in which the transfer of custody of children has been found desirable. Dr. Barnardos has taken seven of these into his Homes, while two sisters have been to the Church of England Society for Waifs and Strays, and another child placed in a Roman Catholic Institution. In addition to these a girl has been placed in service, and a boy returned to his parents. So far as is possible the parents of these children are induced to contribute to their maintenance. (NSPCC Stockton, 1899, p. 15.)

The eleven children involved here were members of a group of 81 local children admitted to the shelter during the year, 'thirty-seven in respect of offences, and forty-four found wandering or lost'. Thus Amy Pearson's experience of being returned home from the place of safety after five weeks, and after the prosecution of her parents, represented the normative content of the casework practice in 1898.

A key to making sense of this lies in examining the shifting historical context of meanings and ideologies that lay behind legal and punitive interventions and how this connected with child protective practice. Earlier in the decade, for example, we find reformers convir.ced that prosecutions had a significance far beyond the contours of the individual lives that they so drastically tried to affect:

> We feel that the success of the work in our district is very largely due to the exemplary sentences which have ever characterised our magistrates' sense of a child's wrong. In the Appendix are given details of some of the cases dealt with in the past year, and also a list of the convictions obtained. (NSPCC Stockton, 1893–4, p. 14)

Punishment as represented here was a profoundly symbolic process tied strongly to the religious vernacular of a Victorian social and moral order. It was designed to effect retribution through the deprivation of liberty and the physical endurance of hard labour. This in turn had a moral aspect to it as offenders were expected to reflect upon, amend, and repent their wrongs. Such a process of moral reform with women, for example, was encouraged through the nineteenth century by philanthropic visits from women caseworkers who counselled 'offenders' in their prison cells (Dobash, Dobash, and Gutteridge, 1986). And, finally, punishment was designed to work as a deterrent by showing to local communities the power of the state as it flexes its disciplinary muscles (Foucault, 1977). It worked to induce fear in local citizens and thereby deter through a spectacular display of the retributive power of the local state.

Such representations were part of a distinctly social process as they reached well beyond the private relations between reformers, social workers, and clients and into communities via a compliant media. Equally visible in the local press, besides detailed reports of the discourse of NSPCC committee meetings, were widely reported cases of child abuse that passed through the courts. 'CRUELTY TO CHILDREN – A WRETCHED HOME AND A DISGRACE TO YORK', headlined the *York Evening Press* in October 1898. '. . . and this at the end of the 19th century in York', the report goes on!

The Pearsons' incarcerations in 1891 can almost certainly be understood on these terms. They were motivated by these elements of 'deterrence', 'retribution', and 'moral reform' which went to make up Victorian penal–welfare strategies (see Garland, 1985, ch. 2). In this sense, they demonstrated a negative use of state power, one that sought to exclude the Pearsons from society. This was both symbolic and real as they were incarcerated in 'total' institutions placed on the edge of cities and society. Here no especial interest would have been shown in responding to them as 'child abusers' as such. They were part of a generalized population of criminals and 'rebels' responded to in a uniform way by the penal law, social practice, and the judicial process of this Victorian period.

Undoubtedly, many remnants of this welfare ideology persisted in their case management in 1898, but crucial differences were unfolding as part of a major transformation in punishment, social practices, and welfare ideologies which occurred in England across the 1890–1914 period. Two major effects of this can be stressed here. First, the prison ceased to be the central institution and the predominant sanction in social practice and became just one institution among many in an extended network of practices that pervaded the 'social' body. The NSPCC is a classic example of this shift: it represents a practice that was constituted and legitimated through the disciplinary power of the penal sanction yet operated socially in and amongst communities. Secondly, it was the principle of moral reformation that defined the core goal of these reconstituted social practices. The goals of deterrence and retribution remained within the system, but, in contrast to the largely symbolic processes outlined above, 'disciplinary practices are henceforth to place their emphasis upon the positive incentives of "hope", with its possibilities of moral regeneration instead of the negative conformity produced by fear' (Garland, 1985, p. 30).

Taken together, the Pearsons' case as it was caught up in these processes of change reflects how a whole modern social and administrative child protection framework and response to child abuse was being set in place. First, they became an individual 'case', which is not a natural development that we should simply take for granted. Administrative processes are central to all 'disciplinary' procedures and practices. Foucault (1977, p. 191) is probably correct to characterize the 'casefile' as an utterly unsentimental utilitarian document, which depicts 'the individual as he [sic] may be described, judged, measured, compared with others, in his very individuality; and it is also the individual who has to be trained or corrected, classified, normalised, excluded etc.'

Secondly, at the same time as they were recognized in their 'individuality', the Pearson parents were no longer 'rebels' but social deviants who could be *reformed* according to the standards of 'normal' parenting and 'good' citizenship defined through the sociopolitical process of which these transformations were a central part. This reformative or 'rehabilitative' ideal was from very early on operationalized in this NSPCC work and represented as a welfare ideology that stressed that: 'The aim of the society is not to relieve parents of their responsibilities, but to enforce them by making idle, neglectful, drunken and cruel parents do their duty to their children' (NSPCC York, 1899).

It was this ideal of the sanctity of 'individual parental responsibility' that led reformers and contemporaries to regard the permanent removal of cruelly treated young people like Amy Pearson from parental custody as both untypical and undesirable in the unfolding character of child protection work. It is quite wrong, in this light, to suggest as some influential commentators have (Holman, 1988) that all child care welfare practice of this period was marked by the absence of a rehabilitative philosophy and dominated by approaches that sought to 'rescue' children from failing parents. As a corollary to such an interpretation, it has been argued that a fixed label of deviancy was then withheld from parents as the weight of the social practice was felt by the rescued child in an attempt to avoid her or him becoming a future threat to social order (Dingwall, Eekelaar, and Murray, 1983, p. 220; Pfohl, 1977).

Casework practice in child protection proceeded upon quite different terms. Cruel parents like the Pearsons could be morally reclaimed through an approach that sought to strengthen and 'enforce' their waning parental responsibility. Power could now be used positively. It began to individualize and mobilize parents in therapeutically oriented practice and treatment programmes. 'Child abusers' were now routinely labelled as social deviants and either institutionalized or supervised around a rehabilitative ideal that sought to correct them *as* parents. By the turn of the century, for example, the NSPCC was writing widely about women like Mrs Pearson in terms of 'inebriate mothers and their reform'. Indeed, in her own locale some women were now being sent for individualized correction to newly established inebriate reformatories for up to three-year incarcerations. 'While in the retreat', it was stressed, 'it is for us to see that she never forgets that she is a *mother*. We recognize that she is where she is in order that she may be restored to her honourable place in the world of mothers' (NSPCC, *Annual Report, 1903)* pp. 13–14; emphasis in original).

Through such positive uses of state powers child protection practices were now tied inexorably to the differentiation and individualization of modern households and subjects at the heart of modern 'case-work', and to the wider social processes of the creative construction of modern identities of motherhood, fatherhood, the 'abused child' and so on. Thus after seven years of casework, with Amy re-injured, rejected, and in care along with her neglected siblings, and with both parents now in gaol, the return of this household to their 'honourable place' in the world of this unfolding social order seemed doomed. Viewed structurally, from the vantage point of the shifting meanings and strategic objectives in practices, it is difficult to avoid the conclusion that, on their own terms, all those involved in the protection of these children had 'failed'. (On this notion of strategic failure in social policy, see Foucault 1980, p. 250.)

Subjective practices: words, opinions, and actions

I have been arguing that the Pearson 'case' can be seen as a historical text that corresponds and gives life to key structural changes and effects that occurred across the late-Victorian/Edwardian period and gave birth to a modern child protection practice much as we know it today. Both the Pearson household and their social workers knew what it was like to live and work in times and ways that were not truly modern at all. Yet here they were having to negotiate new rules and powers and be open to and constitute a whole new mode of professional practice and experience. The Pearsons' casefile must therefore also be read as a text that expresses and displays key dimensions of these new social actions, and it is to this reading that we now turn.

In real terms this meant that across the 1890s various professionals institutionally equipped with 'a new power to judge' (Foucault, 1977, p. 23) were locked in dynamic and even violent struggles with the Pearsons and households like them over parental and children's rights to welfare, privacy, and protection and in general classification struggles over how the household was to be judged, helped, punished, and treated. The changing politics and practices of child protection were deeply felt subjective experiences for the actors involved, and only came to have meaning as they were expressed through these social practices.

Child protection work had become a professional life on the run, as workers followed (and perhaps even chased) the Pearsons around their various addresses. Most often, these struggles were played out on doorsteps or – sometimes invited, often not – in their home as workers demanded to get to know them better as abusive parents and regulate and understand their torrid domestic relations with their abused children. We must now attempt to follow them through these encounters.

Workers took to their task with an alacrity that left households like the Pearsons perhaps feeling unduly invaded and that the odds were stacked against them. Of all new cases opened in 1898, 28 per cent were reported to the Pearsons' NSPCC Inspector by 'police and other officials'. In the same year the Inspector himself unearthed and instigated 29 new cases (17.5 per cent) from the 165 new openings. Child protection workers had taken to the task of developing the social practice on the streets with alarming vigour. They tore into localities, literally patrolling slums. Earlier in the decade, as the practice was establishing itself in this district, the number of new cases 'discovered by Inspector' out of a total of 193 was a remarkable 51 (26 per cent) (NSPCC, Stockton, 1894–5). By 1911 the proportion had dropped to a steady 5.5 per cent.

In addition, child protection practice proceeded from the outset upon major collaborations with other state agencies not only in defining its object of intervention but in the pragmatics of ongoing casework. Two police officers, a general practitioner, and the 'school board man' all rubbed shoulders with the Inspector in the Pearson home in 1898. Add to this the involvement of the judiciary in the public sphere, and the 'child at risk' had already become a focal point of a variety of social practices, all claiming different levels of expertise which would constitute increasingly competitive 'claims to know better' (Dunn, 1985) as the social and administrative child abuse 'system' entered the twentieth century (see Corby, 1987b; Chapter 10 in this volume).

Having torn their way into local communities, workers were powerfully symbolic figures. Like all NSPCC officers, the Pearsons' Inspector was a man and he wore a distinctive uniform. As Behlmer (1982, p. 162) notes, the organization particularly liked to recruit men from the services with proven abilities to respect and carry out orders. The uniform nicely symbolizes the 'disciplined' character of these men, which has two aspects to it. As Giddens (1985, p. 114) observes, within welfare/punishment organizational settings the uniform has the same implications for disciplinary power as in the services, helping strip individuals of those traits that might interfere with routinized patterns of obedience. Second, the uniform is a potent signifier, which indicates to local populations the distinctiveness of its bearer as a specialist purveyor of state disciplinary powers.

NSPCC workers literally embodied both these contradictory processes. Attempts were made to strip them of autonomy and individuality and develop a homogeneous organizational response to child protection. Yet, they were at the same time responsible social actors who had the specialist powers – like none other of these social practitioners beside whom they laboured – to enter people's homes and lives and separate them. However, given the character of these unfolding state powers and their modes of cultural and inter-personal expression, these workers also embodied the social and legal resources and strengths that could enable and enforce households to stay living together, to struggle on to fight each other and bureaucracy another day.

Like all tensions, ambiguities, and vulnerabilities in their practice, these contradictions forced their way into contention and into the casefile writings of these workers, almost against their best utilitarian intentions. In 1898 a York Inspector, in an unguarded moment, found himself doubting a 'neglectful' mother's 'dubious' account of herself, and drew back to rationalize, 'I am allowed to form an opinion, so long as I do not express it in words'!

For all that, of course, the Pearson file, like all others, is constituted almost entirely through the written words of formed and expressed opinions. The essence of this administrative process being to redescribe the social practice and reflect judgements and classifications of household situations and parental culpabilities, there is no sense in which a file describes an 'objective' truth or reality. The key issue becomes not if opinions are expressed, but whose and on what basis.

As these ambiguities strike the NSPCC worker he cannot easily make these distinctions between the demands of organizational philosophy and routine and his own thoughts, actions, and writings. He has received a training for his job and so, like all social workers, has been socialized into a professional occupational culture. This experience can involve a kind of 'deformation of the self', which can affect not only attitudes and beliefs, but the character structure itself. As he loses sight of how, as a professional person, he has a particular view of the world and child abuse, he is apt to become an idealist. He may lose sight of the centrality of his own self and actions in identifying the problem. From within this professional culture, in other words, he comes to see the world, or so he thinks, as it is (Pearson, 1975, p. 127).

Here is the Pearsons' Inspector grappling with these tensions and much more besides. Pearson has called on him on his release from prison in November 1898. The results of the meeting were recorded by the Inspector in a letter to his legal department requesting advice on case management:

> . . . please note that the man is now out of gaol and has been to see me regarding the custody of [Amy]. He is anxious to have a further chance and promised that if allowed to retain custody of the child he will do what he can for her and to

reform his character. I am aware it is an old standing case and he has had ample warnings but I should be glad if you will give him this chance which he asks for. He has signed the temperance pledge with me and if he can manage to keep it I have hope he may do better.

I do not urge the matter beyond what you may consider the best interest of the child and have not brought the matter before my committee and this is only my personal suggestion.

These remarks illustrate how child protection casework was constituted from the outset through complex social and human relationships. The worker here struggles to reconcile and situate his own desires and practical actions and to represent those of his client within the legal–bureaucratic structure that makes their encounter possible. We see an immediate symmetry between the reformative welfare ideology that came to dominate practice over his period and the caseworker's ideals. Having taken steps to 'enforce' parental responsibility, the punishment complete, the caseworker now wants to believe the best of the client. In contemporary idioms, he is an optimistic practitioner. He regards the parents of children – especially it seems those like Amy Pearson who have had to go into care following strong interventions – as his primary clients. He believes in the new power of reform and the emerging rehabilitative ideal, which both he and his client want to invoke. He has 'hope' that even after all these years (and no apparent objective improvements), he can now help to rebuild these tragic broken lives.

What gives this rehabilitative ideal a special reality and authenticity here is how, in its formative phase, the practitioners themselves seem to have been caught up in the enthusiasm for it. It shows workers not only keeping up with the pace of reform but outpacing their managers, their 'hope' driving them on to make 'personal suggestions'. They take initiatives, develop ideas, and begin to conceive of new and varied forms of therapies and ways of helping to reconstruct these lives. This seems to enable them to find meaning and excitement in labour that was invariably emotionally gruelling and always contentious. While the nature of their own subjective experience would always be difficult to assess, these practitioners were no mere organizational dupes or lackeys of a bourgeois state, but social actors actively constructing the foundations of modern forms of knowledge, of therapeutic and cultural practice: in short, a professional culture that would take child protection into the twentieth century. And they seemed inspired to do this because they had some vision of the work as a whole and its value to the emerging liberal social order and community of which it was a central part. (For

aspects of the contemporary relevance of these remarks to child
protection, see Chapter 5 in this volume. More generally, on the
nature of 'modernist' experience, see Berman, 1983.)

Local communities played their part too in shaping a social
practice permeated with an enormous sociability. 'I know the
family by living opposite,' professed the female neighbour whose
statement so indicted Mrs Pearson. 'We can see nicely what goes
on.' On a more general level, local communities were often
more reticent, suspicious, and prepared to resist cooperating.
'The locality in which this family live is very low and neighbours
evidence worth little even if it could be obtained,' the Pearsons'
Inspector complained of a neighbouring household. Workers
clearly built such local knowledge into their casework strategies
and used it as a basis for deciphering the validity of the evidence
that they so rapaciously tried to gather about the community.

In other respects, the flow of initiative from communities was
impressive. Fifty-four per cent of new referrals in 1898 were
from the 'general public' (NSPCC, Stockton, 1899). Behlmer
(1982, ch. 6) argues that deprived working-class neighbourhoods
were prepared to report their neighbours because of a grudging
respect for the 'cruelty men' whose child-centred mission lent to
their work a mystique of classlessness, which seemed to place
it above the rule of bourgeois law and practice. Moreover, he
avers, organized working-class labour supported the anti-cruelty
campaign actively with donations and symbolically through
appearance at national meetings. These are important observations, impressive not least because of their attempt to do justice
to the rationality of the poor in shaping the social practice.

Ultimately, however, because they are pre-eminently social
class oriented interpretations, they stop short of an adequate
account. The Pearson case itself invokes us to seek more complex
meanings and interpretations, primarily because of the extent of
intra-familial conflict it reveals. It was Amy Pearson's 17-year-old
sister who made the second complaint to the Inspector in 1898 (the
source of the first is not given on the file). She went to his office
seeking help in the early hours of the morning after her father
had terrorized her, turned her out of the house, and assaulted
Amy. By responding to such invitations, child protection practice
was fundamentally conceived through arbitrating between the
weak and the strong in familial domestic relations. To refer
unproblematically to 'the' working-class family obscures the
prevalence of intra-familial oppressions of age and gender and
speaks only to the 'needs' of its head: men (see Gordon, 1986).

Thus, in responding to referrals, workers were at all times
encouraged to display tact and discretion. 'Two can play at
the game of bounce,' NSPCC workers were advised in their

training and practice manual of agency rules and manners, 'and the owner of the house plays it with all the odds on his side' (*NSPCC Inspectors' Directory*, 1904, p. 8). In practice, the 'owner of the house', as in the Pearson case, was male, in both real and symbolic terms. Social workers went to great pains to acknowledge men's domestic rights. 'With the permission of [Pearson] I examined the house in company with P. C. H . . . who came round on his beat.' On seeing the Inspector at the address in March 1898, the police constable testifies, 'I went with him and examined the man [Pearson's] house (with his permission) and found it in a filthy condition'.

Workers themselves were emphasizing the acutely sensitive nature of this new social power and some of the rituals and conventions involved in establishing a child protection practice in the domestic domain. Home visiting was from the outset the *modus operandi* of this practice. It had to be. Invited or not, the extension of disciplinary powers and social practice into this spatial context was a fundamental prerequisite to gaining access to children and regulating parental conduct. There was, in fact, almost a literal sense in which other professionals followed after the 'cruelty men' – doctors, for example, as in the Pearson case, routinely home-visiting to examine children at NSPCC request after the latter had made their momentous interventions. The Pearsons' 'supervisions' were among 523 home visits made by their worker that year. Ongoing casework, as well as new interventions, it was noted, 'continues to form an important part of the Inspectors' duties' (NSPCC, Stockton, 1899, p. 15).

A most conspicuous feature of the Pearson case was how this 'game of bounce' was played out almost entirely by men. There may well be some secrets of men's history hidden here (Filene, 1987), as all the professionals who called on this household were men. In addition, an all-male judiciary had heard of Pearson's 'artfully' stated 'misfortune to have a bad wife' and they acted accordingly. In this case and locality there is little evidence of women visitors, who are, conventionally, believed to have played the predominant role in opening up the historical means to state intervention into the family in their role as prodigious philanthropic visitors (Prochaska, 1980). Women were involved in the local child protection practice as fund-raisers, and more actively through a schedule of voluntary work that helped to run the children's 'shelter'. They were, in other words, discharging the class-gendered role of ladies, in the historical sense of the term (Davidoff and Hall, 1987).

Given such gendered assumptions, child protection work was perhaps not surprisingly regarded as men's social practice. This observation may apply more generally to the kinds of social work that developed from the 1880s, conceived as they often were through very different flows of state initiative and power-laden interventions from those typical of traditional charity work. But given the ideals of manhood and a public spirit of masculinity that was embodied in this practice, men did not escape state regulation. Indeed, it was precisely *because* of these ideals that this was so, as this was a period of general 'crisis' in masculinity (Kimmel, 1987) and redefinition of patriarchal powers and relations (Gordon, 1986). As is generally the case (Hearn, 1987), patriarchal power returned to visit men here in the form of the enforcing of modern ideals of respectable fatherhood. Pearson was not rendered morally culpable for the abuse of Amy and her siblings in any simple or straightforward sense associated with his masculine domestic tyranny. This itself was framed in the following terms: 'Instead of spending his earnings upon his home and children he preferred to enjoy himself at Theatres and getting tipsy.'

Professional men scrutinized the characters of male agency clients for evidence of irresponsible manhood. They reinforced an ideal of 'normal' paternal responsibility that saw men as distanced from domestic life since the 'honourable place' for fathers to be was in the public sphere of paid work and indirect familial duty.

By definition, this left women, as primary child carers, open to an almost indeterminate range of interventions by a male-dominated social practice into the domestic arena – one that on its own terms is implicated as profoundly ignorant of this domestic domain and the demands of child care within which child abuse must always be contextualized (Ferguson, 1986). For these public men laboured away here utterly distanced and alienated from *their own* domestic domains. Equipped with little or no knowledge of child care, here they were rapaciously describing and producing a knowledge of child abuse.

Mrs Pearson's relative absence from the narrative of this discussion reflects her silence in the discourse of the file. She speaks twice (both illustrated above), both times as a 'child abuser', never as a woman struggling with the demands of child care in difficult circumstances (see Chapter 3 in this volume). Disciplinary steps were taken to remind her of her failing motherhood, which here, as throughout the period, was regarded as a natural, instinctual phenomenon. Children's 'rights' and entry into the discourse of the file and citizenship were then negotiated on this basis – radical in its time – as an entitlement to strong parental care, not freedom from it.

Professional men sought to remake male agency clients in the image of upright industrious masculinity they saw themselves as embodying, and female agency clients in the image of maternal domesticity so beloved of the prescriptions of the renewed patriarchal powers they embodied (see also Chapter 4 in this volume). Such class-gendered assumptions were the basis of the social worker's optimistic practice and the emerging 'normality' of the liberal order and the terms upon which the meanings and outcomes of practice were negotiated in the evolving routines of child protection work. In this crucial regard, workers can be seen not only to have formed and expressed their opinions, but to have lived by them and acted upon them too.

Finally, children, women, and men clients were far from passive in all this. They resisted not only their own intra-familial oppressions of each other, as it were, but pervasively also the attentions of social workers. Mr Pearson soon got fed up with cooperating with uninvited surveillances. Things came to a head during the course of the investigation into the second complaint – initiated by his daughter – in June 1898. At 9.30 a.m. the Inspector visited and explains:

> I asked to see the beds, but [Pearson] refused to allow me. He again became very abusive and threatened violence. I left the house and again visited at 10.15 a.m. and was followed by Police Sgt M... Whilst the Sgt and I was there [Pearson] behaved as though he was mad – he appeared to be suffering with drink. I saw the sleeping apartment which is fearfully filthy and stinking with accumulated dirt.

Highly emotional confrontations such as these were typical of this early work. At moments such as these, workers were constantly made aware of how none of their casework could be regarded as predetermined in its outcomes. Every background assumption, every rule, every law that they embodied had to be operationalized and put to work through social actions and practices that were then constituted through intensely complex encounters and relations.

The worker goes on to explain what he found upon reaching his objective:

> I saw 4 children lying on a mattress and a broken flock bed. There was a dirty quilt for covering. I lifted up the quilt which exposed the children. They were absolutely naked. They had, it is true, fragments of undershirts, but these were so torn and worn, they would not reach a third down the body if they were pulled.
>
> I searched the house for food but could not find a particle ...

Vivid descriptions such as these were a hallmark of interventions. Practitioners groped to find a language for what they were experiencing. They could barely believe what they saw, or smelled, or touched, and they struggled to contain the sensations it evoked – the risk, the adventure, the tragedy and the awfulness of it all. A whole new professional *experience* had opened up before them. They had torn down the walls of privacy and silences that surrounded the Victorian bourgeois family, stepped into the holes they had made, and so were key actors in constituting a whole new social practice of child protection. In doing so they helped – however conditionally – to make real the misery of hermetically sealed Victorian poverty and human decay that was once a mystery. More than this, they helped create a real and symbolic social practice that would enable practitioners to search round people's houses and enter their most intimate spaces and desires. Even a decade before, such a taking of children from their beds was unthinkable. But they did not do this in any absolute or final sense, of course. For better or for worse, they created the conditions that have made possible the re-enactment of these kinds of struggles and encounters as practitioners have been stepping through the spaces that they made between family and state ever since.

Like so many of its kind, the Pearson case ended uncertainly and without resolution. We are told nothing of Mrs Pearson after she went to prison. Mr Pearson's and the worker's requests to reunite Amy with home were curtly refused. Amy ran away from her new foster home after three days. Found 'wandering the streets' she was brought to the Inspector who placed her in the workhouse with her siblings. The latter would return home; she would not. Hope had turned to resignation. Within the administrative code of the file, what more needed to be said? The case at least could now be closed.

Concluding remarks

'I leave it to you to say', wrote an NSPCC worker in 1899 when seeking legal advice, 'what is to be done to make the lives of these children worth living.' In this chapter I have presented a historical case study that illustrates just how coherently these kinds of questions and the answers to them were formulated a century ago. One of the distinctive features of these case histories of the first child protection work is that, in their attempts to form opinions and find a language and words through which to describe their actions, the questioners leave their questions and their answers echoing in the air long after they, themselves, have left the scene.

Clearly an awful lot has changed since the Pearsons and their many social workers fought out their struggles and sought their own answers. And we may be closer now to answering them more adequately than they were then. I have not sought to make such direct comparisons, but rather to present a case for history which shows implicitly how, in our own search for answers today, we seem peculiarly distanced and out of touch with these early struggles and the times when these questions were first formulated across the 1880–1914 period.

Without an adequate comprehension of historical perspective we are in danger today of trying to develop a child protection practice and policy that misunderstands and takes for granted the origins, scope, and nature of powers invested in state agents to practise at all; to judge others and develop various therapies, techniques, and professional (mis-)collaborations – such as have marked, for example, the recent history of child sexual abuse – and then to work these into knowledge, into theories and images of 'dangerousness', 'abuse', 'normality', and so on. We are apt to lose sight of the wider assumptions concerning gender, class, and ethnicity upon which these views of 'normality' and 'deviance' have been historically and socially built even in the most extreme cases of child abuse. And, crucially, we lose our connections with how practices have historically been experienced and given meaning in the context of some of the most mundane features of child protection work. We have seen how this is so in relation to the foundations of ideologies of 'hope' and rehabilitation and to core practice issues such as trying to gain access to a child, to a home, and how these are constituted through complex struggles and encounters of a long historical duration and character and cannot simply be laid at the door of some simplistic notion of individualized professional 'failure' or post-1970s' malaise in practice common to most contemporary interpretations (for example, London Borough of Greenwich, 1987; London Borough of Brent, 1985).

In sum, we seem to have lost our grip on the nature of the contradictions and experiences these early workers and households had to grasp when these powers and practices were first opening out and with which they had to grapple in order to get through their lives and work. More serious attention to this history will not resolve all, or perhaps many, of these contradictions, which continue to pervade our child protection practice. But it might help us to understand them for what they are. For the lives and work of these workers and households constitute the crucial historical construction site upon which all those who want to take child abuse seriously today must stake out and build a humane child protection practice – one that seeks

8 Dangerousness: a complex practice issue

BARRIE CLARK, WENDY PARKIN
and MARTIN RICHARDS

The primary purpose of this chapter is, at one level, to provide an insight into the skills, methods, and techniques used by the workers in a local authority Family Centre where sessional work is undertaken with families in distress. However, at another level, we discuss our approach to the work and the way the thinking and analysis of it has developed since the start of the Centre. Most crucial is the awareness of how wider economic, social, and organizational factors have influenced both the nature of this work and our responses to it. We wish not simply to locate practice in a wider context but to illustrate how the wider context affects practice at virtually every point.

Put another way, we not only recognize the personal as political but also see the political as personal, and this personal/political dimension is increasingly acknowledged in practice. The writing of this chapter has in itself been an important contribution to the recognition of this process, so that the 'description' of our work, which provides the main body of the chapter, can only reflect our approaches at the time of writing. However, we will be indicating some of the changes in approach and how they illustrate the way changing policies and politics change our practice as workers and the personal lives of families. We feel that many of the issues and tensions in current child care practice are sharply focused in Family Centre work but also have relevance to practitioners in other settings.

In discussion with other members of the study group we have reconsidered how the core of our work has been heavily influenced by the way child care practice has been reconstructed in terms of 'child protection'. The assessment of dangerousness and the legal framework are essential to an understanding of the concept of child protection (see Chapters 1, 4 and 5 in this volume, Parton, 1985a, and, perhaps most significantly, Parton and Parton, 1989).

The dominant influence on current social work practice with children and families has been the pervasive influence of new child abuse policies arising from inquiries and the wider socioeconomic climate. As a consequence, the primary concern and hence priority has become child protection work, with key features being (a) the need to recognize the central significance of the law and not be afraid to use statutory-based authority in professional work; (b) a central focus on the needs of the child rather than the rights of parents; (c) the crucial task of identifying 'high-risk' cases or, as we have now come to understand it, the assessment of dangerousness.

This concept of dangerousness, whilst not new, has in recent years become an important influence on policy and practice in social control strategies generally but is now central in child abuse policy and, as we will demonstrate, in our own day-to-day practice. The essential assumption of dangerousness is that there are a few individuals, or combinations of individuals, in the population prone to causing serious and lasting violence, whether physical, sexual, or psychological. The propensity for violence and dangerousness becomes the central focus in any decision about disposal. In the area of child abuse the focus is on the assessment of past, present, and future dangerousness, which can result in the long-term or permanent removal of children from a family. In this assessment process, the idea of prevention becomes reframed in terms of the identification of 'high-risk' or dangerous cases, with the possible consequence of material and personal resources being directed into this specific area rather than towards wider social changes. It is essentially a narrow and conservative approach to child care and family problems.

Thus, it is one where a family seeking help from social services for apparently minor problems can quickly move up the 'dangerousness tariff system' and be designated a high-risk case. The tariff system is a way of describing a process that begins when a family receives social work intervention in a child care climate where such intervention is from a framework of child protection. Preventive work is redefined and, combined with a need for worker protection, subsequent to the various inquiries, along with child protection, can result in an escalation of the case in terms of the 'dangerousness tariff'. A referral to the Family Centre is often for assessment, but is part of the escalation in that it is about whether children should stay at or return home. A paradox within this is that the existence of such a Centre can offer a last chance to families already designated as dangerous, through either convictions or permanent removal of children (see also Dale *et al.*, 1986), to show they can change and be redesignated as less dangerous.

Such an approach is given further legitimacy with a focus in child care policy on permanency planning for children. Permanency planning is an approach within child care practice that recognizes that early decisions need to be made after a child's admission to care. Such planning is about returning a child to its natural family or for the child to become a permanent member of a substitute family. It was a response to concern about children who remained waiting in care without any specific plans for permanency (Rowe and Lambert, 1973). Thus, assessment of dangerousness alongside this permanency planning in a period of reduced and restricted departmental resources become major factors in making decisions about children's futures: a process we recognize in our practice.

However, we have become increasingly sceptical as to whether such assessments and decisions can be as clear cut as is sometimes assumed. We are acutely aware of the major difficulties related to predictions of future dangerousness in theory, research, and practice (Parton, 1985a; Dingwall, 1989) and the considerable problems of making the wrong decision either way, especially pertinent when comparing the Jasmine Beckford, Tyra Henry, and Kimberley Carlile inquiries with the Cleveland one (see Chapters 5 and 6 in this volume). Also, we have to appreciate the significance of wider social inequalities related to race, class, and gender. What has been important to us has been to acknowledge explicitly the changing nature of our work and to be sensitive to its tensions in developing a practice that honestly spells this out to families and professional colleagues. At the same time we have recognized this reformulation of our work in terms of child protection and how we are now seen as a service for abusing families rather than for families in distress. We have tried to remain true to our original values and principles as we have accommodated to the changing reality of child care practice.

The changing role of the Family Centre

We now wish to outline how the focus and nature of our work has changed, and consequently the function of the Family Centre. This has developed in ways of which we were only partially aware at the time but which would seem to corroborate the preceding discussion on the prime importance of dangerousness and child protection rather than prevention.

The Family Centre in which we work evolved against the backdrop of the 'Family Centre movement' of the 1970s, when the predominant model was one of community-based neighbour-hood centres. Our centre was originally envisaged in this way but the unavailability of adequate accommodation, changing management, staff backgrounds, and philosophy soon contributed to a different model resulting from that initially envisaged in the planning stages. The staff group were, and still are, a combination of social work and NNEB (Nursery Nurse Education Board) trained personnel with administrative support. Though located organizationally with Residential and Day Care Services, the day-to-day work is with fieldwork social workers in area offices. The focus of the work is intensive, planned programmes for families with children under 5 years of age.

The literature on Family Centres illustrates the variety of size, purpose, and philosophy, with the only uniting factor being the vogue title 'Family Centre' (DHSS, 1986; McKechnie, 1986; Warren, 1986; Downie and Forshaw, 1987; Open University, 1987). The title can give rise to certain expectations, such as the desirability of parents and the children staying together, thus leading to an emphasis on the prevention of family breakdown: 'All [Family Centres] were seen to have a common focus on the family with young pre-school children and shared common commitment to enabling parents under stress to care better for their children, prevention of reception into care and strengthening of the family seen as common aims' (Open University, 1987).

Certainly, the Family Centre had, at the outset, the remit of 'prevention', thus fitting into the ideology of children being with natural parents, so that the original policy document statement (1984) stated, 'The ultimate aim of the Centre is to reduce the need for children to be admitted to care or remain in residential care and thus be separated from their natural family.'

Our original practice was also aimed towards preventing children being brought into care; lessening physical and psychological damage to children; and treating the family as a whole unit (Kirklees Social Services Department, 1984). We thought of ourselves developing a preventive practice (see Holman, 1988) using in-depth individual and family work. The first key feature of child protection work was present from the start in that statutory-based authority has always been used. However, work was also undertaken on a voluntary basis and, whether voluntary or statutory, there has always been an attempt to negotiate with families some mutual agreement about the work to be undertaken. On occasions, this work was on an agreed brief to provide a permanent future for a child.

We also began to recognize that one outcome of our intervention was an increasing number of adoptions, and a survey of referrals confirmed and highlighted this fact.

Between October 1984 and February 1988, of the nineteen children in care for whom we attempted rehabilitation, nine were adopted and another two were recommended for adoption. These figures led us seriously to question whether we could be seen as a centre for keeping natural families together when over 50 per cent of attempted rehabilitation finished up as adoptions. We also examined figures for thirty-three children not in care but seen as needing intensive service to avoid family breakdown. These showed that 25 per cent of all the children dealt with by the Family Centre during the period October 1984 to February 1988 were adopted or recommended for adoption. It would appear that the focus of work is not on preventing breakdown but on securing futures for children whether with their natural family or not.

It could be argued that the preventive work has not been about preventing family breakdown but rather about preventing 'waiting' in care and preventing the avoidance of decision-making. No case, except those currently being worked or withdrawals by family or the area social worker, was allowed to drift, and decisions about futures for children were made in all cases. Although the balance of rights was seen initially as being with the parents, a change of focus to the needs of the child took place, again locating the Centre within the field of child protection work.

Another reformulation of the term 'prevention' has been a recognition of the amount of work undertaken with families where abuse or neglect had already occurred. In these cases the prevention becomes the prevention of re-injury. This involves different criteria for the assessment of future risk, but is still located very firmly in the assessment of dangerousness, the third feature of child protection work.

In our experience we have reviewed how we see preventive work. Formerly we saw it as defining which were the soft, low-risk cases with which social workers did preventive work. The hard, high-risk group were dealt with in a more legalistic framework. We believe this to be a false separation of questionable categories. Now at the Centre we work to prevent drift and re-abuse.

Writing this chapter has clarified this process for us and helped us to recognize that it was not just our preference for working with complex, high-risk cases that had led to our present situation; it was also the changing climate of opinion about child care work within which area teams had to also work. Thus resources such as the Family Centre would be used as a resource for high-risk work. At one point the Family Centre offered a service where the NNEB-trained workers could work with children's behaviour problems in the home. This service was never taken up by area teams and only now can we understand why the offer was not accepted – we were firmly into child protection and assessment of dangerousness. The work at the Centre is defined by being part of the tariff system, so that families are scrutinized and subject to surveillance. It is not just public inquiry reports that have seen such intervention as 'social policing'. Clients themselves have been more aware than the workers of the nature of the work. To quote one parent, 'I'm really under threat, by coming here, of having my children removed.'

Input from state agencies occurs in all families, but the amount varies widely in both volume and intensity. Where children are 'at risk', interventions may be made by many different agencies. This input is perceived differently by workers and families, workers often seeing such input as 'helpful' and 'supportive', although they also recognize the need for monitoring and surveillance. The families at the receiving end seem clear, as these varied comments from four parents illustrate:

'They are really watching me to see whether I am a fit mother.'

'They ask us to sit in a room along with our children and play. They watched us taking our child to the toilet but we did not know. Once we caught them watching us and began to understand them. They think they are spies like James Bond.'

'You can set up a bed and come and live with me.'

'Once they get their hands on you they don't let go.'

When we assessed the professional interventions within families who were referred, we observed that the amount of input did not appear to differ between statutory and voluntary cases. In fact some supposedly 'lower-risk' cases seemed to have more professional resources than those designated 'higher risk', possibly again highlighting the spurious distinction between the two and leading us once again to confirm the analysis that all such cases are about assessment of dangerousness. Thus there has been an increasing awareness of the impossibility of seeing 'a family in distress' or one where abuse had occurred in purely personal terms.

Such families are politicized by the changing emphasis at the Centre, which was itself dependent on the changing political and public climate, the nature of referrals, and the expectations of other professionals (see the Pearson case cited in Chapter 7 in this volume). In retrospect we now feel our response to cases was changing in ways that were imperceptible at the time. For example, in the early days of the Centre one particular child was returned home as the parents were seen to achieve an adequate level of child care, despite concern about longer-term prospects. We feel that such a recommendation would now be unlikely, bearing in mind the concerns about future dangerousness. It will be interesting to reassess our changes in thinking, policy, and practice following the rather different concerns reflected in the Cleveland Report (Secretary of State for Social Services, 1988). However, we should not conclude that, because the focus of our work and decision-making has shifted, this is inherently for the better or worse. What is important is that we explicitly recognize how this has come about and the responses that will take place in our practice.

The process of our practice

Before outlining the process and detail of our work there are certain basic principles and values which we see as fundamental to our practice. These include being clear with families and professionals about the focus of our work; working alongside area team colleagues and other professionals; creative use of a variety of means of communication with families; giving clients their own records of sessions; regular reviews of initial aims and progress towards these.

Every family referred to the Family Centre already has an allocated social worker within the local authority social services department area team. This area team social worker, who will already know the family, is asked to supply information about the family circumstances. In addition, we require organizational information such as the legal position; whether the principal social worker is in agreement with referral; whether other agencies are involved and if they are aware of this referral. After receiving this referral, two social workers from the Family Centre work together to identify the family and professional network and decide whether the two networks should be seen separately or together. The process of co-working with these networks is for the purpose of an initial assessment of the case. We begin by planning on the basis of our knowledge of the case; planning our role, and planning the preparation of the room and materials. It is essential to have an understanding of each other's style and philosophy and an ability to be 'tuned in' during the meeting to changes of emphasis from the other worker. Through this co-working we initially attempt to identify the level of cohesion within the worker network (defined as those in direct contact with the family plus line managers) (see also Dale *et al.*, 1986; Rochdale NSPCC, 1986). Frequently families are at the receiving end of confused and conflicting professional relationships which, when played out in front of them, move the focus of work from them to the organization (see Chapter 10 in this volume).

Such network meetings focus on the different ways the various agencies perceive the families and the professional roles. The basic aims of this initial meeting are to clarify fact, opinion, and issues; openly to face differences, and accurately to record decisions made. The information is collated on a chart to high-light the issues and contrast different agency inputs. Table 8.1 is an example of information collated from a family where there were concerns about the child's development and behaviour with input from five agencies. As the chart illustrates the value of having all agencies together is not only to obtain a com-prehensive picture of the family but to contrast and compare observations.

Table 8.1   *Sample chart with information from initial network meeting*

	Social worker	Health visitor	Home care assistant	Psychologist	Day nursery staff
Develop-ment	Speech delay	Failed 3 year test	Wets during day Gestures not speaks	Speech delay	Speech delay Not toilet trained
Child's behaviour	Wary at home, not at nursery		Poor eater	Poor communi-cation	Poor concentration Poor eater
Attachments	Goes to social worker for cuddles and stands next to her			Goes to her instead of mum	

At this initial network meeting, we have on occasions recognized that our involvement would be superfluous and would only cause further confusion, so we did not proceed. However, once we are involved, we have to accept that we too are part of the network and strive to be clear as to our role. There can be three possible outcomes: no offer of work, because the referral was not appropriate; no offer of work, because it was already being done by the existing professional network, thus there was no justification for introducing another agency; and information sorting with family. At an 'information sorting' the family is the focus of the meeting, together with a core group of professionals with input to the family and the Family Centre staff. Its purpose is to give the parents an opportunity to say how they see their family circumstances and to hear how the professionals view them. In our experience, families often handle these meetings better than the professionals and can avail themselves of this opportunity to be heard. Information emerges in the meeting and is dependent on the quality and quantity of the material offered by the family, and on the willingness of professionals to be honest in front of them. This intervention is shaped by the forward planning and intervention of the co-workers within a framework that highlights issues and difficulties. Sometimes these focus on tensions between the family and agencies as well as on intra-family difficulties. These meetings can last up to two hours. We discourage professional colleagues from attempting to express concerns behind parents' backs, or using 'jargon', preferring a model of openness with families about what the concerns are.

The starting point is always identifying the family size and shape, put into the form of a family diagram onto which is added information brought to the meeting by the participants. This diagram is based upon information from the family and shaped by them; for example, a divorced woman refused to have her violent husband recorded on the diagram. At the same time, the significance of a still-born baby became strikingly apparent – we had a mother of two children, not one. A mother was giving her child's history omitting several hospital admissions. However, this information was supplied by the health visitor. Her prompts, with dates and hospital names, led the meeting to view the history differently and the mother to exclaim, 'It looks as if he has been in hospital more than he has been at home.'

Within this information sorting meeting we try to gain information about various aspects of the family and how they relate to published risk factors (Kempe and Kempe, 1978; Greenland, 1987; Corby, 1987b). At the end of the meeting we often have a list of areas of difficulty, which may or may not correlate with known risk factors. While we acknowledge the importance of being familiar with these risk factors, we recognize their limitations as direct predictors of abuse. At this session, we always attempt to draw out the strengths and positives within the family to give a more rounded picture of the family rather than just concentrating on negative aspects. The final question we ask, first of the parents and then of the professionals, is 'Why are the family here?'

In the information we seek we place less obvious emphasis on predictors such as material conditions, housing, criminality, and suicide attempts. However, we have additional categories that we have found to be significant when trying to establish the level of concerns about parenting. These include the nature of the relationship between the parents or parenting group: 'I know the moment I wake up and see the mood she is in and I go to work with things bottled up inside me'. 'I'm jealous when he goes out and we say hurtful things to each other.' Also, spontaneous feelings about a child immediately after birth: 'I did not feel I had a baby;' '"Ugh no" because of the way he looked;' 'Felt close.' and, the way the child/children's development is described: 'She never seemed a baby, she was walking at nine months;' 'He is withdrawn and quiet;' 'speech is not good, not clear.'

The words used by parents to describe their children are also informative. For example, whilst a couple both described one child as 'withdrawn', the mother described another as 'spoilt' whilst the father described the same child as 'devious'. In listing parents' words describing their children, it becomes clear that *affect* is an important factor to recognize within abusing situations. Physical injury to children has, then, two parameters, Smith (1984) suggests:

> The first is the degree of injury. The second is the *affect* which accompanies the abusing act. The affect may contain malicious or sadistic qualities directed towards an unloved or unwanted child, or it may be intended to meet discipline needs. If the context is disciplinary, there may be an *intention* to hurt the child within certain limits whilst the child is otherwise loved and wanted.
>
> Confusion is compounded here because the disciplinary act may be either controlled and purposeful – a calculated punishment for a specific misdeed carried out with love or malice; or, uncontrolled – stress causing a parent to hurt the child more than intended.
>
> Therefore, in trying to define physical abuse we should be trying to ascertain the degree of injury in relation

to the age of the child, the circumstances in which it occurred and the local community norms about discipline *and* the affect with which the abusive act was endowed.

At the end of the information sorting, the workers have a family diagram with a large amount of written material often including substantial verbatim quotes from families. Previously, families and networks were asked to identify areas to be worked on for change, whereas now we prefer to have time for reflection by all parties. We spend the time collating and presenting the information in a variety of chart forms, bearing in mind the family's ability to absorb information, and hold a feedback meeting where the written information can be read (or heard) with workers, feelings acknowledged, and corrections made by the family.

If it is decided to make an offer of work to the family, this is done at the feedback meeting detailing the areas to be worked upon; sometimes this offer is made within a contract. We always share the long-term aims with the family and recognize the need for short-term goals that are achievable.

The work is structured into three areas: that with parent group; parent/child interaction; and work with the child alone. We will discuss these three areas in depth. However, we again emphasize that the philosophy underpinning this structure is one of clarity and honesty with families and professionals about the reasons for referral and the focus of the work. Records of contact with families are always made available to them and some families choose to keep their own files. Within this we have to respect information from third parties and that given by a child alone. The importance of the central role of the referring area social worker is recognized, particularly as he/she continues to hold case accountability. In addition, the area worker needs to recognize change and respond accordingly, rather than be sidelined or continue to respond in a historical manner to the family. One form of involving the area team social worker is co-working with them in counselling sessions with the family.

In beginning work with a family, a recurring theme is that of 'engagement', that is, are the parents really committed to working for change or just paying 'lip service'? They might be doing this for a variety of reasons, including legal ones – 'My solicitor told me to just go along with "the rehabilitation plan"'. In addressing this issue of 'engagement', another related factor is whether families are more likely to be committed if subject to an order (Dale *et al.*, 1986). Dingwall *et al.* (1985) suggested that research on this point is both needed and feasible. Irueste-Montes and Montes' (1988) study indicates that

court-mandated treatment does not necessarily render abusive
and neglectful parents less amenable to treatment. Whether a
family is 'engaged' is a recurring dilemma, which we struggle
to overcome and sometimes never answer at all. Often, this
can only be assessed with hindsight. Regularity of attendance
on its own is meaningless without attitudinal and behavioural
changes. However, we do not have a strong view on the relative
merits of the value of statutory control. Families are accepted
without any legal order over them, but the threat of legal action
is often a feature in the case. For example, 'They will come to
the Centre the same way as they took their children to the day
nursery. If they refused we would have gone to Court' (worker
about a family).

The first area of work is with the parent group, and
concentrates on change and not on undertaking a long-term
nurturing/re-parenting role. For example, a family where there
had been a very serious injury were clearly told that there
needed to be fundamental changes, such as improved marital
communication and a more equal distribution of power between
the parents, if their daughter was to be returned from foster
care. If these changes were not forthcoming she would be
adopted. Obviously, there is resistance to this approach and
resistance to such fundamental changes in family functioning
(Dale et al., 1983). This is manifested, for example, by missed
appointments, hostility to workers, wanting quick change, and
debunking when we are unable to give quick, easy and magic
answers.

The change we are seeking is a safer family environment for
a child. In doing so we have always found it necessary for
parents eventually to face the abusive or neglectful situation
and have an understanding of the circumstances leading up
to it. Non-verbal communication is crucial in this work. For
instance, when a mother, who had witnessed her first baby
being shut in a drawer following a marital argument, played
out the situation with the worker in the role of the abuser, she
demonstrated her part in the process and allowed the observing
co-worker to witness this also.

Figure 8.1 illustrates one example of the use of non-verbal communication. The barrier between a couple was explored with the
use of labelled bricks with 'his' and 'hers' showing their different
perceptions of the situation. Figure 8.2 is another example of non-
verbal communication. Here two parents were invited to illustrate
their own perception of the 'family atmosphere' over a period of
months. We used their own descriptions for one dimension of
the graph and time for the other. Yet another example is that
of an overloaded mother who understood more clearly why a

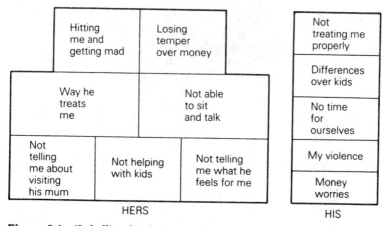

Figure 8.1 'Labelling bricks' example

third child could not be returned to her when she saw a plastic boat float with two coins in it but sink with a third, which paralleled her own experience of coping with two children but not three.

In addition to the non-verbal communication being a way of illustrating important issues, it also assists in speeding up identification of key issues, which can be lost in overwhelming amounts of verbal information. An example of such a key issue that frequently emerges is that of early separation and loss. In this area of work with parents we have become familiar with, and challenging of, fundamental blocks, defensive ploys, and the avoidance of painful issues, such as 'don't know', 'can't remember', 'not bothered', and body language such as 'hand twiddling' which conflicted with statements.

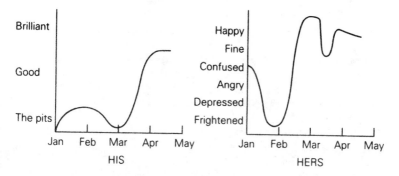

Figure 8.2 Change graph

The second area of work is parent/child interaction, which has assumed increasing importance within the Centre in the work of securing futures for children, as it has been increasingly recognized in recent research (Bentovim; 1987; Furniss, 1988; Dunn–Smith, 1987). Rivara (1985, p. 86) comments: 'Child abusive parents do seem to differ in their sensitivity to their infants' cues and in the greater proportion of their interaction with their children which is negative or aversive. There is little evidence that traditional parenting classes would effectively change parenting patterns.'

The gathering body of research on the importance of parent/child interaction has informed our own development in this area of work. The aim of the work is to intervene on several levels for behavioural changes achieved through positive reinforcement through to the more fundamental issue of attitudinal change.

There are distinct stages in the work, starting with observation, which can be at home and/or at the Centre, sometimes over a long period. Workers do not parent the children, apart from exceptional circumstances, as the aim is to observe what happens between parents and children. The next step is to make sense of the observations and interpret them along with the parent. This is then followed by intervention for change. An important measure of change is when the balance of work moves from the Centre to the family home, which offers an opportunity to assess whether behavioural changes can be continued and sustained in a less structured environment.

An important and developing method of work is the use of video. One observation was of a father bringing up wind in his baby son in an insensitive and heavy-handed way, obviously distressing the child. The man was impervious to persuasion, and his interpretation and that of the workers were in conflict. The way he brought up the wind by banging him on the back was videoed and played back to the father. At first the disbelieving father accused us of turning up the sound and he had to see the video again, but he subsequently modified his behaviour. Parents are often wary of the use of the video, which raises a number of issues related to surveillance and evidence-gathering on which it is difficult to formulate policy. Currently we have decided to use video for 'therapeutic use' only, and the video tapes are no longer stored. This means their use can be confined to parents being able to observe and interpret both positive and negative interactions for themselves and to be more fully involved in the process of intervention.

We have also used charts as a similar aid in order to record interactions, parents sometimes completing charts themselves. An example of this is when a parent was asked to fill in a chart when a tantrum occurred, and it was subsequently used as a way of changing behaviour. A further example of a chart is one where the parent spoke of some of the sessions being 'brilliant' during access with her child. This language of the parent was incorporated into a chart (Figure 8.3) designed to measure quality of interaction and frequency of attendance for parental access sessions. This was shared with the parent after each session – worker and parent together did the rating.

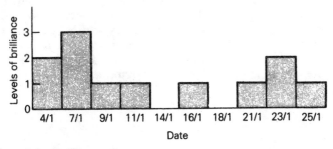

Figure 8.3   Brilliance chart

Behaviourist interventions such as a 'care line' (Scott, 1987; see Table 8.2) have been used in order to clarify to parents worrying behaviours that need changing if a child is to return home safely. This particular care line was a baseline drawn up for the parenting of a child following periods of observation that highlighted certain areas of difficulty that needed to change. Each one is drawn up

Table 8.2   *Example of a care line*

Safety pin closed and out of reach
Using reins in high chair if unattended
Rinsing baby's bottles before use
Baby given regular drinks
When dressing baby, hold wrist when pulling arm through sleeve
Giving baby soft toys
Changing baby's nappy when wet or soiled

Care Line

Baby overwhelmed with noise or toys
Hot drinks within reach of baby
Too hot foods (steaming)
Too big lumps in the food (has he choked?)
Taking anger out on baby
Rough handling

individually, with behaviours above the care line being encouraged and those below giving rise to concern. Parents are involved in the drawing up and measuring of the care line on a regular basis.

In spite of the intensive work undertaken in these interaction sessions, parents often find them less threatening than work on their own. These sessions can be a crucial component of the work in the process of 'engaging' families in the work at the Centre, and helping parents into the counselling work on difficult areas.

The third area of work undertaken is with children on their own, but only for specific reasons. Children need explanation for moves such as to an adoptive family or into care, but first we have to attempt to understand the child's view of what has happened to them. This is done through play, with a recognition that children often feel they have been very 'naughty' and caused traumatic events in their lives. They also often feel they don't belong to anyone. There is recognition of this emotional

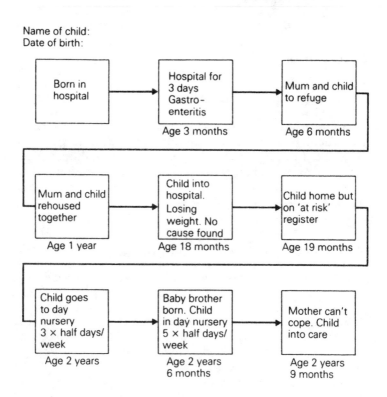

Figure 8.4 Flow chart

damage, and of the need to work with the feelings that go with it and to attempt long-term repair work whilst trying to build towards current or future secure attachments. A useful starting point is the compilation of a flow chart (Figure 8.4), which should incorporate as much information as is available concerning moves, separations, and other changes in circumstances.

In face-to-face work with children, a variety of media, introduced by the worker and chosen by the child, are used as imaginatively as possible. Forward planning is essential but so is an ability to 'think on your feet' or 'seize the moment' as the child takes you into unexpected areas that present opportunities for expression of feeling or finding out what a child thinks. For instance, a child refusing to acknowledge anger gave us an opening when singing a song in the back of the car. 'If you are happy and you know it, clap your hands' quickly led in the session to 'If you are angry and you know it, clap your hands'. After this she started to put angry faces on her pictures, which she had refused to do before.

In another instance we discovered that a child saw herself as having three mothers when a Mother's Day card in the worker's car led to questions about it and a game of 'I pretend' about who the child would send Mother's Day cards to. We obtained not only information about her multiple attachments and her confusion, but also an indication of the quality of those attachments from her descriptions of each mother and the messages she put in each card.

To explain things to children who are already confused by a variety of moves and often feel to blame, we have used stories that mirror the child's experience, using a 'third object' such as fish, squirrels, plants, soft toys, clouds, and so on. Very young children seem to understand that these stories are about them by repeating them back and putting their own names in.

In order to coordinate these three areas of work it is essential that there is close communication amongst the workers by use of notes, meetings, and supervision. Supervision of all the workers within the unit takes place weekly. Alongside this, specific cases have supervisory sessions including area team social workers as well as Centre workers. A variety of models of supervision are used to enable workers to be clear about aims and objectives; to prevent workers becoming neutralized by over-identifying with clients; to plan future sessions using a range of materials; to ensure that communication and liaison are taking place within the three areas of work. One model used is (a) to look for clarity of thinking and good decision-making with forward planning rather than reactive responses; (b) to recognize that this clarity often arises in contentious situations so differences that exist must be dealt with and communication should not remain on safe areas of agreement; therefore (c) to present the opposite point of view to test the validity of the argument (Sands, 1988). Another frequently used model arises from the familiar problems of areas of unclarity in a case and workers becoming lost in detail. One method of handling this is for the supervisor to 'float' particular points of view, however extreme, for which the worker provides evidence for or against. From this process questions are formulated that require answering and give direction for subsequent sessions.

Frequently the Centre is involved in assessing the feasibility of rehabilitation of a child back to its parents, and Bentovim (1987) provides a useful framework as to whether the workers are addressing all the relevant issues. Bayley (1988) provides yet another useful supervisory model whereby workers identify (a) their feelings following a session, (b) the problems arising from these feelings, and (c) the issues in the case. Another important aspect of supervision is when workers are encouraged to identify repeated themes and issues by reading records of past sessions. The Centre uses outside consultants for supervision when appropriate.

The process of supervision can include talking-through sessions; self-critical process recordings with supervisor's comment added and then used as focus for discussion; using diagrams, analogies, and materials as described for use in sessions; joint planning for the next session; and experimenting with ideas. However, we have had to face missed sessions; interruptions; lack of ideas; flatness; loss of direction; unproductive conflict; struggle with worker blocks; late write-ups; and other frustrations. Yet, at its best, supervision can be challenging, enhancing of creativity, and produce more skilled and focused work with families.

Dilemmas and tensions

Within the work there are many unresolved practice dilemmas, which are constantly faced and force an examination of practice and the seeking out of appropriate research.

When working with young children there are often timescales that conflict with their need for security. These include delays in court hearings, and procedural and organizational delays, such as awaiting severance of access decisions. In intensive therapeutic work with adults who have entrenched, long-standing and unresolved difficulties, the timescale for change to be achieved may not be compatible with that of the child.

Large amounts of information from families can confuse and overwhelm workers, hide key issues, and, therefore, delay working for change. Within this is the difficulty of measuring change (Dallos and Aldridge, 1986), which is especially hard when assessing whether to return a child to the natural family. This again links with the difficulties in predicting dangerousness, as does the recognition that some parents who have lost their children need further therapeutic work to prevent replays of children coming into care. In some cases decisions are made that parents should never parent again, but research in this field is limited as to what is effective (D. P. H. Jones, 1987).

The philosophy of the Centre emphasizes quality of work rather than volume, and a successful outcome is one in which a decision is made about a child's future, which often entails intensive input to a case over a long period. This does not obviously fit easily into the current climate of cost-effectiveness of units.

There was earlier reference to the work of Dunn-Smith (1987), who points out the apparent short-term nature of behaviour change without attitudinal change. Other research information (Cohn and Daro, 1987; Ferleger *et al.*, 1988) demonstrates the importance of self-help groups and community support for successful long-term outcomes in work with children who have been abused and are with their parents.

Finally the power imbalance between clients and worker has to be recognized as an inhibiting factor in the way parents respond to the work–for example, a mother feeling there is no point in trying to get her child returned to her because the workers have already made the decision before the assessment. This can be a very difficult attitude to overcome and sometimes is not.

Part of the nature of child abuse work is holding these tensions within day-to-day practice whilst recognizing broader theoretical perspectives and insights. These unresolved tensions are wider than practice dilemmas and we now explore them in relation to the concept of the 'rule of optimism'. One obvious example is the name 'Family Centre' as outlined earlier. This view of the 'family' is itself a component of the rule of optimism and, therefore, can define and influence the role of Family Centres in 'preventive' work. For example, a young mother wanted her son adopted and then changed her mind. On referral to the Family Centre it was recognized that all the support and resources on offer were conditional on her remaining a mother. The professionals involved had assumed 'maternal love' and ignored much of the negative interactional behaviour between mother and child. We had to make clear to her how many adoptions had taken place and that we were there to plan the best outcome for the child and not necessarily keep them together.

In our work we meet families that seem unsafe for children. We have to consider the concept of 'untreatableness'

(Cohn and Daro 1987; D. Jones, 1987) and the intractable nature of child abuse and its tendency to recur (Ferleger *et al.*, 1988). This can locate the work within the deviance/disease/treatment model, but at the same time we are aware of structural analyses suggesting that all families are capable of violence given certain circumstances. There is evidence for this from a number of studies on corporal punishment in families (Newsom and Newsom, 1968; Korsch *et al.*, 1965; Straus, Gelles, and Steinmetz, 1980; Gough and Boddy, 1986). Twenty-five per cent of a sample of mothers had 'spanked' their child within the first six months of life, and 4 per cent of 3–17 year olds had suffered abusive violence, including kicking, biting, punching, hitting with an object, threat or use of knife or gun.

Another tension arises out of a gender analysis of violence in families, which is addressed more fully elsewhere in this text (Chapters 3, 4, and 7). We frequently have evidence of male violence towards powerless women and children. At the same time we face the fact that women can also be perpetrators of violence and accessories to it. However, the major tension is caused by the 'failure to protect' role of women. Here the tension is between seeing the child as 'subject' and requiring acceptable levels of child care and the women as subject and their powerlessness in the face of male violence (see Chapter 5 in this volume).

An example is a couple who were in a repeating cycle of violence, where the workers recognized the difficulty of the woman's role when she had to leave home and possessions and enter homeless units, the problems of being a single parent and her mixture of fear for herself and concern for the man, who became suicidal. Figure 8.5 was used with the family to describe the repetitive cycles of behaviours in an attempt to help the couple decide whether they wished the cycles to continue and, if not, how and where to break.

This circle of violence and instability led to low standards of child care, exemplified by the failure of one child to thrive in this atmosphere and the fear of both children in the presence of the man. The woman herself stated, 'Am I doing the best for my kids by returning?'

Tension also arises out of sociological understanding of middle-class workers facing clients who experience gender, structural, and class inequalities and who ask workers why they were targeted when all the other families in the street behave the same way towards their children and all are in poor material and financial circumstances. These tensions and a desire to redress the balance can lead workers to interpret parental behaviour

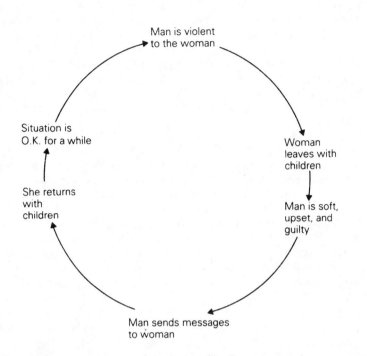

Figure 8.5 Circle of violence

positively, the other component of the rule of optimism along with the assumption of maternal love. An example is that of a rehabilitation plan designed to test out the motivation of a single parent on minimum state benefit who had a child in care. Money was given to cover the costs of travelling to visit the child; this was spent on other things. The plan of testing out her motivation was jeopardized when we had to consider whether it was harsh and unfair to expect her to walk or whether to give her more money and another chance.

There is tension too between the emerging children's rights movement (Children's Legal Centre, 1988), with suggestions that children should, for example, have the right to refuse a medical in suspected sexual abuse cases, and the knowledge that threats towards children can render them too frightened to speak of their experience.

Long-held social work values, such as client self-determination, conflict with the emerging new practice. This new practice is based on an awareness of the dangers of viewing parental behaviour within the 'rule of optimism'. If workers are to avoid being pilloried at inquiries and by the media, there is a need to recognize the increasing emphasis on dangerousness, risk factors, and more objective views of parental behaviour. Such self-determination may no longer be seen as appropriate in the climate of child protection and, arguably, worker protection, and it feels as if such practice is going beyond existing conflict with clients when statutory powers are invoked.

The value base of practice changes when the child is the main subject. For example, a mentally ill couple had intensive, long-term, daily input of resources to keep them and their children together. The social worker, a mental health specialist, was concerned about their mental health as his 'subjects' and did not want them to lose their children. The children were exhibiting some disturbed behaviour suggesting some abuse or neglect; however, small unsustained changes on the part of the parents were amplified to be seen in an optimistic light and preserve their mental health. When these 'allowances' stopped, the damaging environment for the children was recognized.

There are further practice tensions when white workers face black families and are told they do not understand the way black families bring up their children (Chapter 6 in this volume). One obvious tension is when assumptions are made that different sets of norms and values exist between cultures as to what is good enough parenting. This highlights the need to understand the difference between cultural relativism and ethnically sensitive practice. If a culturally relative stance is taken when assessing acceptable levels of child care, this can also feed into the rule of optimism.

An additional factor affecting worker judgement can be an awareness of the current difficulties in finding black adoptive families for black children in care. Thus there is a reluctance to take any steps that may lead to an admission into care if the waiting time for a permanent placement can be considerably longer for a black child than a white child. This reluctance may result in further unacceptable behaviour being tolerated, leading to dual standards in practice. The level of abuse and possibility of re-abuse could be equivalent in two instances. For the black child, when looking at the least detrimental alternative, it is difficult to avoid taking into account the length of waiting in care with its emotional consequence. This could result in the black child being returned home rather than being allowed to drift in care, whereas the white child remains in care with the prospect of a speedier permanent placement. Is this a further manifestation of the rule of optimism?

In practice we have found that all the tensions outlined *can* lead to 'worker immobilization', but we have been *most* immobilized when faced with black families saying we do not understand them. One example was when a mother was questioned about her children under 5 roaming the streets at night and being allowed to wander, unsupervised, across busy roads. Another example was an Asian mother stating that Asian children do not play with toys. Ethnically sensitive practice requires workers to seek advice from other representatives of the ethnic groups about child care norms; to continue to address the issue of why the care of the children was so poor and to take action to safeguard them; while working with the mothers on their unwillingness to do so.

Organizational constraints

The writing of this chapter has led us to recognize repeatedly the way organizational factors affect practice and its outcomes in the work with families. However creative and imaginative the work undertaken, it is to no avail if the place of the workers and the unit within the organization and wider institution of society is not appreciated. Thus workers are politicized as are the families with whom they work, and personal distress cannot be kept private.

We are attempting to address this issue of politicization of families, workers, and the unit by examining the influences on an area team social worker when considering a referral to the Family Centre. One hypothesis is that referrals are because of worker and organizational need rather than specific family need. This hypothesis is being tested by a survey of workers who referred cases and is to be published in full later (Clark *et al.*, 1989).

There are many intra-and inter-departmental and societal influences on practice over which we have little or no control, yet have a major influence on our work. These range from different area teams having different philosophies, through delays in appointing a guardian-ad-litem, to government guidelines with regard to child protection.

Having highlighted some important organizational issues, we are concerned that the concept of dangerous organizations should be explained rather than focusing on dangerous families and dangerous individual workers.

Conclusion

This chapter has addressed the issue of dangerousness, how it is flawed by being based on misconceived assumptions yet is central to current practice in child protection and thus inevitably affects the practice and philosophy of the Family Centre. The division between high-risk and low-risk cases has also been discussed with the subsequent questioning of the concept of preventive work. In addition, we recognize we have a place within the local child abuse tariff system whereby referral to the Centre may be part of the process of a case becoming a high-risk one.

Finally, we are concerned that the full complexity of child abuse practice cannot emerge when families and individual workers are labelled as dangerous. This over-simplification ignores the tensions and dilemmas of working in organizations within the wider institutional and societal structure.

9   The family systems approach: a help or a hindrance?

HELEN MASSON and PATRICK O'BYRNE

Introduction

In this chapter we will explain our view that family systems ideas have a useful role to play in terms of understanding and treating child physical and sexual abuse in situations where abuse has already been established. The chapter will not have anything substantial to say about the investigative stage of child protection work, a large area of study in its own right. Family systems ideas are not diagnostic in terms of proving that abuse has occurred though clearly, looking at family patterns, resistances, and boundaries, for example, will provide useful information about the dynamics of the family and hence what may be the nature of the child's experience in it. We will be focusing instead on the usefulness of systems ideas to the post-abuse assessment and treatment phases of the work.

Such usefulness will be demonstrated via a brief historical view of the development of family therapy and family systems theory. We will also, however, be explaining that the approach does have its limitations and that as of today there are only a few centres in the country where such ideas are in regular use. We shall consider why this is so and we shall also be stressing that if child physical abuse and child sexual abuse and their treatment are to be taken seriously then further attention should be paid to the appropriate resourcing of such treatment services, so they can be more widely available to families in need.

This is not, however, a chapter on family therapy, though we will be referring to the main schools. (For a description of our approach to family work, which draws on a number of schools, we refer the reader to Masson and O'Byrne, 1984.) In family work, the term 'systems approach' is used to cover three main models:

(a) The 'systemic' model developed by the Milan group (Palazzoli *et al.*, 1978 and 1980) uses principles of worker neutrality, hypothesizing about the nature of problems and family dynamics, and circular questioning of system members. This produces a systemic assessment leading to an often positively reframed message and/or a task that aims at fundamental change in the way family members interact with each other and deal with difficulties. They also draw on communication theory, which suggests that warped communications can result in double-binds. To counter these they have developed therapeutic double-binds in the form of paradoxical messages.

(b) Next there is the 'structural' model of Minuchin (Minuchin, 1974 and Minuchin and Fishman, 1981), where notions of sub-systems, boundaries, enmeshment, or over-involvement and disengagement or emotional distance and the normal difficulties of negotiating family life-cycle tasks are central. A wide range of techniques are used to 'join with' the family and 'kick and stroke' the system into restructuring itself. For Minuchin, family problems are associated with problematic family structures where, for example, the intergenerational boundaries have been infringed and the focus of work is on sorting out these structural confusions.

(c) In contrast, the 'strategic' model of family therapy (Haley, 1976 and 1980), which contains elements of the previous two models, such as notions of boundaries, emphasizes the importance of power and hierarchy in families and argues that family problems are typically a comment on some unresolved issues in the family – they are a message about family dysfunction. Strategic family therapy involves sorting out issues of power and hierarchy and unresolved and often feared hidden agendas through a variety of straight and paradoxical interventions and reframes.

For all these models or schools resistance is a primary issue. Systems such as a family system seek to establish and maintain a steady state or homeostasis based on rules and beliefs and, in the face of the prospect of change, resistance is normal. This is so even if the steady state is dysfunctional, either to individual family members and/or to the family as a whole in its interaction with systems outside itself. In other words change is feared. Such resistance has to be addressed in work with families and the various models of family therapy offer strategies for negotiating this reluctance to change. When working in situations where child abuse has occurred it is highly likely that one is dealing with involuntary clients. Resistance is likely to be heightened and needs to be acknowledged and tackled (see, for example, Dale *et al.*, 1983). As we shall indicate later on too, the resistance may be mirrored also in the family–agency system and, for work to progress, this needs to be identified and acknowledged.

As we shall be discussing families and wider systems in this chapter, it is important next to make clear what we mean by the family. We do not define the family purely on the basis of a marriage or a living-in relationship, nor do we define it purely on the basis of blood ties or shared property ownership. Neither do we define the family in terms of idealized neo-liberal images of the modern nuclear family in its castle. For us, a family exists when people related to one another by blood or the sharing of a home consider themselves as resources for each other on a more comprehensive basis and at a higher degree of intensity that they consider other people. So we are interested in the patterns of interaction or the transactions that develop as a result of the everyday life experiences of such groups.

We see the family also as in constant interaction with systems outside itself, such as the school, the workplace, political institutions, religious institutions, and so on, and we conceive of the family as being in a constant state of change in response to changes outside it and in response to changes in the developmental tasks being faced by the individual members of the family.

It is crucial to be aware of the vast variety of family structures and styles that such a definition allows for and we believe that our definition is relevant to the full spectrum of families that make up a multicultural society. Our definition does not seek to define what is normal about family life, though, as we shall indicate later on, some schools of family therapy are being criticized for trying to do just that. We prefer the kind of definition of normality that is offered by Goldberg (1965, p. 27), who suggests that normality 'consists in a tolerable fit between what members of a family seek from each other and receive in return, and also perhaps in a fit between their values and ways of living and those of the social group or network to which they belong'. This view of normality is, however, problematic if it means that issues of power and dependency in families are ignored, something that we will be arguing family theorists have tended to do, particularly in relation to their analysis of child sexual abuse.

Family therapy and family systems ideas – from Utopia to reality

In his editorial in the *Journal of Family Therapy*, Bryan Lask (1987, p. 303), introducing an article by Kaffman in the same edition of the journal, writes:

> Kaffman describes the four phases in the development of any therapeutic modality, starting with what he calls the pioneering phase, followed by what I hope he will excuse us for calling 'the bandwagon phase' and then the phase of omnipotence. Each phase, lasting for about ten years, claims ever greater success. But after thirty years reality strikes and the sobering-up begins. The fourth phase is that of disillusionment, when therapists stop making amazing claims and even start describing failures.

We believe that this greater realism and modesty is in evidence in family systems thinking now. Later in the chapter we will be showing how such ideas do have a useful contribution to make to the understanding of families where abuse has occurred and to working with them. But in this section our aim is to highlight the general criticisms of family therapy theory, particularly as it was presented in the early decades, and then to make some statements about when family systems ideas are potentially useful, and specifically in relation to child protection work of all kinds.

There are two main criticisms of family systems thinking: first, that the social context is neglected and, secondly, that basic issues of patriarchy are ignored. Concerning the first criticism, other chapters in this book discuss the social context of families and family issues in various ways and we will be looking later on at the work of Justice and Justice (1976), family workers who are strong on the stresses created by the societal context, and at the work of Dale *et al.*, (1986), who do not focus on them. Dale *et al.* comment, for example, in relation to the serious abuse cases that they are discussing (p. 82): 'Overall, surprisingly few of the families we see following serious child abuse have significant financial or material problems.' Despite this comment, which is based on one team's experience, there does nevertheless seem to be considerable research evidence that social inequality and powerlessness are associated with child physical abuse and this needs to be explored for its significance in any assessment. Jordan (1981) and Kingston (1979) have discussed policy and organizational aspects of family problems and have suggested that practitioners underestimate the potential to pursue change in organizational, policy, and resource areas. Similarly, Mayhall and Norgaard (1983) have advocated the need to consider the provision of community care, self-help groups, better schools, and medical services. As they say, 'people live in families, but families live in communities and communities live in districts and states'. Certainly some family theory has not done justice to the impact of the supra-system, beyond the immediate family.

Turning now to the second criticism, very few books on family systems ideas address the abuse of male power within families, a fact that is taken up elsewhere in this book. Clearly the powerlessness of women and the accusation that they 'fail to protect' children are, for example, two central issues. We think (as Christine Parton suggests in Chapter 3 in this volume) that there is possibly a meeting point between radical feminism, which sees women's problems as caused by men (therefore power and gender issues are to the fore, and the family is not *per se* a healthy institution), and socialist feminism, which sees the situation of men and women within its larger context, the economic structure of society (therefore there is no choice or negotiation, and men and women are forced into certain role relationships). Pilalis and Anderton (1986) argue that feminist family work is possible if socialist feminism is taken on board. This means empowering people, 'raising consciousness', of women in particular, placing behaviour in its social context, and encouraging people to make choices and negotiate for what they want out of family life. Marianne Walters (Roys, 1987) discusses the importance of validating people and creating a context in which people can feel they are competent and have power to change. When women enter therapy they are usually thinking 'what did I do wrong?' whereas men are wondering 'what went wrong?' Women will feel they have failed and they are more likely to be in touch with their feelings. For these reasons, therefore, it is tempting to design interventions based on the assumption that it is the woman in a family who needs to change and that men cannot.

Sue Beecher, writing in *Gender Reclaimed* (Marchant and Waring, 1986), challenges current family therapy practice and argues for some new practice strategies. She sees systems thinkers as assuming that the family's relationship with the rest of society is irrelevant, as assuming that the prevailing culture is just and non-damaging. She comments, for example, that 'there is no consideration of class or gender as important factors operating in families [and] no explanation of the non-provision of services is seen to be called for.' She points out that the structural school as exemplified by Minuchin (1974) and Minuchin and Fishman (1981) and the strategic school as exemplified by Haley (1976 and 1980) condone the seeking of solutions within current ideologies and structures, failing to distinguish, for example, between the power and roles of male and female parents, roles that are entirely different in our patriarchal society. The systemic school of the Milan group (Palazzoli *et al.*, 1980) offers a 'neutrality' that likewise misses this difference and indeed denies access to feminist issues. There is a general assumption that fathers are breadwinners and mothers nurture the children while having little autonomy. Sexist language is to be found in the works of the 'masters'.

Yet Beecher finds in family therapy the roots of a way forward out of all this, for example, in the distinction between first- and second-order change, gender-sensitive work being an application of the latter. Women can be encouraged to draw 'boundaries' around themselves rather than seeing themselves only in terms of their relationships to others, and their place in the 'hierarchy' can be squarely addressed, 'making explicit what has been implicit' (Madanes, 1981). Likewise the Milan notion of 'circularity' can be applied to a notion of family–society, rather than 'punctuating' intrafamilial relationships only. So systemic ideas can be used to integrate feminist principles with family therapy and thereby improve it. Roles can be expanded and changed. For example, fathers can be involved more in the care of their children in an empathizing way and women's roles can be correspondingly widened, for example, via paid work, so that they become less guilty about traditional gender roles. What needs to change, however, is the *way* fathers relate to their children, not just that they spend more time with them. This is about shifts in the way men are socialized so that they can better understand a child's world and feelings. We agree with Jeff Hearn (see Chapter 4 in this volume) that, without this kind of second-order change, putting fathers and children together more will probably result only in more abuse.

All the above seem eminently timely suggestions and family workers are ideally placed to confront sexist ideas such as 'ownership' of wife or children, and also to empower women, for example by shaking hands with both adults, not just with the male, by their use of language, by confronting gender stereotypes, and by expecting men to look at feelings and their need to make changes.

A family systems approach is therefore potentially useful if it does not assume that all families, simply by being families, are safe and satisfying for all their members. In other words, families should not be assumed to be a 'good thing' as much current conservative thinking would try to have us believe. Functionalist arguments about families being a haven of emotional warmth, stability, and nuture have been strongly criticized by sociologists such as Sennett (1970) and psychologists such as Laing (1971) and Cooper (1970), who see the family as increasingly isolated from the rest of society and characterized by tense, destructive relationships that deny individual autonomy and identity. A family in harmony provides deep security, satisfaction, and growth towards individuality but, in disorder, it possesses a potential for terrible damage. It can indeed be argued that the fact of child abuse questions the viability of family life *per se* and demands a neutrality on the part of professionals who are trying to establish whether any particular family is a safe, viable setting in which a child's needs can be met.

Similarly the family systems approach is useful if it does not ignore the social structure and societal context. *First*, a society (supra-system in family systems language) that fails to confront men over the abuse of male power is itself a sick system and certainly 'dysfunctional' for women and children, failing to meet their needs. Any systems approach that assumes that the adult/child generations and the genders possess equal powers, that ignores the differences, thereby supports and perpetuates the inequality that is itself conducive of abusive situations. *Secondly*, a social system that encourages the ideal of individual achievement via self-assertion, at the expense of developing the sense of community or empathy for others, is conducive to abuse. People become objects, means to an end. *Thirdly*, a system that allows a lack of support for families – leaving them isolated, lacking communications (via facilities such as telephones and transport), living in poverty, in unemployment, short of child-care services such as day nurseries and pre-school play groups – is neglectful. Rearing children is a most important and interdependent task; but interdependence, mutuality, and vulnerability are not held in great esteem, especially by men. All the above features are, in our view, characteristic of Britain in the 1980s. *Fourthly*, in its lack of education and consciousness raising about the tasks of parenthood, society is negligent. (See Devore and Schlesinger, 1981, on the universal life-tasks of families.) An educational system that trains people for jobs, for financial success, to the neglect of values relating to giving and caring, loyalty, commitment and respect, and to the neglect of valuing child rearing, must not be surprised at the cruel results. *Fifthly*, a society where there is little interest in analysing the secondary damage caused by legal, medical, and social work responses to families where abuse is alleged is a society where it is all too easy for such responses to become as abusive as the original family-located abuse. For example, in this society, there is now considerable agreement that quite often the responses to a child who discloses that she has been sexually abused can actually be just as abusive to the victim as the trauma she disclosed. Such experiences include insensitively handled medical examinations, the removal of the girl rather than the perpetrator from the home, the trauma of having to give evidence in an adult-centred court, and getting no therapy for her distress.

The above features of the supra-system that characterize British society today do have an enormous stress impact on families. In our view, it is crucial that family workers try to distinguish between the problems that society and its institutions induce and those that arise from within the family itself, and also the relationship between the two, including the differing timescales for action attached to these differing aspects. We do not underestimate the difficulty of trying to make these judgements, but we believe it is part and parcel of the social worker's role. While family work should certainly not be a matter of experts diagnosing and manoeuvring people who are out of line, and assuming a harmony and fairness in the rest of society, nevertheless the judgements that have to be made are complex.

As we will hope to show in later sections of this chapter, family theorists in the field of both child physical abuse and child sexual abuse are trying to develop frameworks that help practitioners to identify the various systems levels that are in operation in the generation and maintenance of an abusive situation. But here special knowledge and skills are not enough. Having to make value judgements, dealing with ethical dilemmas, having to make choices often between the lesser of two evils, are an integral part of the job of being a welfare professional and of the functions of a child protection agency. The whole area of values and rights (for example, in relation to children) is a complex and contradictory one and there are no simple guidelines or clear solutions to the dilemmas that face practitioners. What is important is that such professionals realize this and develop self-awareness, as well as practice skills, so that they can appreciate and explore how their assessments and decisions are affected by more or less conscious personal and professional values, feelings, and attitudes, which are themselves not divorced from the social, legal, and political minefield of the time. Although, as we have made clear, this chapter is focusing on post-abuse work, and although in this area ethical dilemmas abound, we acknowledge too that in the *investigative* stage the waters are still more muddy in a society that upholds parental responsibility and family privacy and yet expects workers to prevent abuse when it can seldom be clearly identified in advance.

Perhaps the above is particularly well illustrated in relation to multicultural-based practice. Ellen Gray and John Cosgrove (1985, p. 389) comment that:

> When different cultures come into contact with one another, the potential for confusion and conflict multiplies. Under such conditions perceptions of the relative value and harm of different child rearing practices will unavoidably depend on the background of the observer. The official view of those practices that are harmful to children and that require intervention will probably be biased in favour of the dominant culture. This in turn sets up the possibility that those official judgements may be in error resulting in the violation of the cultural integrity of a family and community, when there is no real harm or threat of harm to a child.

Nevertheless the issues are also evident within any one culture. For example, Elaine Arnold (1988, p. 32) points out that:

> some professionals in this country who operate from a middle class culture are not comfortable with the culture of the poor working class of their own ethnic group let alone other groups. Socialized in a white society where racial prejudice exists, cultural or ethnic differences add to the complexity of working with child abuse.

We believe that the nature of this complexity makes it even more imperative that sufficient time and space are made available on training courses and in agencies for reflection and consultation on personal and professional values, ethical issues, and the layers of factors that impinge on any given 'incident' of abuse.

In addition to all the above, family systems thinking must not consider the question '*Who* abused the child?' as irrelevant, and must not attribute the cause of the abuse solely to some dysfunction in the family system, for example, in a case of child sexual abuse. Blame should not be spread over the whole group when responsibility should be laid squarely at the feet of the (usually male) perpetrator.

Arising out of the previous paragraph, the family systems approach, to be useful, should individuate and respond to individuals' special needs. Some family therapists give the impression of being so 'systemic' in approach that they would work only with the whole family group. Fortunately it has become recognized that in the treatment of families a range of approaches is needed, including individual, dyad, and group work. Family therapy methods as such, therefore, form only part of the assessment and treatment process and must also operate in collaboration with other workers and resources such as family centres and foster parents. (Taking a systems approach means thinking systemically, even when working with individuals; it does not mean seeing the whole system together.)

Finally, a family systems approach has validity if it keeps the child as the first client, in so far as protection and security are the prime issues. Where abuse has occurred, not even family assessments of the kind we are going to describe should begin until investigations are complete and the risk of further abuse is removed. Moreover, in the post-abuse work, practitioners need to be able to approach treatment without being hooked on the notion that rehabilitation home would be the only successful outcome. Until the adult caretakers can show the ability to protect their children from abuse in the future because of changes they have made, any wish to have the family reunited must be questioned. Hence the focus of worker interventions or change efforts is mainly the parents, but primarily in the interest of the child. One could say the child is the 'client' (the person who is expected to benefit) and the parents the 'targets' (the people who need to change). If they agree to be helped they could be said to become the 'secondary client' system. The sad fact is, however, that even if parents are making changes, it may be judged that the pace of progress is too slow and that the child's developmental needs mean that rehabilitation is still out of the question. Then, as suggested by David Jones (1987), the work should focus on helping parents to let go of their children, sad and difficult though this situation is for everyone involved. In this sense, family therapists cannot be neutral, but have to function from the principles that the child's right to protection is paramount and that the use of authority or control on behalf of the child has to be integrated within therapeutic skills and approaches.

Family systems ideas, child physical and sexual abuse

Given the context outlined in the previous section we will now seek to analyse the contribution of the family systems approach to child abuse. We acknowledge that there are many forms of abuse:

physical abuse or non-accidental injury (NAI)
physical neglect and failure to thrive
emotional abuse
emotional neglect
sexual abuse

but in terms of analysing the potential of a family systems approach we intend to make a distinction between only two forms, child physical abuse and neglect and child sexual abuse. Probably the explanations of the two phenomena are somewhat different – physical abuse and neglect being more associated with societally and personally induced stress in some way (Brown *et al.*, 1988), and sexual abuse having more links with issues of patriarchy. Ray Wyre (1988) has emphasized this difference from a somewhat different perspective. He argues that in relation to child sexual abuse the abusive behaviour is addictive and enjoyed by the perpetrator and may well involve the entrapment of youngsters outside the family if victims within the family are unavailable. Little of this applies to physical abuse. Nevertheless we believe that these differences have barely begun to be explored. It may well be that gender issues do also have significance in relation to forms of abuse other than sexual abuse. What is clear is that simple explanations of the 'causes' of child abuse are totally inadequate as regards the complexity of the reality of abusive situations.

The family systems approach and the physical abuse of children

Olive Stevenson (1986) criticizes *The politics of child abuse* (Parton, 1985a) because it does not explain 'why some very poor disadvantaged parents abuse their children and others do not ... indeed, it is insulting to many poor people to impute to them *all* the possibility of behaving in such an aberrant way as we have seen reported recently in the press'. We would suggest that, in order to understand why some poor families abuse rather than others, we need not only to consider structural theories but also to look at family history and dynamics as important pieces in the jigsaw that contribute to the whole understanding of why people abuse their children.

In this section we are going to concentrate on two texts, one American and one British, which try to analyse the dynamics of families where serious abuse has occurred. It may be that cases of serious abuse are not representative of the full range of abusive situations but nevertheless they cause great concern to practitioners and so we make no apology for focusing on them. It may also be the case that similar dynamics exist in situations where the physical abuse is less severe and that by looking at extreme cases it is easier to spot the patterns of interaction that are at play.

As we have already made clear, we are restricting our analysis of family systems thinking and child abuse to situations where abuse has been established. We acknowledge that a great deal of time and concern is also invested in the uncertain, 'grey' areas of *investigation* of child physical abuse. Identification and prediction of abuse are often very difficult and there is considerable ambiguity in the literature and in research (Brown *et al.*, 1988). Indeed, as Dingwall (1986) comments, 'the more familiar one is . . . the more one doubts'. Investigative work is, in our view, a specialist set of skills, which needs to be taught as such and which should not be attempted without appropriate consultation and back-up resources. Once investigations are concluded and a protection plan for the child(ren) formulated and agreed by those agencies involved, then treatment becomes a possibility, and family systems ideas may well have a more important role to play.

So, focusing on post-investigative treatment and assessment work, let us first consider the work of Rita and Blair Justice in the USA. They have tried to look at abusive situations from a number of systemic levels. In their book *The Abusing Family* (Justice and Justice, 1976) they concentrate on the idea of group therapy with abusing parents, but they put forward a theory about why abuse occurs which emphasizes the systems aspects of it – dysfunctional interactional patterns within families, supra-systems that may both create and maintain stress, and societal systems that paint unrealistic pictures of child rearing and the ease of parenting. The Justices argue that most abusing families are ones where there have been a series of life crises, some self-induced but not all by any means, which create intolerable stress, and where parents exhibit various problematic behaviours. Parents are often isolated and mistrustful of the outside world, having a symbiotic relationship with each other (each seeking to be taken care of by the other) and/or with a child (expecting the child to take care of the parent), which leads to unrealistic demands and inevitable disappointment and frustration. They have poor self-images and tend to deny problems and feelings; and to cap it all, often the abused child is especially irritable and temperamentally difficult.

To digress briefly, this 'interaction with the child' aspect has been closely studied by Kadushin and Martin (1981), who found that many parents first tried to warn/threaten, reason with, or cuddle the child and only 8 per cent were violent straight off. As the first non-violent response failed, frustration was heightened and, with the child persisting (for example in crying), what might have been 'controlled' violence now gets seriously out of hand, though this was frequently limited to when the abuser had had a worse than usual day (68 per cent) or had been drinking (12 per cent). While there is no excuse for the abuse even under the greatest provocation, it is worth noting that none of the parents had attacked a passive child – they all perceived the child as non-passive and wilful. Kadushin and Martin suggest that unless workers begin by accepting the parents' definition of their problems with the child, meeting them on their own ground in order to engage with them, no meeting of minds can occur, nor a dialogue that can lead to change. When Giovannoni and Becerra (1979) offered professional workers 313 vignettes of aversive behaviour by children, all of the workers moved their assessments of the situation closer to that of the parents! We also need to bear in mind that behaviour described by some parents as 'terrible' is hardly noticed by others; in other words, people's levels of tolerance and images of acceptable behaviour vary enormously.

At the biological (or age) level, parents are responsible in a linear, causal way for the protection of their children, have the power that derives from being physically more mature, and possess abilities to protect (for example, to lock a window), to control their own emotions, and to contain children safely. However, at the interactional level the parent and the child may feel equally powerless and both may feel guilty. (See Minuchin's discussion of pleading versus coercive violence, 1984.) Thus parents can be viewed as being simultaneously powerful and powerless. It is this very combination that we would argue leads to situations where the child may be in danger. Attributing blame at the interactional level helps no one (though the nature of the interactional patterns has to be clearly understood); acknowledgement of responsibility at the linear level does.

As well as looking at difficulties of parent–child interactions, the Justices draw on concepts such as systems, subsystems, and supra-systems; they use ideas of hierarchy, boundaries, and enmeshment, notions of alliances and coalitions, and of closeness and distance. Families are seen as open or closed systems, depending on the rigidity of their boundary with neighbourhood systems. The Justices work a good deal, however, with the couples involved because of their symbiosis, and in the work they focus on what they see as six key areas: symbiosis, isolation, employment, talking and sharing with mate, handling impatience and temper, and educating and coaching about child development and management. They work with a maximum of five couples per group over a four to five month period on a weekly basis of one and a half hour sessions. They use a variety of therapeutic approaches, such as transactional analysis, behaviour modification, hypnosis/relaxation, and group work therapies. They find the group context particularly valuable as these isolated people are thereby often helped to trust, to express feelings and needs, to experience non-rejection, and to discover that their opinions are valued. Some of the techniques they use have a very task-centred flavour on the lines we adopt in our work with families (Masson and O'Byrne, 1984).

Now we go on to look at the work of Dale and his colleagues (1986) in Britain. In their book *Dangerous Families*, describing their work in the NSPCC Child Protection Team in Rochdale, the authors offer a brief historical backcloth to their current practice, including some illustrations of how concepts of care and control have been acted upon over the last couple of decades. In particular, they comment on how the earlier nurturing approach adopted by the NSPCC Denver House team (Baher *et al.*, 1976) clearly failed to reduce the risk for children. They go on to argue that parents, not social workers, have to be responsible for making changes and securing safety, and that therapy is about providing the right context for change. This context involves a marriage, on the one hand, of social control functions, clarity about contracts, engagement issues and resistance, and goals to be achieved and, on the other, of traditional social work values of warmth, genuineness, and well-communicated empathy. Workers assess the rate and quality of progress towards a safe environment for the child as well as assisting the parents' change efforts.

In their work the team now use a combination of family therapy and Gestalt ideas to help abusing parents. They are interested in family processes (patterns of role relationships, communication, homeostasis, and so on), and in the interactional dynamics that result in abuse (in the processes involving the victim, the aggressor, and the non-abusing parent). They pluck ideas from the different family therapy schools of systemic work already mentioned, and from these models the NSPCC team have developed assessment and treatment exercises such as the use of family trees or genograms to help people understand their history and unfinished business, and active approaches like role-plays and sculpts; from Gestalt they have developed experiential exercises of various kinds such as talking through unfinished business to an 'empty' chair.

Dale *et al.* emphasize the need to protect the child as the first priority before assessment or treatment can begin. They offer some facts on the incidence of child abuse and reiterate their view that some families are dangerous places for children. They also discuss the potential dangerousness of workers who fail to notice or will not acknowledge what is happening in a family and what needs to be done – a failure that is often the result of stress, they add – and the need for workers to have supervision and consultation and to work at constructive case conferences and network meetings (the latter including family members and all the professionals involved). One point they make very clearly in their book is that very often the professional system (the network of professionals from various agencies) mirrors what is happening in the family system and that it is very important to pay attention to the process in the professional system in order to understand the family process better and in order to prevent the work becoming stuck and the inter-agency system itself becoming dangerous.

Engagement with often involuntary clients is always likely to be problematic. Frank discussions about the team's role and power are offered, contracts are emphasized, the options available to parents are identified as well as the likely consequences arising out of each option choice, and clear expectations of parents are outlined. Resistance, a concept used in the systems approach, is discussed at length in their book, and advice is offered on ways of responding to its different forms. The authors describe various aspects of their assessment work – using genograms; assessing the spouse relationship (the viability of which is seen as crucial to any ideas of rehabilitation); discussing and analysing the abuse and how it occurred; assessing the impact of the extended family; discovering people's reactions to events subsequent to the abuse (for example, court hearings); current attitudes; structural considerations; and so on. The team mainly work with the parents, but whole family sessions are scheduled as appropriate (for example, to assess current attitudes to rehabilitation plans) if this is what is recommended. Separate, direct work with the children may also be necessary and is given high priority.

We recognize that there are difficulties with the notion of 'dangerousness' as applied to families by Dale *et al.*. What we want to add to the debate is our view that dangerousness, like power and powerlessness, needs to be understood at various levels. Whilst working at the NSPCC one of us heard of several cases of child abuse where it was clear that the abusive parents were relatively powerless, pathetic, and victimized individuals. (As we have already argued, it is powerlessness at the interactional level that makes linear power over children dangerous, especially where the powerlessness is not understood and the power/responsibility is not acknowledged.) Parents often came from miserable home backgrounds themselves and had often been subject to physical and/or sexual abuse during their childhoods. They had very little going for them psychologically or materially and it was hardly surprising if the tasks of parenting had been too much for them. However, as parents of their children they were in a very powerful position (in the linear sense), as we have already outlined, and from the child's point of view the behaviour they exhibited was dangerous.

Consider, for example, a recent case we heard about of a mother who had a childhood history of physical and sexual abuse. She ended up in a relationship with a man who continued to abuse her in a most appalling manner, a man who exerted a tremendous power over her as well as over many professionals. Between them the couple brought four children to their relationship and it is suspected that he sexually abused one of them. They lived in a council property that they did not like and they pressed for a housing transfer. Presumably not getting the move as fast as they wanted, they hatched a plot to set fire to the house; in order to make the event realistic they decided to start the fire whilst the children were asleep in their bedrooms. The parents had agreed that he would make sure that two of the children got out and she would get the other two out before the fire reached them. She gave him the matches, which he used to set the fire. As planned she got her two children out, but to her horror he failed to get to the other two. They both died as a result of burns sustained in the fire. One of the children who died was the youngster whom he was thought to have sexually abused. That, to us, is about dangerous behaviour from dangerous people – dangerous from the point of view of their ability and motivation to protect their children.

However, even in horrendous situations like this people do not necessarily forfeit the right to be responsible for the care of children for ever in the future. Given parental motivation and the appropriate treatment context, we are optimists about the ability of people to change. Thus, in the case described, the mother (who separated from the father) has been involved in intensive work on her personal and parenting issues and has made such progress that the remaining two children have been rehabilitated to her care. In contrast, the father has refused all offers of help and accepts no responsibility for what happened. He remains in the community, convicted of manslaughter and a suspected sex offender, and in our view a potential danger to other children.

As regards 'cause', we will never be able to say whether these parents were dangerous because of any one factor or a particular combination of factors, but in working towards securing the future of the children we use various criteria (such as those described in Chapter 8 in this volume) to assess the level of danger and the parents' ability to protect and nurture, so that children can grow up in physical and emotional security.

The work of the Rochdale team (Dale *et al.*, 1986) is also criticized for being extremely authoritative and undermining of parents. In our view all social workers have authority and power arising out of legislation and all that Dale *et al.* are doing is being clear about that. At one level this fits with Blom-Cooper's idea (London Borough of Brent, 1985) that social workers should be more like probation officers in living more comfortably with their statutory powers, but more significantly we agree with the view of Vizard (1987, BBC Childwatch programme) that therapeutic use of the law is underestimated in the confrontation of abuse. The clarity of Dale and his colleagues is almost shocking because very often practitioners fudge on their power and are rarely straight with parents about the legal context in which they are involved with them. Mike Horne asks, 'Is this social work?' – we suggest that, given the alternatives, it is. It *is* good social work provided that there is a marriage between open, honest, unambiguous use of the law and work that is supportive yet change oriented. This work needs to be realistic, wanted, and agreed to by the parties. Thus seemingly conflicting issues – legal control and therapeutic intervention – can be reconciled. (See also Bentovim, 1987.)

In post-abuse treatment work, parents need to be clear about the context in which they are being asked whether or not they want to look at themselves and what they need to change in order for the professionals to come to a decision about whether or not they are people with whom it is safe to leave children. In this respect the findings of Corby (1987b) are interesting and supportive of Dale *et al.* (1986). He reports from his study of 'the child abuse system' in Britain that, while most social workers wanted to be helpers and supporters and a few of these carved out a therapeutic role, once reviews and assessments had passed many gave ongoing work a much lower priority than initial work, and there seemed to be few guidelines as to how to conduct such ongoing work. As Sainsbury, Nixon, and Phillips (1982) found, social workers were seen as having something to hide (hidden agendas), which made families angry and hostile; they were able to accept the *open* use of authority more easily. Corby found a general lack of explicitness concerning roles carried by social workers, which led to unstructured and amorphous interventions (partly as a result of liberal views of freedom – or half-baked 'self-determination' ideas, we would suggest). He makes a connection with Jordan's view (1976) that when problems are not brought out into the open the social worker becomes part of the nightmare. As a result,

Corby recommends that there be open and clear communication with families over the social worker's concerns, no equivocation about the social worker's roles and duties, openness about the necessary checks, and more use of contracts and task-centred work. Regular evaluation of interventions, with a clear structure concerning length of time allocated to the treatment work and clear limits to confidentiality, is also needed.

The fact that parents respond better when they are clear about the duties of the worker in social control issues (because the worker has been open about it), and find this much easier to deal with than being 'betrayed' by people who engage their trust on a false basis, should encourage workers towards the synthesis we are discussing. We feel also that this clear, firm model is the best escape from what Corby found, namely that the system as it is simply operates as a managerial check on social workers who worry about their 'over-intrusiveness' but in a climate that is oppressive for both them and the families.

It has been our experience in both investigative and treatment work in this field that being straight with people is the way forward. What of course it means is that people one is being straight with may well feel straight about expressing their anger and resistance to one's authority. It is up to the worker, with the support of competent supervision, to be able to handle this and take it. Who wouldn't feel angry being placed in the kind of situation in which many abusive parents find themselves? It is our view that often social workers are not straight about their power because they are fearful about people's natural reactions. We recognize that this is nevertheless extremely difficult work and Dale *et al.* (1986) would never attempt it on an individual basis without full consultation and support. This is about taking the work seriously and taking child abuse seriously.

The family systems approach and child sexual abuse

Early family systems thinking focused in particular on understanding the dynamics within families where father–daughter incest had occurred. In this section we will briefly introduce these ideas and then show how thinking has developed more recently about sexual abuse generally.

In relation to intrafamilial sexual abuse, family systems ideas such as 'closed' systems have been used, for example by Alexander (1985), to describe such families (though observing such patterns is not diagnostic; it is possible that such patterns may be found where no abuse is occurring). However, feminist writers make a crucial point that it is not the family that is incestuous but the (usually male) perpetrator. Nevertheless many family workers would still argue that such men often live in family systems that are closed to the community. Even though such men may be upheld as 'pillars of the community' there may, in fact, be a high level of conflict, violence and neglect, and secrecy between family and community. Furniss (1985) calls them the 'conflict-regulating' type of family. In contrast to this type there is what he calls the 'conflict-avoiding' group. These show certain internal patterns/structure such as weak intergenerational boundaries and role differentiation. Bentovim *et al.* (1988) have identified a number of family patterns that seem predisposed to abuse – high secrecy, avoidance of conflict between marital partners, intense fears of separation so that the child is called upon/sacrificed to maintain a togetherness at the expense of the child's needs. Furniss (1983b) has outlined work with various dyads within such families focusing on, for instance, mother– daughter distance or the parental coalition.

Trepper and Barrett (1986) list five types of family structure often found in cases of intrafamily child sexual abuse (though again this is not proof of abuse):

(a) 'Father Executive' – daughter reversing roles with mother, often in a family with rigid stereotyped views of male–female relationships, and with aggressive fathers.

(b) 'Mother Executive' – mother having responsibility (but not power), father being parented and like a peer to the children in some ways.

(c) 'Third Generation' – mother interacting more like a grandmother, having a polar relationship with the children but periodically moving in closely with executive force.

(d) 'Chaotic' – no executive subsystem, little impulse control, immature need for immediate gratification.

(e) 'Estranged Father' – who in some ways is lower in the hierarchy than the children.

All five types can be high up in the spectrum of 'closedness', having a rigid external boundary and confused/weak internal boundaries.

However, as Finkelhor (1986b) and Will (1989) point out, there are serious criticisms of the type of family systems thinking just outlined. First, the theory has limited scope in that it looks only at father–daughter incest, which amounted to 7 per cent of all child sexual abuse in one study, and totally neglects the fact that boys can also be victims, as well as being abusers. Secondly, the theory overemphasizes the difference between intrafamilial and extrafamilial child sexual abuse. Evidence is now accumulating (as outlined elsewhere in this volume) that links intrafamilial abuse with rape, sexual harassment at work, and so on – the link being the abuse of male power. Thirdly, the theory does not account adequately for sources of offending behaviour. It emphasizes a matrix of dysfunctional family dynamics rather than the deviant tendencies of the father. In one study, 45 per cent of fathers involved were also involved in abusing children outside the family. Fourthly, as some critics have maintained, the analysis often puts 'moral responsibility' for the abuse on the mothers, who are seen sometimes as 'the corner-stone in the pathological family system'. As Finkelhor (1986b) comments:

> In the context of a situation where a father has violated one of society's most serious legal and cultural prohibitions, such statements do seem to represent a harsh, inverted value judgement. Few experts in the field would disagree that in some cases of sex abuse mothers may have poor relationships with their daughters, may be eager to have daughter take on some of their role responsibilities, may ignore signs that incest is occurring or may even fail to act when confronted with irrefutable evidence of the incest. It is not clear in what proportion of father–daughter incest these dynamics exist but even when they do they are open to a variety of explanations . . . these circumstances do not warrant holding mothers morally responsible for the incest. The behaviour of mothers in incest situations can be just as easily accounted for by seeing the mother as a victim herself – trapped in an oppressive role to begin with and then faced with an impossible dilemma which is easy to deal with by denial . . . [However] not all analyses from the family systems point of view endorse the idea that mothers are the corner-stone of the incestuous family. The question is whether because of its focus on the contribution of the whole family, the analysis has an inevitable tendency to exaggerate the role of the mother.

Glaser and Frosh (1988), who believe that such problematic family systems as described above may be apparent in cases of repeated sexual abuse inside or outside the family (though they may also characterize non-abusive situations), are also careful to make clear that the fact that alienated mother–daughter relationships are often apparent should not lead to the conclusion that mothers are causal agents in abuse. They quote Ward (1984, p. 174) who puts the matter bluntly: 'Even if a Daughter does experience her Mother as rejecting, neither she nor the Mother are asking for the Father to rape her.'

Nelson (1987) also strongly challenges 'mother-blame theories' in their numerous forms and argues that 'current professional theory and practice discourages "collusive wives" from even starting to move towards such dangerous and unwifely notions', such as that women deserve the same respect, independence and sexual fulfilment as men; that they should value themselves and their daughters as much as their husband. In challenging the family systems approach, which fails to take into account power structures reinforced by society, she rightly points out that 'families don't assault children sexually. Men do'. (See also Chapter 3 in this volume on this issue.)

When it comes to locating the 'cause' of incest, we recommend the work of Finkelhor (Trepper and Barrett, 1986, p. 53), who offers a diagram to show that there has to be a motivation to abuse plus the overcoming of internal and external inhibitors and the resistance of the child (see Figure 9.1). Finkelhor then goes on to look at these four preconditions in so far as they explain abuse outside as well as inside the family. For example, a father, himself abused as a child and seeking to be powerful

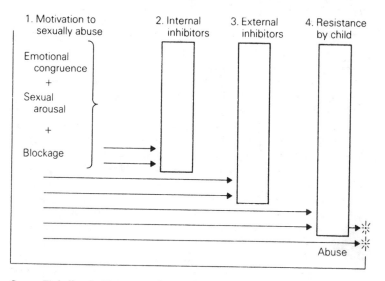

Source: Finkelhor in Trepper and Barrett (1986)

Figure 9.1 Four preconditions of sex abuse

in sexual relationships, fantasizes about his daughter; alcohol may have lowered his internal inhibitions or he may rationalize that it is an expression of love for his daughter; external inhibitors are low because mother is not present or able to prevent it or mother and daughter are not close and daughter is unable to confide; and finally father, by using force or fear, exploiting trust, or making daughter feel guilty about holding the family together, overcomes the child's resistance.

Given these levels of analysis, then interventions too have to be pitched at different levels, However, before moving on to treatment approaches, a word of support for the impact of family systems ideas in relation to child sexual abuse. Trepper and Barrett (1986) argue that the family systems approach and the women's movement together have helped to get child sexual abuse recognized professionally. The contribution of the systems approach, they believe, is threefold: (a) in its assumption that symptomatic children may be expressing problems in the parents: (b) in being an important antidote to psychoanalytic theory by emphasizing that adults have sexual fantasies about children rather than vice versa; and (c) its models of classical abusive families have been influential and used as a basis for family and groupwork treatment by such people as Giarretto (1982) and Sgroi (1981).

Turning to treatment approaches, which should only be offered after the investigative and immediate post-disclosure work is completed, Bentovim and his colleagues (1988), for example, have published a series of papers outlining current family treatment models. In meeting with the family, usually along with various workers, a family systems approach is taken in so far as techniques such as circular questioning are employed, and not only is the family system a focus but also the family-and-professionals system. Systemic thinking helps the worker to remain meta or objective to the client system and avoid dangerous involvement. It is also conducive to positive reframing – for example, reframing the system in order to 'name the game' that is being denied. (Note that a positive connotation is put *not* on the abusive event but on the wider game.)

Thus family systems thinking offers some useful theory, but it does not offer a complete explanation, protection, or treatment for child sexual abuse, and a multi-systems model is much to be preferred. Nevertheless such concepts as boundaries and enmeshment are useful in assessing families (for treatment) and for deciding whether family dynamics are playing a part in the maintenance of sexually abusive situations. For example, Bentovim *et al.* (1987), in setting out criteria for assessing a hopeful prognosis, look for an absence of scapegoating and the presence of generational boundaries so that the parents take responsibility for the state of the child. Where there is a chronic denial of this responsibility, where boundaries are broken down, where there is long-term scapegoating of the child and poor communication in the system, then the prognosis is seen as 'hopeless' so far as family rehabilitation is concerned. Then other treatment approaches are needed. What seems to have been one of the problems in Cleveland was that social work practitioners lacked confidence in their ability to contribute to the assessment of abusive situations, did not tackle family assessments drawing on these ideas, and relied solely on medical examinations/tests, the validity of which, as a diagnostic tool, has been subject to much debate. Neither, we would add, did they seem to understand the needs of children or work to empower mothers in the families concerned.

It is most important to stress, however, that family therapy ideas play only a relatively small part in the treatment of sexual abuse. Much of the work with victims is done individually and increasingly in small groups. The same applies to work with perpetrators, where the stress is on their genuine taking of responsibility for the abuse. There is also important work with mothers, empowering them to protect the child. Kolko's (1987) finding that the most optimistic outcomes come from multidisciplinary programmes that include family involvement is important. A good example of family involvement is to be found in the work of Lucy Berliner and her colleagues in Seattle (Berliner, 1988). First, the perpetrator is excluded from the family for a lengthy period during which (in keeping with the feminist approach outlined in Chapter 3 in this volume) a new system is built with the mother in charge, being supported in developing a clear set of rules to protect the child or children when or if the man is to be rehabilitated back into the family. Meanwhile 'the other things that are wrong' in the family are addressed: the mother learns to cope with her feelings, such as a sense of failure; possibly her own abuse is an issue to be faced and worked with; she and the victim/s get individual and group help; the offender is helped/treated while away from the family; the mother gradually gains power – the man will return only on her terms. The thinking with the children may include statements such as 'Daddy has a weakness, so he is not allowed to have physical contact, or to initiate discipline or sex education any more'. *If* the man returns, it is to a new system, as a spouse but to a different sort of partnership and with a different parenting role, constrained by very firm rules. In addition, the mother becomes an ally of the therapist in supporting the victim, in empowering the victim to use her/his experience to 'read' the web of deceit, betrayal, and rationalization, and in reducing stigmatization in the child (who needs to talk and share). This is 'working with the family' to help it restructure in a special way to cope with a special danger.

At the supra-system level too, there are important changes that can and must be made, particularly in the socialization of men and in how boys are trained to be men. There is a need for a less traditional sex-role differentiation. Macleod and Saraga (1987) argue that there is some evidence that the risk of abuse may be greater in traditional families – those that adopt strict sex roles – and that men involved in nurturing their children may be less likely to abuse. Long-term prevention therefore requires changing our expectations of men. This work, they suggest, needs to go on alongside the work of empowering women and children. We would add that expensive treatment work with perpetrators does need to be attempted because it is quite clear that unless treated (if they are not to be locked away for a lifetime) such men drift from one vulnerable woman to another wreaking havoc in their families. At the Sexual Behavior Clinic, New York, in an impressive treatment programme, they were able to reduce the reoffending rate to 13 per cent at one year after completion (albeit a very short follow-up period), whereas imprisonment alone had little if any effect (Becker, 1988). That is not to say that offenders should not be punished, but Finkelhor (1988) has said that realistic treatment centres for perpetrators could well be the most useful policy step society could take in this area. (He is probably assuming that in Britain we already have treatment centres for victims, but we know of children who, abused by their father or stepfather and sometimes rejected by their mother, are left in the care of foster parents or the staff of children's homes who have to try and deal with their acting out-behaviour without appropriate support.) Lastly, without placing any responsibility on them, children should be taught to say 'no', teachers and other workers using 'Kids can say no' videos and literature of the type produced by 'Kidscape'.

Systems ideas generally also help us to understand the impact of the professional system on abuse in families and the impact of the abusive families on the professional system or network. As Furniss (1987a) comments:

> In the societal context where taking responsibility for the sexual abuse of a child may lead to punishment or major family disruption without therapeutic response, the activation of professional conflicts and differences may ensue. Parents, paediatricians, the police, police surgeons, social workers, legal

experts, politicians and the media become pitted one against the other in an escalating run-away fashion.

This smacks of what happened in Cleveland. Furniss argues that 'conflicts by proxy' occur when professionals take on conflicts from the family and begin to mirror aspects of family dynamics. If the mirroring is unrecognized, these conflicts are unresolvable because they are conflicts that belong not just to the professionals but to the family. Moreover, the conflicts within a family are often mirroring those of wider society where the rights of children and women, male power, and values supporting the sanctity of the family versus state intervention are in competition for supremacy. Furniss (1987b) has developed systemic techniques that managers, supervisors, and consultants can use in order to deal with inter-agency conflicts of this kind, but there are no easy solutions, given that professionals have to function within a context of societal ambivalence about child sexual abuse and what should be done about it.

The way forward

If the reader is thinking that precious little of the sort of therapeutic work described in this chapter actually goes on in social services departments, whether in respect of child physical abuse and neglect or child sexual abuse, then she or he is right. In over thirty child abuse inquiry reports no mention of family therapy is made, though we note that it does receive a mention in the Cleveland Report (Secretary of State for Social Services, 1988). We believe that this is because treatment is not on anyone's political agenda, whereas identification, self-protection, and surveillance are, and in Cleveland it appears that investigation and treatment work became hopelessly muddled. Even where family centres are set up, they are sometimes less about treatment and more about taking the pressure off social workers (see Chapter 8 in this volume).

In addition, there is a depressing level of ignorance of the family systems approach among social workers, particularly in relation to process issues, compounded by a general agency resistance towards moving on from traditional ideals of personal caseloads. Co-working pairs for example are still difficult to find. We have argued (Masson and O'Byrne, 1987) that in order to improve this situation training must seek to make theory more useful to prac-titioners, among whom there is considerable interest and enthu-siasm for useful practice theory, taught by people who remain in touch with practice and who are given time and space to operate a workshop, experiential style of teaching. This is expensive and time-consuming, but if work with families is to improve so that planned, ongoing intervention and constructive engagement can take place, the volume and quality of training (pre-qualifying and post-qualifying) must change.

If child sexual abuse is to be taken seriously, we must take on board what treatment involves, not only for victims but for perpetrators, for non-abusing partners, and for survivors of abuse generally. Locking away perpetrators is not more than first aid – if we stop there, perpetrators will re-abuse. We have given Finkelhor's view on the need for treatment centres: he argues that they could greatly affect the whole system, including disclosure problems, the responses of spouses and families, the level of secondary damage to children, the practice in courts, and so on. We note that the report into child abuse in Cleveland proposes that 'different arrangements' might be made for abusers who admit their guilt, cooperate with arrangements made for the child (for example, leave home so that the child need not do so), and submit to a programme of control. Similarly, survivors of abuse who have not been offered treatment are more likely as adults to have children who are vulnerable to being abused and, especially if they are boys, to become abusers.

We hope it will be clear from this chapter that large inputs of resources – in terms of teams, equipment, premises, consultation, and multidisciplinary approaches – are also required if child abuse is to be effectively tackled. At the moment the necessary resources are available in only a few specialized settings and we want to make it clear to practitioners in other situations, such as in most social services departments, that they should not feel guilty, if given the resources available to them, they feel they are able to do little more than monitor and survey. Their first priority must be to protect children and, given the position they are often in, it is likely that this is all they can do. However, there are some lessons to be learned, from management levels upwards, about avoiding the creation of 'paranoid systems', as Minuchin (1984) describes in relation to what happened in the Maria Colwell case. In this case, he believes the hundred or so professionals and others involved in surveilling Maria and the Kepples increased the stress on Maria's parents to make the situation more dangerous for her, as they blamed her for this surveillance. This is another instance of linearly powerful adults feeling powerless and victimizing the child as the cause of their predicament.

Family systems theory can help in understanding some parts of the processes that lead to abusive situations and to secondary abuse resulting from poor efforts to intervene. It can be useful too as a part of a programme for treatment. It can help us to think about the complexity of the total therapeutic system and of its relationship to the family. Understanding that complexity may provide points for future action on various fronts such as in relation to family courts, the laws of evidence, specialized foster parents' training, the involvement of self-help groups and para-professionals, and the need for joint training of professionals, such as police and social workers. We worry, however, about the growth overnight of 'child abuse experts'. While the difficulty of this work makes specialization in agency organization most desirable, in this complex and uncertain world we learn more by being uncertain. Those who take a 'one-up' position that is dismissive of other viewpoints are likely to end by doing the greatest secondary damage. As Kee MacFarlane (1988) has said, regarding sexual abuse in particular, many 'experts' are learning that the longer they deal with the problem the more they have to eat their words.

10 The process of inter-agency work

ERIC BLYTH and JUDITH MILNER

Introduction

In the helping professions, the failure of different agencies to work effectively together has emerged as a significant hallmark of past and current practice, being identified as a major culprit in virtually every single inquiry into child abuse in this country. The committee inquiring into the death of Lisa Godfrey (London Borough of Lambeth, 1975) made a typical comment:

> Whether the life of Lisa Godfrey could have been safeguarded without her removal from her home had there been better co-ordination between the social, the probation, the medical and health services can only be a matter of opinion. There can be no doubt, however, that if co-ordination and communication between these services had been effective then on the information and evidence available to one or more of the services, the degree of risk of repeated serious, non-accidental injury to Lisa should have been clearly recognized and acted upon.

So, whilst the DHSS (1986, p. 10) asserts that 'Interdisciplinary and inter-agency work is an essential process in the professional task of attempting to protect children from abuse by their parents or carers', Dale and his colleagues in the NSPCC (1986, p. 41) can more realistically acknowledge that professional workers can unwittingly add to the 'existing dynamics of dangerousness . . . Perhaps the most dangerous aspect of inter-agency functioning lies in the ways in which agencies relate to one another . . . on many occasions multi-agency involvement can become totally confused and competitive.'

However, the problem of effective inter-agency work is not specific to child protection. Reporting on services for disturbed adolescents, the Health Advisory Service (HAS)(1986) found that there were 'many instances in which lack of interprofessional collaboration had resulted in poor services', there was 'unwillingness to share knowledge and skill', and 'stereotyped perceptions of other professions were frequently encountered'. Like those responsible for many of the child abuse inquiries, the HAS team asserted that without inter-agency coordination 'no comprehensive solutions can be found'.

Failure of both exhortations to agencies to work together more effectively and elaborate bureaucratic arrangements indicate that the problem is not an easy one to resolve. It is probably no coincidence that, when we have conducted experiential training sessions on inter-agency work, agency groupings quickly emerge exhibiting very strong feelings of anger and frustration, reflecting what we believe characterizes the reality of much inter-agency work.

In this chapter we propose to examine agency function in relation to child protection and the need for inter-agency work, what prevents agencies from working effectively together, and how problems of poor collaboration can be overcome. Finally, we identify what we mean by effective partnership and how it can be recognized.

Agency function

The perorations of central government and the media simply to 'get on' with inter-agency work are less than helpful. Given the opportunity, professionals would probably work better alone. However, management of child abuse dictates that professional isolationism is not an available option because of the interdependence of agency functions, the fragmentation of responsibility, and the multi-faceted nature of problems. Quite simply, workers from many different agencies have to find ways of working together.

The importance of recognizing particular agency functions and their implications has been one of the most significant developments in public welfare work over the past few years. Agency responsibility and accountability dictate (or at least shape) the activities of other professionals operating within the field of child protection – teachers, health visitors, police officers, NSPCC workers, education welfare officers, and doctors.

Failure to appreciate the nature of specific agency functions has been perceived as contributing to (usually well-publicized) tragedies in child care, including the Cleveland controversy (Secretary of State for Social Services, 1988). An official DHSS report of child abuse inquiries observed: 'Agency functions are to a very large extent shaped, if not actually determined by the law ... [Therefore] professionals with the same basic professional orientation and training may have very different parts to play, depending on the objectives and responsibilities of their employing agency' (DHSS, 1982, p. 5), a theme tersely echoed two years later by the panel of inquiry established by the London Borough of Brent following the death of Jasmine Beckford (London Borough of Brent, 1985).

On the other hand, social agencies have much in common, presenting a very clear dilemma for welfare professionals, which is articulated by the Health Advisory Service (1986, p. 26):

> Professional integrity depends on clear definitions of responsibility and accountability. A range of styles and approaches is essential to a lively reactive service. But many skills are interchangeable between professions and the needs of patients/clients invariably overlap and exceed the boundaries of responsibility of one group,

and by the Commission of Inquiry into the death of Kimberley Carlile (London Borough of Greenwich, 1987): 'The existing child abuse system is a fudge of divided responsibilities between the relevant authorities ... At various stages during the management of the Kimberley case, the system spluttered and malfunctioned because other agencies did not act fully in accepting responsibility.'

Much as social workers might prefer to see themselves as autonomous 'therapists', they are more appropriately perceived as 'welfare bureaucrats' and good practice defined in terms of organizational flair. Weissman, Epstein, and Savage (1983) have exposed the sterility of much of the debate about the nature of social work. Quite simply 'the agency is the hidden reality of social work'.

Traditional perspectives on the social work task, which either ignored the agency dimension altogether or conceived of the employing agency as merely a fortuitous accident, imposing unwelcome constraints on the social worker, totally miss the point. Without the agency there is no client/worker relationship. For social workers employed in welfare bureaucracies the issue is that well-emphasized social work values (for example, respect for individuals and respect for human dignity) can influence *how* they perform their statutorily derived tasks, but cannot define *what* they do (Howe, 1986). Neither, when such fundamentals are expressed at a high level of abstraction, are they unique to social work.

As Horne has argued in Chapter 5 in this book, whilst social work principles may insist that what social workers do is commensurate with the human dignity of the client, the essential mandate of social workers employed by the state is to oversee the maintenance of standards across a broad spectrum of human endeavour, and to intervene when those standards appear not to have been met, or when individuals fail to avail themselves of services. The development of the 'problem' of child abuse is a good example of this. The distinction between those who deserve sympathy and help and those who are not so deserving and should be punished is rarely clear – so the boundaries between state help and control are rarely distinguishable. Invariably such intervention, whether through welfare or overtly controlling agencies, is characterized by stigmatization (Parton, 1986).

Child abuse and dirty work

In the literature, and from our own work with practitioners, a number of significant factors militating against effective inter-agency work emerge. A major one is the very nature of child abuse itself. In sociological terms child abuse work is an excellent illustration of 'dirty work'. According to Hughes (1958, p. 49): 'Dirty work includes those activities which have to be done but are nevertheless distasteful in the doing and those which ought not to be done but unfortunately seem unavoidable.'

Those whose role in life is to perform 'dirty work' are 'increasingly caught between the silent middle class which wants them to do the work and keep quiet about it and the objects of that work who refuse to continue to take it lying down' (Rainwater, 1974, p. 335).

Hughes also notes that workers attempt to make their labours meaningful, tolerable, and predictable. This can lead to them setting objectives that can be achieved by defining their own role and that of others in a way that enables them to 'ditch the dirty work' on to other people. Social workers who wish to break out of the straitjacket of their social policing role are clearly in difficulties (Satyamurti, 1981).

The pressures imposed on welfare and health services to recognize child abuse, predict, and prevent it have been examined in Chapter 1 by Nigel Parton. In essence we do not know how prevalent it is, we cannot successfully predict it, and we do not always know whether it is there or not. Confidence in medical diagnoses of both physical and sexual abuse of children has been undermined (Hobbs and Wynne, 1986; Roberts, 1986; Wynne and Hobbs, 1986; Clayden, 1987; Dyer, 1987; Hobbs and Wynne, 1987; Sharron, 1987). In the absence of social criteria for assessing the likelihood of both physical and sexual abuse, social workers have readily accepted over-confident medical diagnoses, which Sharron 1987, p. 13) refers to as 'a collapse of social work theory and practice before medical expertise and the moral panic over child abuse'.

The current contradictory perspectives on sexual abuse illus-trated in the Cleveland debate pose challenges to preconceived ideas, undermining the certainty and confidence of workers. As Christine Parton has shown in Chapter 3, one aspect of the development of feminist analyses, exposing the culpability of patriarchy, threatens to deskill *all* male workers. Social workers have come to accept that, whatever they do in relation to child abuse, they are likely to get it wrong. Following the Kimberley Carlile murder trial, most of the popular press considered social workers fair game. One of the most extreme indictments came from Lynda Lee-Potter (1987), writing in the *Daily Mail*: 'I truly believe social workers are too often the wrong peo-ple in the wrong job, effecting only cosmetic support to the most at risk. They are hamstrung to red-tape, convoluted by gibberish, stuffed up with psychological drivel and terrified to act.'

Burnout

Burnout and stress amongst workers in the helping professions, particularly in relation to child abuse, has been noted (Blyth, 1986; Moore, 1982). The Commission investigating the death of Kimberley Carlile (London Borough of Greenwich, 1987) observed that the system is insufficiently supportive of individual workers and places too much reliance on individuals. Martin Ruddock, the social worker in the case, said in his evidence to the Commission: 'Undiluted and uncontrollable pressure is incompatible with thoughtful work.' Dale *et al.* (1986) make the point that 'dangerous' professionals who need to be seen as 'friendly and helpful' tend to collude with abusers by becom-ing over-involved and over-identifying with them, and that relationships between professional workers experiencing stress mirror those that exist within the pressurized, abusing family, echoing traditional psychodynamic themes of transference and counter-transference.

Similarly, we might consider that organizations under pressure, like families in similar circumstances, may abuse their own junior powerless members, a point emphasized by Hodgkin (1987, p. 21), who dismisses clients and their problems as the main source of stress in social work. Rather it 'comes from within the local authority or from the social work setting. In all my twelve years' experience, I can't remember any client who has given me as much stress as co-ordinating different points of view within case conferences and so on'. Masson and O'Byrne touch on this issue in Chapter 9 and it has been clearly expressed by Tilman Furniss (1988), who refers to 'conflict by proxy' in child protection work, meaning that the professional system often mirrors the conflict in the family system, thus increasing the workers' feeling of conflict, impotence and stuckness, the latter defined by the Rochdale NSPCC Child Protection Team as 'the process of going round and round in circles without getting anywhere and each major participant blaming others for the failure to achieve change', where more and more 'solutions' are applied in the absence of a real understanding of the 'problem' (Dale *et al.*, 1986).

And, of course, social workers are not the only ones to experience job-related stress. Recent research analysing occupational stress in general practice (Baker, 1988) indicates that GPs working single-handedly experienced comparatively little job-related stress, whilst those in group practices reported feeling pressurized in areas of their work where it could be assumed that their partners would help to ease the burden. This conclusion is not surprising in the light of studies of occupational stress which indicate that it is considerably more stressful to have to work with individuals in other organizations (Kahn *et al*, 1964; Cooper and Payne, 1980). People who occupy 'boundary-spanning' positions have constantly to assume the delicate task of resolving conflicts of objectives and demands between their own organization and others that they have to deal with (Tung and Koch, 1980). Mettlin and Woelfel (1974) concluded that the more extensive and diverse an individual's interpersonal communications network, the more stress symptoms (s)he displayed. *So the organizational role that is at the boundary between the organization and the 'outside world' is by definition characterized by extensive communication networks and high role conflict.*

Although we do not wish to present a parody of reality, we need to recognize the potential difficulties when a number of burnt-out workers in different agencies are obliged to work with each other.

Working in confusion

Lack of necessary knowledge on the part of concerned workers has been identified as a major issue at various levels. For example, the Hillingdon Area Review Committee inquiry into the death of Heidi Koseda discovered 'alarming lack of knowledge of the roles of the professionals involved' (Croale, 1986). However, whilst individual workers are normally pilloried for their lapses, we have to take account of not only the fragmentation of agency policies, perceptions, priorities, and responsibilities in relation to child abuse, but also the complexity of child care legislation, all of which confuse rather than clarify. At present there are seven major statutes, some of which are only partly implemented, and all have been modified by subsequent legislation. Yet, according to the panel inquiring into the death of Jasmine Beckford (London Borough of Brent, 1985), the law is supposed to provide the bedrock of agency practice.

In this context all organizations claiming some degree of ownership need to take others into account in order to achieve their own objectives (Litwak and Hylton, 1962). We tend not to give too much credence to the notion of agencies cooperating in order to better serve the interests of their mutual clients, since this largely founders on the basic prerequisite that a consensus exists about clients' 'best interests' and that serving the interests of clients is necessarily a principal organizational objective.

Much of what takes place between organizations in these contexts can be understood in terms of reciprocating needs. Homans' notion of exchange theory (1958) suggests that individuals and groups engage with each other with the intention of obtaining certain pay-offs. Every interaction is an exchange in which somebody gives something in order to receive something in return. As a minimum, all parties will be attempting to achieve some balance between costs and rewards – some will be attempting to give less and take more. Cooperation costs. At its most simple level, it consumes the time and energy of agency staff. However, when (as invariably happens) the allocation of resources becomes the subject of inter-agency negotiation, each agency relinquishes some control over its own resources. One of the more 'sensitive' costs is that agency practice 'becomes visible to other agencies, increasing the organization's vulnerability to outside scrutiny and evaluation' (Weissman *et al.*, 1983).

Collusion and preservation

Duplication of functions between agencies often encourages a diffusion of roles and too heavy dependence on each other, such as occurred markedly in the case of Maria Colwell. In a context in which everyone is overworked, such arrangements may easily lull agencies and workers into thinking that someone else has done the job or is in a better position to do so (Waterhouse, 1987). 'The existence of more than one agency with power to intervene can, instead of increasing the protection available, lead to children falling through the net because each agency is relying on another' (DHSS, 1983, p. 47).

Paradoxically, effective inter-agency communication may be impeded by ostensibly 'good' working relationships. The relationship between paediatricians in Middlesbrough and the Cleveland social services department's child abuse consultant was denigrated by critics as collusive (Secretary of State for Social Services, 1988). Too-cosy links not only generate collusion rather than cooperation, but the need to have one's own perceptions challenged and tested may be lost by excessively uncritical professional colleagues in other disciplines. The search for consensus might well hinder the search for alternative perceptions. The panel inquiring into the death of Malcolm Page (Essex County Council, 1981) highlighted the importance of different 'views of the world'. It noted that social workers' standards may be adjusted downwards to an unacceptable level by constant exposure to a deprived population, and that the value of views of those who are routinely working with a more representative sample of the general population, such as health visitors and teachers, should be more generally recognized. Yet, when everyone professes to be acting in 'the child's best interests', it is hard to accept the legitimacy of other conflicting perspectives. As Ferguson comments in Chapter 7 in this volume, these perspectives become deeply embedded expertises, with each agency worker claiming to 'know better'.

The right-wing press in both its 'popular' and 'serious' guises has attacked child abuse workers. Foot (1987) writing in the *Daily Mail* (18 July), has accused workers in the child protection 'pseudo industry' of empire building and power grabbing, whilst Amiel (1988), writing in *The Times*, asserted: 'We are giving arbitrary powers over our children to social workers and doctors who may well have a philosophical stake in the discovery of child abuse.'

Our inherent reluctance to take seriously any pronouncement from such sources has had to give way to more reasoned thought. When common sense dictated that the best course of action would be to place as much professional distance as possible between oneself and child protection work, a letter in a national education magazine made us realize that some people not hitherto perceived as part of the 'front-line troops' might actively seek an involvement: 'The school nurse can and should be contacted immediately whenever there is any suspicion, however slight, that this is a case of child abuse' (Kendrick, 1987, p. 4).

It appears to us that such assertions have much to do with professional power and professional survival. Statutory agencies cannot abrogate their responsibilities, even if they have no answers to the problems. Any wholesale admission of defeat would render the profession open to scrutiny in other areas of functioning – where it might also be found wanting. Emerging professional groups, such as social workers, whose professional survival is precarious to say the least, can at least protect their existence by claiming competence or indispensability in relation to an activity about which society wants 'something' done. And doctors have been used to being experts on everything under the sun, along with prescribing the activities of other, less-established occupations, so why not child abuse as well?

The relative power of different professional groups and 'ownership' of both problems and potential solutions is important. For example, in the case of Jasmine Beckford, a female health visitor's views were disregarded in favour of those of a male doctor. Different professional groups attempt to control both their own work and that of others in the desire to maintain professional integrity. As Webb (1975, p. 5) notes, 'the main barrier to collaboration is ... the very powerful need to protect organizational interests, philosophies, priorities and a satisfactory professional self-image'. Brandon (1987, p. 2) makes much the same point, speaking specifically about child abuse:

> There is buck passing, scapegoating and boundary disputes. There are a number of cases in which police surgeons are not on speaking terms with the paediatricians, who in turn are not on speaking terms with social workers . . . some agencies wish to select cases and exclude others from involvement. Others pass on or ignore any sexual abuse problems which come near them.

In the absence of well-tested perceptions of others through extensive experience we all tend to resort to the use of stereotypical assumptions (which are likely to be based on a range of half-truths) about others. Stereotypes provide a basis upon which we can relate to others, albeit in an oversimplified way. They also help to reinforce agency group solidarity by highlighting the similarities between people as well as emphasizing the differences. In situations where a particular group of professionals come together relatively infrequently (e.g. in relation to child protection), reliance on stereotypes is likely to be prevalent. Stereotyping can be a useful mechanism though, and only becomes a liability when its persistent use contributes to labelling and 'self-fulfilling prophecies' or we refuse to alter our perceptions to take account of new information based on 'real' experience.

Differences in training and professional orientation may also be a factor perpetuating inter-agency barriers, although within any single professional group there is likely to be a wide range of values and views. We could argue, for example, that traditional training in medicine encourages the perception of the patient as the object of medical technique – and too much consideration of the patient as someone with feelings could well be a distraction (if not a downright liability) to the prime task. So, for example, it may be an indication of the success of the professionalization process that Dr Alistair Irvine, the senior police surgeon in Cleveland, was able to state to the judicial inquiry that an internal anal investigation of alleged child victims was a 'gentle examination'.

Different work settings and organizational constraints will also have a significant impact on inter-agency relationships. Workers who are employed in hierarchically organized agencies (including most professional welfare staff) will rarely have the autonomy possessed by other professionals, who may well find the hierarchical control of decision-making irksome. The inability to make a decision is not infrequently perceived by others as a major identifying personality attribute of social workers rather than an organizationally inspired constraint. Similarly, class teachers have very limited discretion in decision-making, whilst many *head* teachers exercise the autonomy characteristic of medical consultants. The teacher's day is fairly extensively regulated by the timetable (and compared to many other workers teachers get long holidays – affecting the level of their 'availability'). General practitioners have their routine surgeries. On the other hand, police work is regulated by 24-hour rotas. Social workers are rarely to be found in their offices and are, consequently, difficult to get hold of.

Case conference problems

Later in this chapter we outline some of the developments in good practice that relate to case conferences, but first we wish to identify some of the problematic areas here, especially where they relate to inter-agency issues. The basic issue of who attends case conferences is a convenient starting point. Too often those who have direct knowledge of the child and family under discussion, such as school teachers and GPs, as well as the family themselves, are not present (Family Rights Group, 1986; Hallett and Stevenson, 1980; Holman, 1987; McGloin and Turnbull, 1986; Parents against Injustice, 1986). A. Jones (1987, p. 9), Birmingham's Director of Social Services, commenting on accusations that social workers had mishandled a child abuse allegation concerning an Asian family, observes: 'The composition of case conferences is also highlighted in this report. A police representative with information about Mr. X's previous convictions was in favour of court proceedings. A school who had formed a positive opinion of the child and her family sent their apologies for absence.' All too often those who attend conferences and make the significant decisions not only lack first-hand information and are unable to make a constructive contribution to the debate (Desborough and Stevenson, 1977) but are also mainly male and white.

The second major issue has to do with the dynamics of conferences and attitudes of those participating. Given that case conferences represent the formal forum for inter-agency liaison in child protection, much of what we have noted earlier (for example, reliance on stereotypical perceptions) will apply. Whilst official literature and guidance (DHSS, 1974, 1976a, 1982, 1986) are unambiguous in outlining the ostensible purposes of conferences, the authority of conference decisions is less clear (Hallett and Stevenson, 1980; Jones et al., 1978). In addition, Dale et al. (1986) and Furniss (1983a) recognize that the explicit 'top of the table' business may be effectively undermined by simultaneous 'below the table' business. This is particularly evident in agencies that have explicit policies to keep children out of care at all costs, a policy that limits case conference discussions concerned with older children at risk as it minimizes the possible range of outcomes. Waterhouse (1987) notes a growing tendency for professionals to go into case conferences with their minds already made up, and Hallett and Stevenson (1980, pp. 104–5) observe: 'Sadly we must ... take into account the anxiety and guilt which may cause participants to hold back contributions which might call in question their handling of the case.'

Finally, the effective chairing of case conferences has been highlighted as a major determinant of their success or failure (Hallett and Stevenson, 1980; Jones *et al.*, 1978). It quite clearly behoves the effective chairperson of any child protection case conference to recognize their essential inter-agency dynamics and to be alert to the danger of one agency group 'hijacking' the proceedings.

In the same way that case conferences are designed to enhance inter-agency effectiveness, so too are child protection registers. According to the DHSS (1986), the essential purposes of the Child Protection Register are to provide:

> a record of all children in the area who are currently the subject of an 'inter-agency protection plan' and to ensure the outline periodic review of such plans, and a central point of 'speedy inquiry for professional staff' who are 'worried' about the child and want to know whether the child is subject to an inter-agency protection plan. In addition the Register will provided statistical information about current trends in the area.

However, the day-to-day effectiveness and relevance of the child protection registers have been subject to widespread criticism. The anxiety of agencies to protect themselves from public opprobrium has resulted in the inclusion of an excessively high number of names on registers, rendering them meaningless and impractical (Corpe, 1987; Geach, 1980). Sutton (1980) argues that the ways in which children are labelled 'at risk' are based on dubious empirical grounds. In addition, Geach (1980) claims that the vague and inconsistent criteria used as the basis for registration represent an infringement of civil liberties.

How can problems of poor collaboration be overcome?

As accurate prediction in the area of child protection eludes each agency, the first essential requirement is that individual workers understand and feel confident in their own role and functions, avoiding the pitfalls of 'dangerous' practice highlighted by Dale *et al.* (1986). Social workers were criticized in the Jasmine Beckford inquiry for failing to understand the essential nature of their job and its statutory context – unlike the police and NSPCC workers. Similarly the pressure group Parents against Injustice (1987) has indicated that many parents suspected of abusing their children prefer investigations to be carried out by the police rather than social workers.

Weissman, Epstein, and Savage (1983) identify a range of roles that practitioners may perform in welfare agencies. It is on the basis of a clear understanding of the nature of such roles that workers can more readily make sense of the organizational structures in which they operate. They also recognize that on occasions performance of some roles may conflict with other tasks. Whilst they do not pretend that their model offers a panacea for effective agency employment, they argue that it helps clarify the tensions and potential flashpoints. Workers in boundary roles may be continually exposed to new and often inconsistent information, but they can also exert the main influence in clarifying these inconsistencies.

Secondly, it is important to establish intra- and inter-agency lines of responsibility and accountability. The DHSS attempts to clarify the role of the *key worker* in child abuse work and recognition of this individual's crucial role in inter-agency coordination (1986) are welcome in this respect. Within schools the DES response to the Cleveland inquiry has been to concentrate responsibility for such coordination in a senior member of staff (DES, 1988). Elsewhere we have argued against the efficacy of such procedures (Milner and Blyth, 1988). The Rochdale NSPCC child protection team (Dale *et al.*, 1986; Waters, 1987) have pioneered a novel way of dealing with the complexity of multi-agency involvement. They have made use of 'network meetings' when professionals become 'stuck'.

A network meeting involves the family and its agency helpers getting together to identify and work on its problems. Waters observes that the largest network meeting was attended by thirty-five people. The two major achievements of such meetings are that they encourage a high rate of attendance by both family members and professional workers and that the group is enabled to emerge from the 'stuckness', making definite decisions about future action. Of the twenty network meetings referred to, thirteen resulted in taking 'statutory protection measures', in six instances the case was closed, whilst in the remaining case everyone remained 'stuck'. Networking has continued to be successful, with Waters reporting that in all cases where the legal mandate was sought the network was a significant punctuation of the process of a turning point in work or intervention in the family (personal communication, 1987).

However, when all else fails the team simply take over and exclude other agencies from active involvement, a move referred to as 'clearing the ring'. There is currently limited independent empirical evidence to validate this particular way of working, which at first glance appears both deceptively simple and elitist, and it might be no more than yet another manifestation of workers avoiding the reality of inter-agency work. For example, Cornick (1988) tries to avoid possible conflicts by arguing that 'too early' multidisciplinary work can be confusing and counter-productive, and Kelville (1988, p. 12), whilst recognizing the need for joint work between police and social workers in child sexual abuse investigations, fears that 'finding the common ground necessary for shared professional practice can turn out to be a long and sometimes destructive process'.

Thirdly, it is essential that practitioners, managers, and policy makers develop an adequate understanding of the functions, philosophy, ideology, and aims of workers in other agencies.

> It is not enough for individual agencies to have a clear view of what they are doing. There will be no comprehensive service ... unless there is an agreed joint philosophy and an agreed joint strategy to put it into effect. Reaching such agreements may well cause some professional pain, and may lead to 'sacred cows' being investigated and even slaughtered. (HAS, 1986, p. 39)

Many of the inter-agency difficulties, as we have observed, surround the limited resources available to individual agencies, and the explicit or implicit mandate for agency workers to resolve client problems by conserving their own agency's resources whilst utilizing those of others. In the area of child protection, such problems have been aggravated by the persistent refusal of the government to acknowledge that implementing its proposals for more effective effort requires more than simply re-jigging existing resources (DHSS, 1986).

Where there are conflicting or divergent aims or perspectives it is not at all helpful to dismiss such differences as simply obstructive, irrelevant, or the result of personality clashes. After all, all actions appear reasonable when seen from the other individual's agency's perspective!

This brings us to the fourth point – working constructively with difference. As we have noted earlier, differences of opinion in child care are especially difficult to handle, although we believe that conflicts of perspective in child protection can be used constructively. As Furniss (1988) argues, such conflicts can help workers to understand the family process better if they are acknowledged and examined rather than if workers try to outwit each other and prove the other professionals wrong.

As Ferguson has emphasized in Chapter 7, no one professional group – or individual – has a monopoly on wisdom. The validity of separate viewpoints is important. Being able to accept another's perspective requires a firm, although not inflexible, confidence in one's own abilities. Otherwise any alternative perspective is seen not as a helpful corrective, but as a fundamental challenge.

Personal acquaintance with other key individuals, awareness of individual perspectives and values, recognition of their skills and personal qualities, help dispel the myths and establish both personal and working relationships (Lewin, 1986; Frosh, 1987a). There is obviously no substitute for actually meeting other people and, basic to the point of naivety as it may seem, in our experience it is preferable to do this before the need to meet formally over a specific case arises. As the evidence on child abuse case conferences all too often shows, participants to these meetings are virtual strangers to each other and are prepared to display only their formal 'professional selves'.

As Weissman, Epstein, and Savage (1983) observe, being an effective team member requires constant awareness that teamwork is a means to an end and not an end in its own right, otherwise excessive focus on members of the team getting on with each other may detract from the team's real business and possibly encourage cosiness and collusion.

Earlier, we highlighted some of the problems of case conferences, although the DHSS (1986) asserts that inter-agency meetings may be extremely effective and there are, of course, references to these in the literature. For example, Gray (1987, p. 22) describes a project designed to encourage GPs to take a more active part in child abuse conferences and concludes: 'GPs can be involved, particularly if their work patterns are taken into account.'

We must also be prepared to expand our perception of who can make a positive contribution to case conferences. As David Pithers of National Children's Home (NCH) has observed: 'with child abuse you often can't determine who is the most expert person. In many cases it's the childminder or the foster parent' (Tonkin, 1987, p. 17).

Perhaps the most controversial development in case conference management has been the issue of parental involvement, which has been addressed with surprisingly positive results in view of conventional wisdom (Dale *et al.*, 1986; DHSS, 1986) in the London Boroughs of Greenwich (McGloin and Turnbull, 1986) and Sutton (Burningham, 1988). According to McGloin and Turnbull, the Greenwich experience showed evidence that, whilst both professional workers and the parents themselves felt inhibited and anxious, these problems seemed relatively insignificant when compared with the positive spin-offs, which improved the operation of the case conferences themselves and enhanced necessary information gathering and effective professional decision-making. As for the parents, 'irrespective of the decisions made, [they] appeared to feel that in participating at a review conference they had some say and control in the power being exercised on themselves and their children' (p. 44).

More recently, Sutton won a Campaign for Freedom of Information Award for involving parents in child abuse case conferences. David Monk, the social services department area manager who pioneered the authority's practice, commented:

> We are no longer deluged with unsubstantiated gossip and unclear allegations. If parents are there professionals are forced to be specific about just what is fact and what is only rumour . . . Moreover we have been able to clear up countless examples of mistaken information from agencies simply because parents are on the spot. (Burningham, 1988, p. 13)

Contrast these perceptions with Corby's (1987a) research, which indicated that official attitudes generally presumed that 'having regard to parental rights actually impedes the protection of children and is, therefore, a practice to be avoided', and that social work practice consistently disregarding parents' rights seemed to have little positive impact on children's rights.

Summary: What do we mean by effective partnership and how would we recognize good practice if we saw it?

Effective partnership involves hard work and a fundamental appraisal of the effects of power differentials on agency workers in child protection. Male violence, the ownership of expertise, the subordinate position of women and black people, have all been explored in previous chapters. Hearn, particularly, makes some positive suggestions in Chapter 4 for men working in this area to help them recognize and understand how welfare agencies replicate and mirror power disparities in families and society. There can be no effective partnership unless these areas are addressed.

Secondly, good communications are essential if inter-agency work is to avoid the pitfalls of the past and the only-too-regular tragedies that haunt social workers. Conflicting views and opinions should be embraced rather than fought over or avoided. They are most appropriately considered as helpful rather than a hindrance. The interchange of ideas not only illumines the debate and aids an understanding of family dynamics, but it also prevents the establishment of cosy and collusive relationships. Excessive familiarity and interdependence can lead to blurring of roles, duplication of roles, duplication of functions between agencies and the lack of constructive criticism – all notable features of the relationships between the members of a number of agencies involved with Maria Colwell and her family.

It is also important that the notion of 'care' is examined more closely. As Phillipson (1988) reminds us, too often care involves 'caring about' as opposed to 'caring for'. Agency managers tend to talk about 'caring about' and make decisions, whilst more junior members of welfare agencies (usually female) end up doing the 'caring for'. Unless this issue is resolved and primary carers such as foster parents and teachers are given a voice in decision-making, there can be no reciprocity and no effective partnership.

Making clear, explicit, and equitable arrangements about tasks and objectives should be a primary aim of inter-agency cooperation. Reciprocity means that all parties should feel they are getting a fair deal and that, irrespective of professional status, everyone with a contribution to make is encouraged to make it. No one should be precious about their knowledge or skills. As Weissman, Savage, and Epstein (1983, p. 112) have noted: 'to be a good colleague, one must understand and be sensitive to the values and skills of other professions as well as the demand of their roles and tasks. There is nothing more destructive to collegiality than a suggestion by one profession, such as social work, that its mission is to humanise other professions.'

Our own experience and work with practitioners in a range of agencies emphasize that success in simple activities and performing inherently minor tasks can lead to more substantial achievements. The occasional informal lunchtime meeting between different professional groups has been a well-tried and useful means of meeting others and even the expedient invitation of a key individual for a cup of coffee may pay greater long-term dividends than the most prescriptive directive to cooperate. How much more effective this might be if the person to boil the kettle and get out the cups were the area manager or consultant paediatrician?

There are also simple and effective ways of improving communications at case conferences. For instance, punctual starts would help emphasize that everyone's time is valuable. Lessons could be learned from education practice. Formal seating around a table might well be replaced with informal seating, and flip-charts used to enable participants' contributions to be visually presented. Conferences of this sort could be held without the need to always book conference rooms – an unconscious display of who controls the territory and wields the greatest power.

If workers fail to make a start on developing effective partnerships, the spectre raised by recent inquiries suggests that they might be forced to do so by statute. The panel investigating the death of Jasmine Beckford (chaired by Louis Blom-Cooper) noted that health authorities and local authorities already have a 'duty' under Section 22 of the National Health Service Act, 1977, to 'cooperate with each other in the discharge of their respective functions'. The report went on to recommend a statutory duty to report concerns to a child protection agency on the grounds that this 'would give expression to society's deep concern that health professionals should play their part in bringing child abuse cases to the notice of Social Services' (London Borough of Brent, 1985, p. 145).

The Commission of Inquiry into the death of Kimberley Carlile (also chaired by Blom-Cooper) took this a stage further, asserting that 'Nothing short of a joint organisation incorporating child care and child health will suffice' (London Borough of Greenwich, 1987). The Commission suggested two possible alternatives to achieve this objective:

(1) legal responsibility for child protection should rest with a single authority (Child Protection Service) with necessary powers, or
(2) management of the child protection system should be shared statutorily by all the relevant agencies.

Both these alternatives have received further endorsement from the judicial inquiry into child abuse in Cleveland, which further recommended the establishment of specialist assessment teams comprising a doctor, police officer, and social worker (Secretary of State for Social Services, 1988). The DHSS (1988e) has now produced a guide to arrangements for inter-agency cooperation for the protection of children from abuse, which emphasizes the need to understand other professionals' agency function and information sharing. But, whilst reorganization may appear a superficially attractive remedy, it cannot, of itself, provide a convincing resolution of the problems we have identified. We believe that the only effective way forward is to begin to pay attention to the *process* of partnership and to be a little less bound up with procedures and power.

Bibliography

Ageton, S. (1983), *Sexual Assault among Adolescents* (Lexington Books).

Ahmed, S., Cheetham, J. and Small, J. (eds) (1986), *Social Work with Black Children and their Families* (Batsford).

Alexander, P. C. (1985), 'A systems theory conceptualisation of incest', *Family Process*, 24, pp. 79–87.

Althusser, L. (1971), 'Ideology and ideological state apparatuses', in *Lenin and Philosophy and Other Essays* (New Left Books).

Amiel, B. (1988), 'The problem facing us now is a philosophical divide', *The Times*, 8 July, p. 17.

Amphlett, S. (1987), Letter in *Social Work Today*, 8 June.

Anderson, M. L. (1988), *Thinking about Women: Sociological Perspectives on Sex and Gender* (Macmillan).

Arditti, R., Duelli Klein, R. and Minden, S. (eds) (1984), *Test Tube Women* (Pandora).

Arnold, E. (1988), 'Cross cultural aspects of physical abuse', *Child Abuse Review*, 2 (1), pp. 31–3.

Bagarozzi, D. and Giddings, C. W. (1983), 'Conjugal violence: A critical review of current research and clinical practices', *The American Journal of Family Therapy*, 11, pp. 3–15.

Baher, E., Hyman, C., Jones, C., Jones, R., Kerr, A. and Mitchell, R. (1976), *At Risk: An Account of the Battered Child Research Department* (Routledge & Kegan Paul).

Baker, A. W. and Duncan, S. P. (1986), 'Child sexual abuse: a study of prevalence in Great Britain', *Child Abuse and Neglect*, 9 (4), pp. 457–67.

Baker, B. (1988), 'GPs in group practices are under more stress', *Pulse*, 88 (6), 6 February, p. 1.

Barker, W. (1984), *Child Development Programme* (University of Bristol).

Batta, I. D. and Mawby, R. I. (1981), 'Children in local authority care: a monitoring of racial differences in Bradford', *Policy and Politics*, 9 (2), pp. 137–50.

Bayley, A. T. (1988), *Staff Development Seminar* (Kirklees Family Centre, 15 April).

Becker, H. (1963), *Outsiders: Studies in the Sociology of Deviance* (Free Press).

Becker, J. (1988), Conference on Child Sexual Abuse, Glasgow.

Becker, S. and MacPherson, S. (1986), *Poor Clients: The Extent and Nature of Financial Poverty amongst Consumers of Social Work Services*

(Nottingham University Benefits Research Unit).

Bee, H. (1985), *The Developing Child*, 4th edn (Harper & Row).

Behlmer, G. K. (1982), *Child Abuse and Moral Reform in England 1870–1908* (Stanford University Press).

Bell, P. and Macleod, J. (1988), 'Bridging the gap: feminist development work in Glasgow', *Feminist Review*, no. 28, January, pp. 136–43.

Bell, S. (1988), *When Salem came to the Boro'* (Pan Books).

Bentovim, A. (1987), 'Physical and sexual abuse of children – the role of the family therapist', *Journal of Family Therapy*, 9, pp. 383–8.

Bentovim, A., Elton, A. and Tranter, M. (1987), 'Prognosis for rehabilitation after abuse', *Adoption and Fostering*, 11 (1), pp. 26–31.

Bentovim, A., Elton, A., Hildebrand, J., Tranter, M. and Vizard, E. (eds) (1988), *Child Sexual Abuse in the Family and Related Papers* (Wright).

Berliner, L. (1988), Conference on Child Sexual Abuse, Glasgow.

Berman, M. (1983), *All That Is Solid Melts into Air: The Experience of Modernity* (Verso).

Bernard, J. (1974), *The Future of Motherhood* (The Dial Press).

Birchall, E. M. (1989), 'The frequency of child abuse – what do we know?' in O. Stevenson (ed.), *Child Abuse: Professional Practice and Public Policy* (Wheatsheaf).

Bishop, M. (with A. Fry) (1988), 'The trial of working through a nightmare', *Social Work Today*, 7 July, pp. 12–13.

Blanchard, F. (1983), *Report of the Director General* (Geneva: ILO).

Blaxter, M. (1983), 'Health services as a defence against consequences of poverty in industrialised societies', *Social Science Medicine*, 17, pp. 1139–48.

Blyth, E. (1986), 'Burn out or cop out?', *Social Services Insight*, 1 (6), pp. 18–20.

Blyth, E. and Milner, J. (1987a), 'Reaching potential', *Social Services Insight*, 2 (33), pp. 20–1.

Blyth, E. and Milner, J. (1987b), 'Black and laid back', *Scan*, no. 3, pp. 16–18.

Bogle, M. T. (1988), 'Brixton Black Women's Centre: organizing on child sexual abuse', *Feminist Review*, no. 28, January.

Bouhdiba, A. (1982), *Exploitation of Child Labour* (United Nations).

Boulton, M. (1983), *On Being a Mother* (Tavistock).

Boyden, J. and Hudson, A. (1985), *Children: Rights and Responsibilities*, Minority Rights Group, Report no. 69.

Brandon, S. (1987), *Community Care*, 17 September, p. 2.

Breines, W. and Gordon, L. (1983), 'The new scholarship on family violence', *Signs*, spring, pp. 490–531.

Bristol Child Health and Education Study (1986), 'West Indians: no link between disadvantage and attainment', *Education*, 25 April, p. 383.

British Association of Social Work (1975), *A Code of Ethics for Social Work* (BASW).

Brook, E. and Davis, A. (eds) (1985), *Women, the Family and Social Work* (Tavistock).

Brown, C. (1984), *Black and White Britain: The Third PSI Survey* (Heinemann).

Brown, G. W. and Harris, T. (1978), *The Social Origins of Depression: a study of psychiatric disorder* (Tavistock).

Brown, K., Davies, C. and Stratton, P. (1988), *Early Prediction and Prevention of Child Abuse* (Wiley).

Brownmiller, S. (1975), *Against Our Will* (Penguin).

Bull, D. and Wilding, P. (eds) (1983) *Thatcherism and the Poor* (Child Poverty Action Group).

Burchall, J. (1987), 'The gender benders', *New Society*, 24 July, p. 25.

Burningham, S. (1988), 'Freeing information', *Social Work Today*, 7 April, p. 13.

Burstyn, V. (1983), 'Masculine dominance and the state', in R. Milliband and J. Saville (eds), *The Socialist Register 1983* (Merlin).

Butrym, Z. (1976), *The Nature of Social Work* (Macmillan).

Caines, R. and Mignott, J. (1987), 'Social care in a multi-racial society', SCA Annual Seminar, *Broadening our Horizons*, 27–29 October.

Cameron, D. and Fraser, E. (1987), *The Lust to Kill* (Polity).

Carlson, M. (1979), 'What's behind wife beating?' in E. Shapiro and B. Shapiro (eds), *The Women Say/The Men Say: the Women's Liberation Movement and Men's Consciousness* (Dell).

Cashmore, E. E. and Troyna, B. (1983), *Introduction to Race Relations* (Routledge & Kegan Paul).

Chant, J. (with A. Fry) (1988), 'Time to dim the blue light of dramatic intervention', *Social Work Today*, 7 July, pp. 16–17.

Children's Legal Centre (1986), *Black and in Care*, Conference Report.

Children's Legal Centre (1988), *Child Abuse Procedures – the child's viewpoint* (The Children's Legal Centre).

Chodorow, N. (1978), *The Reproduction of Mothering: Psychoanalysis and the Sociology of Gender* (University of California Press).

Chodorow, N. and Contratto, S. (1982), 'The fantasy of the perfect mother', in B. Thorne with M. Yalom (eds), *Re-thinking the Family: Some Feminist Questions* (Longman; Stanford University Press).

CIBA Foundation (1984), *Child Sexual Abuse Within the Family* (Tavistock).

Clark, B., Parkin, W., Parton, N. and Richards, M. (1989), *How a Family Centre is Seen: A Survey of the Perceptions of Area Team Social Workers*, Research Notes.

Clarke, C. with Asquith, S. (1985), *Social Work and Social Philosophy: A Guide for Practice* (Routledge & Kegan Paul).

Clarke, L. and Lewis, D. (1977), *Rape: The Price of Coercive Sexuality* (The Women's Press).

Clayden, G. (1987), 'Anal appearances and child sexual abuse', letter to *The Lancet*, i, 14 March, pp. 620–1.

Cohen, B. (1988), *Caring for Children. Services and Policies for Childcare and Equal Opportunities in the UK* (Commission of the European Communities, London).

Cohn, A. H. and Daro, D. (1987), 'Is treatment too late: what ten years of evaluative research tell us', *Child Abuse and Neglect*, 11, pp. 433–42.

Coombe, V. and Little, A. (1986), *Race and Social Work. A Guide to Training* (Tavistock).

Cooper, C. L. and Payne, R. (1980) (eds), *Current Concerns in Occupational Stress* (Wiley).

Cooper, D. (1970), *Death of the Family* (Alan Lane).

Corby, B. (1987a), 'Why ignoring the rights of parents in child abuse cases should be avoided, *Social Work Today*, 23 November, pp. 8–9.

Corby, B. (1987b), *Working with Child Abuse. Social Work Practice and the Child Abuse System* (Open University Press).

Corea, G., Duelli Klein, R., Hanmer, J., Holmes, H. B., Hoskins, B., Kishwar, M., Raymond, J., Rowland, R. and Steinbacher, R. (1985), *Man-Made Women* (Hutchinson).

Cornick, B. (1988), 'Proceeding together', *Community Care*, 17 March.

Corpe, G. (1987), 'How can the registration of children protect them from abuse?' *Social Work Today*, 31 August, p. 24.

Coveney, L., Jackson, M., Jeffreys, S., Kay, L. and Mahoney, P. (1984), *The Sexuality Papers: male sexuality and the social control of women* (Hutchinson).

Creighton, S. (1984), *Trends in Child Abuse* (NSPCC).

Creighton, S. J. (1987), 'Child abuse in 1986', *Social Services Research*, 16 (3), pp. 1–10 (Department of Social Administration, Birmingham).

Croale, A. (1986), 'Behind the panel', *Community Care*, 17 April, pp. 24–5.

Curnock, K. and Hardiker, P. (1979), *Towards Practice Theory: Skills and Methods in Social Assessments* (Routledge & Kegan Paul).

Dale, J. and Foster, P. (1986), *Feminists and State Welfare* (Routledge & Kegan Paul).

Dale, P., Morrison, T., Davies, M., Noyes, P. and Roberts, W. (1983), 'A family-therapy approach to child abuse: countering resistance', *Journal of Family Therapy*, 5, pp. 117–43.

Dale, P., Davies, M., Morrison, T. and Waters, J. (1986), *Dangerous Families: Assessment and treatment of child abuse* (Tavistock).

Dallos, R. and Aldridge, D. (1986), 'Change: How do we recognise it?', *Journal of Family Therapy*, 8, pp. 45–59.

Davidoff, L. and Hall, C. (1987), *Family Fortunes: Men and Women of the English Middle Class 1780–1850* (Hutchinson).

Davies, M. (1981), *The Essential Social Worker: A Guide to Positive Practice* (Heinemann Educational Books).

Denney, D. (1983), 'Some dominant perspectives in the literature relating to multi-racial social work', *British Journal of Social Work*, 13 (2), pp. 149–74.

Department of Education and Science (1985), *Young People in the Eighties* (HMSO).

Department of Education and Science (1988), *Working Together for the Protection of Children from Abuse: Procedures within the Education Service*, Circular no. 4/88, 6 July.

Department of Health (1988), *Protecting Children: A Guide to Social Workers Undertaking a Comprehensive Assessment* (HMSO).

Department of Health and Social Security (1974), *Non-accidental Injury to Children*, LASSL(74)13.

Department of Health and Social Security (1976a), *Non-accidental Injury to Children: Area Review Committees*, LASSL(76)2.

Department of Health and Social Security (1976b), *Non-accidental Injury to Children: the Police and Case Conferences*, LASSL(76)26.

Department of Health and Social Security (1980), *Child Abuse: The Central Register System*, LASSL(80)4.

Department of Health and Social Security (1982), *Child Abuse: A Study of Inquiry Reports* (HMSO).

Department of Health and Social Security (1986), *Child Abuse – Working Together: A draft guide for inter-agency co-operation for the protection of children.*

Department of Health and Social Security (1988a), *Child Protection: Guidance for Senior Nurses, Health Visitors and Midwives* (HMSO).

Department of Health and Social Security (1988b), *Diagnosis of Child Sexual Abuse: Guidance for Doctors* (HMSO).

Department of Health and Social Security (1988c), *Private Fostering and Place of Safety*, A/F87/15 (HMSO).

Department of Health and Social Security (1988d), *Working Together for the Protection of Children from Abuse*, LAC(88)10, 6 July.

Department of Health and Social Security (1988e), *Working Together: A guide to arrangements for interagency co-operation for the protection of children from abuse* (HMSO).

Department of Health and Social Security, Department of Education and Science (1976), *Fit for the Future: Report of the Committee on Child Health Services* (HMSO).

Desborough, C. and Stevenson, O. (1977), *Case Conferences: A study of interprofessional communication concerning children at risk* (University of Keele).

Devore, W. (1988), 'Working with Families in Crisis and Accepting Cultural Differences', Lecture, Kirklees Social Services, March.

Devore, W. and Schlesinger, E. G. (1981), *Ethnic Families and Social Work Practice* (C. V. Mosby).

Dingwall, R., Eekelaar, J. M. and Murray, T. (1983), *The Protection of Children* (Blackwell).

Dingwall, R. (1986), 'The Jasmine Beckford affair', *The Modern Law Review*, 49, pp. 489–507.

Dingwall, R. (1989), 'Some problems about predicting child abuse and neglect', in O. Stevenson (ed.) *Child Abuse: Public Policy and Professional Practice* (Wheatsheaf).

Dobash, R. E. and Dobash, R. (1979), *Violence against Wives* (Free Press).

Dobash, E., Dobash, R. and Gutteridge, S. (1986), *The Imprisonment of Women* (Basil Blackwell).

Dominelli, L. (1988), *Anti-racist Social Work: A challenge for white practitioners and educators* (Macmillan).

Donzelot, J. (1979), *The Policing of Families: Welfare versus the State* (Hutchinson).

Doran, C. and Young, J. (1987), 'Child abuse: the real crisis', *New Society*, 82 (1300), 27 November, pp. 12–14.

Downie, A. and Forshaw, P. (1987), 'Family centres', *Practice*, 1 (2), Summer, pp. 140–7.

Driver, G. (1980), *Beyond Underachievement: Case Studies of English, West Indian and Asian School Leavers at Sixteen Plus* (Commission for Racial Equality).

Dunn, J. (1985), 'Identity, modernity and the claim to know better', in *Rethinking Modern Political Theory* (Cambridge University Press).

Dunn-Smith, J. E. (1987), 'Scientific and ethical dilemmas of intervention studies: with particular reference to non-accidental injury', conference paper, Association for Child Psychology and Psychiatry.

Dworkin, A. (1982), *Pornography: Men Possessing Women* (Women's Press).

Dworkin, A. (1987), *Intercourse* (Secker and Warburg).

Dyer, C. (1987), 'First High Court judgement on sex abuse in Cleveland', *British Medical Journal*, 8 August, p. 382.

Edwards, A. (1987), 'Male violence in feminist theory: an analysis of the changing conceptions of sex/gender violence and male dominance', in J. Hanmer and M. Maynard (eds), *Men, Violence and Social Control* (Macmillan).

Egglestone, S. I., Dunn, D. K., Anjali, M. and Wright, C. Y. (1985), *The Educational and Vocational Experiences of 15–18 year old Young People of Minority Ethnic Groups* (DES).

Eisenstein, Z. (ed.) (1979), *Capitalist Patriarchy and the Case for Socialist Feminism* (Monthly Review Press).

Ely, P. and Denney, D. (1987), *Social Work in a Multi-racial Society* (Gower).

EMERGE (1986) 'Do you feel like beating up on someone?' EMERGE pamphlet.

Ennew, J. (1986), *The Sexual Exploitation of Children* (Polity Press).

Essex County Council (1981), *Malcolm Page: Report by the Panel appointed by Essex A.R.C.* (Essex County Council).

Family Rights Group (1986), Response to DHSS draft circular – *Child Abuse – Working Together: A draft guide for inter-agency co-operation for the protection of children.*

Ferguson, H. (1986), 'The faces change but the bruises don't: child care and the growth of child abuse as a social problem', paper presented to the British Sociological Association Conference, Loughborough University.

Ferleger, N., Glenwick, D. S., Gaines, R. R. W. and Green, A. H. (1988), 'Identifying correlates of re-abuse in maltreating parents', *Child Abuse and Neglect*, 12, pp. 41–9.

Fido, J. (1977), 'The charity organisation society and social casework in London 1869–1900', in A. P. Donajgrodski (ed.), *Social Control in Nineteenth Century Britain* (Croom Helm).

Filene, P. (1987), 'The secrets of men's history', in H. Brod (ed.), *The Making of Masculinities: The New Men's Studies* (Allen & Unwin).

Findlay, C. (1987–8), 'Child abuse: the Dutch response', *Practice*, 1 (4), Winter, pp. 374–81.

Finkelhor, D. (1979), *Sexually Victimised Children* (Free Press).

Finkelhor, D. (1983), 'Common features of child abuse', in D. Finkelhor, R. Gelles, G. Hotaling and M. Straus (eds), *The Dark Side of Families: Current Family Violence Research* (Sage).

Finkelhor, D. (1984), *Child Sexual Abuse: New Theory and Research* (Free Press).

Finkelhor, D. (1986a), *A Sourcebook on Child Sexual Abuse* (Sage).

Finkelhor, D. (1986b), in T. S. Trepper and M. J. Barrett (eds), *Treating Incest* (Haworth Press).

Finkelhor, D. (1988), Conference on Child Sexual Abuse, Glasgow, June.

Finnegan, F. (1982), *Poverty and Prejudice: The Irish in Victorian York* (Cork University Press).

Firestone, S. (1970), *The Dialectic of Sex* (William Morrow).

Fitzgerald, T. (1983), 'The New Right and the family' in M. Loney, D. Boswell and J. Clarke, *Social Policy and Social Welfare* (Open University Press).

Fitzherbert, K. (1967), *West Indian Children in London* (J. Bell & Sons).

Foucault, M. (1977), *Discipline and Punish* (Harmondsworth).

Foucault, M. (1979), *The History of Sexuality, Vol. 1: An Introduction* (Allen Lane).

Foucault, M. (1980), *Power/Knowledge* (Harvester).

Fowler, D. A. (1975), 'Ends and means', in H. Jones (ed.), *Towards a New Social Work* (Routledge & Kegan Paul).

Franklin, B. (ed.) (1986), *The Rights of Children* (Blackwell).

Freeman, M. D. A. (1983a), *The Rights and Wrongs of Children* (Francis Pinter).

Freeman, M. D. A. (1983b), 'Freedom and the welfare state: child rearing, parental autonomy and state intervention', *Journal of Social Welfare Law*, March, pp. 70–91.

Freeman, M. D. A. (1987–8), 'Taking children's rights seriously', *Children and Society*, 1 (4), Winter, pp. 299–319.

Frosh, S. (1987a), 'Facing disclosure: Common anxieties when interviewing sexually abused children', *Practice*, 1 (2), pp. 129–36.

Frosh, S. (1987b), 'Issues for men working with sexually abused children', *British Journal of Psychotherapy*, 3 (4), pp. 332–9.

Frude, N. and Goss, A. (1980), 'Maternal anger and the young child', in N. Frude (ed.), *Psychological Approaches to Child Abuse* (Batsford).

Furniss, T. (1983a), 'Mutual influence and interlocking professional-–family process in the treatment of child sexual abuse and incest', *Child Abuse and Neglect*, no. 7, pp. 207–23.

Furniss, T. (1983b), 'Family process in the treatment of intra-familial child sexual abuse', *Journal of Family Therapy*, 5, pp. 263–78.

Furniss, T. (1985), 'Conflict-avoiding and conflict-regulating patterns in infant and child abuse', reprinted in Bentovim *et al.* (1988).

Furniss, T. (1987a), 'Address to the First European Conference on Child Abuse and Neglect', Rhodes, March.

Furniss, T. (1987b), 'Surviving child sexual abuse', in *Child Abuse Review*, 1 (7), pp. 3–5.

Furniss, T. (1988), Child-oriented Family Assessment Workshop held at the Institute for Family Therapy, 4 and 5 March.

Garland, D. (1985), *Punishment and Welfare* (Gower).

Geach, H. (1980), 'When registers lead to abuse', *Community Care*, 12 June, pp. 18–20.

Gelles, R. (ed.) (1979), *Family Violence* (Sage).

Gelles, R. (1983), 'An exchange/social control theory', in D. Finkelhor, R. Gelles, G. Hotaling and M. Straus (eds), *The Dark Side of Families* (Sage).

Giarretto, H. (1982), *Integrated Treatment of Child Sexual Abuse: A treatment and training manual* (Science and Behaviour Books).

Gibson, A. and Barrow, J. (1986), *The Unequal Struggle* (CSS Publications).

Giddens, A. (1985), *The Nation State and Violence: Volume 2 of a Contemporary Critique of Historical Materialism* (Polity Press).

Gil, D. (1970), *Violence against Children* (Harvard University Press).

Gil, D. (1975), 'Unravelling child abuse', *American Journal of Ortho-psychiatry*, 45 (3), pp. 346–56.

Giovannoni, J. M. and Becerra, R. M. (1979), *Defining Child Abuse* (Free Press).

Glaser, D. and Frosh, S. (1988), *Child Sexual Abuse*, BASW/Practical Social Work (Macmillan).

Glendinning, C. and Millar, J. (eds) (1987), *Women and Poverty in Britain* (Wheatsheaf).

Goldberg, M. (1965), 'The normal family – myth or reality?' in E. Younghusband (ed.), *Social Work with Families* (Allen & Unwin).

Goldstein, J., Freud, A. and Solnit, A. (1979), *Beyond the Best Interests of the Child* (Free Press).

Gondolf, E. (1985), *Men Who Batter* (Learning Publications).

Gordon, L. (1985), 'Child abuse, gender and the myth of family independence: a historical critique', *Child Welfare*, 64 (3), May/June, pp. 213–24.

Gordon, L. (1986), 'Feminism and social control: the case of child abuse', in J. Mitchell and A. Oakley (eds), *What Is Feminism?* (Blackwell).

Gough, D. and Boddy, A. (1986), 'Family violence: context and method', in G. Horobin (ed.), *The Family: Context or Client*, Research Highlights in Social Work 12 (Kogan Page).

Graham, H. (1980), 'Women's accounts of anger and aggression towards their babies', in N. Frude (ed.), *Psychological Approaches to Child Abuse* (Batsford).

Graham, H. (1982), 'Coping: or how mothers are seen and not heard', in S. Friedman and E. Sarah (eds), *On the Problems of Men: Two Feminist Conferences* (The Women's Press).

Graham, H. (1984), *Women, Health and the Family* (Harvester).

Graham, P. (1988), 'Social class, social disadvantage and child health', *Children and Society*, 2 (1), pp. 9–19.

Graham, P., Dingwall, R., and Wolkind, S. (1985), 'Research issues in child abuse', *Social Science Medicine*, 21 (11), pp. 1217–28.

Gray, A. (1987), 'A case of time', *Community Care*, 8 October, pp. 21–2.

Gray, E. and Cosgrove, J. (1985), 'Ethnocentric perception of child rearing practices in protection services', *Child Abuse and Neglect*, 9, pp. 389–96.

Greenland, C. (1987), *Preventing CAN Deaths: An international study of deaths due to child abuse and neglect* (Tavistock).

Grounds, A. (1987), 'Caught up in the struggle', *Amnesty*, no. 26, April/May, pp. 12–13.

The Guardian, 7 August 1987, p. 1 and p. 32.

The Guardian, 31 August 1987, p. 4.

The Guardian, 22 September 1987, 'Assault "cost life of unborn child"', p. 2.

Hadley, J. (1987), 'Mum is *not* the word', *Community Care*, 5 November, pp. 24–6.

Hale, J. (1983), 'Feminism and Social Work Practice' in B. Jordan and N. Parton (eds), *The Political Dimensions of Social Work* (Blackwell).

Haley, J. (1976), *Problem Solving Therapy* (Jossey Bass Inc.).

Haley, J. (1980), *Leaving Home* (McGraw-Hill).

Hall, H. S., Critcher, C., Jefferson, T., Clarke, J. and Roberts, B. (1978), *Policing the Crisis: Mugging, the State and Law and Order* (Macmillan).

Hall, H. S. and Jacques, M. (eds) (1983), *The Politics of Thatcherism* (Lawrence & Wishart).

Hall, S. (1979), 'The Great Moving Right Show', *Marxism Today*, 23 (1), pp. 14–20.

Hallett, C. and Stevenson, O. (1980), *Child Abuse: Aspects of Interprofessional Co-operation* (George Allen).

Hamblin, A. and Bowen, R. (1981), 'Sexual abuse of children', *Spare Rib*, 106, pp. 6–9, 31.

Hanmer, J. and Statham, D. (1988), *Women and Social Work. Towards a woman centred social work*, BASW (Macmillan).

Harne, L. (1984), 'Lesbian custody and the new myth of the father', *Trouble and Strife*, no. 3, summer, pp. 12–15.

Hartman, A. (1987), 'Family violence: multiple levels of assessment and intervention', *Journal of Social Work*, May, pp. 62–78.

Health Advisory Service (1986), *Bridges over Troubled Waters* (HMSO).

Hearn, J. (1982), 'Notes on patriarchy, professionalisation and the semi-professions', *Sociology*, 16 (2), May, pp. 184–202.

Hearn, J. (1983), *Birth and Afterbirth. A Materialist Account* (Achilles Heel).

Hearn, J. (1985), 'Progress towards the abolition of corporal punishment', *Forum for the Discussion of New Trends in Education*, 27 (2), spring, pp. 54–6.

Hearn, J. (1987), *The Gender of Oppression. Men, Masculinity and the Critique of Marxism* (Wheatsheaf/St Martin's).

Hearn, J. (1988), 'Child abuse: Violence and sexualities towards young people', *Sociology*, 23 (4), November, pp. 531–44.

Hearn, J. and Parkin, W. (1987), *'Sex' at 'Work'. The Power and Paradox of Organisation Sexuality* (Wheatsheaf/St Martin's).

Heptinstall, D. (1986), 'The Black perspective', *Community Care*, no. 622, pp. 12–14.

Herman, J. with Hirschman, L. (1981), *Father–Daughter Incest* (Harvard University Press).

Hewitt, R. (1986), *White Talk, Black Talk: inter-racial friendship and communication amongst adolescents* (ESRC/Cambridge University Press).

Heywood, J. S. (1959), (third edition, 1978), *Children in Care: The development of the service for the deprived child*, 3rd edn (Routledge & Kegan Paul).

HMSO (1987), *The Law on Child Care and Family Services*, Cmnd 62.

Hobbs, C. J. and Wynne, J. M. (1986), 'Buggery in childhood – a common symptom of child abuse', *The Lancet*, 4 October, pp. 792–6.

Hobbs, C. J. and Wynne, J. M. (1987), 'Child sexual abuse – an increasing rate of diagnosis', *The Lancet*, 10 October, pp. 837–41.

Hodgkin, J. (1987), 'Who helps the helpers?' *New Society*, 1 May, pp. 20–1.

Holdsworth, R. (1987), 'Redefining the boundaries of trust', *Community Care*, 12 November, pp. 22–4.

Holman, B. (1988), *Putting Families First: Prevention and Child Care* (Macmillan).

Holman, D. (1987), 'Parents and procedures', *Community Care*, 5 February, pp. 10–11.

Homans, G. (1958), 'Social behaviour as exchange', *American Journal of Sociology*, 63, pp. 597–606.

Home Office (1988), *The Investigation of Child Sexual Abuse*, Circular 52/1988, 6 July.

Home Office Statistical Bulletin (1986), *The Ethnic Origins of Prisoners*, 17/86, June.

Horne, M. (1987), *Values in Social Work* (Wildwood House).

Howe, D. (1979), 'Agency function and social work principles', *British Journal of Social Work*, 9 (1), pp. 29–47.

Howe, D. (1986), *Social Workers and their Practice in Welfare Bureaucracies* (Gower).

Hughes, E. (1958), *Men and their Work* (Free Press).

Husband, C. (ed.) (1982), *Race in Britain* (Hutchinson).

Inner London Education Authority (1983), *A Policy for Equality: Race* (ILEA Publications).

International Children's Rights Monitor (1984), Special Edition.

Irueste-Montes, A. M. and Montes, F. (1988), 'Court-ordered vs. voluntary treatment of abusive and neglectful parents', *Child Abuse and Neglect*, 12(1), pp. 33–9.

Jagger, A. (1983), *Feminist Politics and Human Nature* (Rowan & Allanheld, The Harvester Press).

Jones, A. (1987), 'The problems we face in dealing with cases like "Family X"', *Social Work Today*, 17 August, p. 9.

Jones, D., McLean, R. and Vobe, R. (1978), 'Case conferences on child abuse: the Nottinghamshire approach', unpublished paper to the second International Congress on Child Abuse and Neglect, London.

Jones, D. (1982) (2nd edn 1987), *Understanding Child Abuse* (1st edn Hodder and Stoughton) (2nd edn Macmillan).

Jones, D. P. H. (1987), 'The untreatable family', *Child Abuse and Neglect*, 11, pp. 409–20.

Jordan, B. (1976), *Freedom and the Welfare State* (Routledge & Kegan Paul).

Jordan, B. (1981), 'Family therapy – an outsider's view', *Journal of Family Therapy*, 3, pp. 269–80.

Justice, B. and Justice, R. (1976), *The Abusing Family* (Human Sciences Press).

Kadushin, A. and Martin, J. A. (1981), *Child Abuse, an Interactional Event* (Columbia University Press).

Kahn, R. L., Wolfe, D. N., Quinn, R. P., Snowk, J. D. and Rosenthal, R. A. (1964), *Organizational Stress* (Wiley).

Kane, P. (1987), 'Police killed my baby', *Daily Mirror*, 27 August.

Kaufman, M. (1987), 'The construction of masculinity and the triad of men's violence', in M. Kaufman (ed.), *Beyond Patriarchy. Essays by Men on Pleasure, Power and Change* (Oxford University Press).

Kellmer Pringle, M. (1977), *The Needs of Children* (Hutchinson).

Kellmer Pringle, M. (1979), *A Fairer Future* (Macmillan).

Kelly, L. (1987), 'The continuum of sexual violence', in J. Hanmer and M. Maynard (eds), *Women, Violence and Social Control* (Macmillan).

Kelly, L. (1988), 'What's in a name? Defining child sexual abuse', *Feminist Review*, no. 28, spring, pp. 65–73.

Kelville, H. (1988), 'Joint venture', *Social Services Insight*, 8 April, pp. 12–14.

Kempe, R. S. and Kempe, C. H. (1978), *Child Abuse* (Fontana/Open Books).

Kendrick, J. M. (1987), letter in *Child Education*, September.

Kimmel, M. S. (1987), 'The contemporary "crisis" of masculinity in historical perspective', in H. Brod (ed.), *The Making of Masculinities: the New Men's Studies* (Allen & Unwin).

Kingston, P. (1979), 'The social context of family therapy', in S. Walrond-Skinner (ed.), *Family and Marital Psychotherapy* (Routledge & Kegan Paul).

Kirklees Social Services Department, draft operational proposal for Milnsbridge Day Nursery and Family Centre (Kirklees Social Services), October, 1984.

Kitzinger, J. (1988), 'Defending innocence: ideologies of childhood', *Feminist Review*, No. 28, spring, pp. 77–87.

Kolko, D. J. (1987), 'Treatment of child sexual abuse: programs, progress and prospects', *Journal of Family Violence*, 2 (4), pp. 303–18.

Korsch, B. *et al.* (1965), 'Infant care and punishment: a pilot study', *American Journal of Public Health*, 55 (12).

Kutek, A. (1987), 'The racial dimension in child protection: some prompts for practice', *Journal of Social Work Practice*, November, pp. 13–18.

La Fontaine, J. (1988), *Child Sexual Abuse* (ESRC).

Lahey, I. A. (1984), 'Research on child abuse in liberal patriarchy', in J. Vickers (ed.), *Taking Sex into Account* (Carlton University Press).

Laing, R. D. (1971), *The Politics of the Family* (Tavistock).

Lambeth Social Services Committee (1981), *Black Children in Care Report* (Lambeth Social Services Department).

Lashley, H. (1987), 'Research and social policy implications for the black community and their education', unpublished paper (University of Warwick).

Lask B. (1987), Editorial – 'From honeymoon to reality', *Journal of Family Therapy*, 9, p. 303.

Lee-Potter, L. (1987), 'Kimberley - how to end the tragedies', *Daily Mail*, 20 May.

Leith, A. (1988), 'Child abuse: groupwork with men', *Practice*, 2 (3), pp. 197–207.

Leith, A. and Handforth, S. (1988), 'Groupwork with sexually abused boys', *Practice*, 2 (2), pp. 166–75.

Lemert, E. (1967), *Human Deviance: Social Problems and Social Control* (Prentice-Hall).

Leonard, E. B. (1982), *Women, Crime and Society* (Longman).

Levidov, L. (1987), 'Free the children from the witches', paper given at Psychoanalysis and the Public Sphere Conference, Free Associations/NELP Conference, October.

Lewin, R. (1986), 'O wad some powr the giftie gie us to see oursels as others see us', *Social Work Today*, 3 March, pp. 12–13.

Lewis, C. and O'Brien, M. O. (1987), *Reassessing Fatherhood* (Sage).

Lewis, J. (1986), 'The working-class mother and state intervention', in J. Lewis (ed.), *Labour and Love – Women's Experiences of Home and Family 1850–1940* (Basil Blackwell).

Litwak, E. and Hylton, L. (1962), 'Interorganizational analysis: a hypothesis on co-ordinating agencies, *Administrative Science Quarterly*, 6, pp. 395–426.

Liverpool, V. (1986), 'When backgrounds clash: understanding cultural norms among non-white clients', *Community Care*, 2 October, pp. 19–21.

London Borough of Brent (1985), *A Child in Trust: Report of the panel of inquiry investigating the circumstances surrounding the death of Jasmine Beckford* (London Borough of Brent).

London Borough of Greenwich (1987), *A Child in Mind: Protection of Children in a Responsible Society. Report of the commission of inquiry into the circumstances surrounding the death of Kimberley Carlile* (London Borough of Greenwich).

London Borough of Lambeth (1975), *Report of the Joint Committee of Inquiry into non-accidental injury to children, with particular reference to the case of Lisa Godfrey* (London Borough of Lambeth).

London Borough of Lambeth (1987), *Whose Child? The report of the panel appointed to inquire into the death of Tyra Henry* (London Borough of Lambeth).

Lukes, S. (1978), 'Power and authority', in T. B. Bottomore and R. Nisbet (eds), *History of Sociological Analysis* (Heinemann).

McAdam, L. (1987), 'Racial analysis of children in care', *Social Services Research* (University of Birmingham) (4), pp. 29–34.

MacFarlane, K., Waterman, J. with Conerly, S., Damon, L., Durfee, M. and Long, S. (1986), *The Sexual Abuse of Young Children* (Holt, Rinehart & Winston).

MacFarlane, K. (1988), Conference on Child Sexual Abuse, Glasgow, June.

McGloin, P. and Turnbull, A. (1986), *Parent Participation in Child Abuse Review Conferences* (London Borough of Greenwich).

McGoldrick, M., Pearce, J. K. and Giordano, J. (eds)(1982), *Ethnicity and Family Therapy* (Gillard Press).

McKechnie, N. (1986), 'Family Centres: a shared preventive relationship with the community', *Child Abuse Review*, 1 (3), summer, pp. 5–9.

MacKinnon, C. A. (1982), 'Feminism, marxism, method and the state: an agenda for theory', *Signs*, 7 (3), pp. 515–44.

MacKinnon, C. A. (1983), 'Feminism, marxism, method and the state; towards feminist jurisprudence', *Signs* 8 (4), pp. 635–58.

MacKinnon, C. (1982), 'Violence against women', *Aegis*, 33.

MacLeod, M. and Saraga, E. (1987), 'The absence of trust', *Journal of Social Work Practice*, November, pp. 71–9.

MacLeod, M. and Saraga, E. (1988), 'Challenging the orthodox: towards a feminist theory and practice', *Feminist Review*, no. 28, spring, pp. 16–55.

Madanes, C. (1981), *Strategic Family Therapy* (Jossey Bass).

Mahoney, P. (1984), *Schools for the Boys? Co-education reassessed* (Hutchinson).

Marchant, H. and Waring, B. (1986), *Gender Reclaimed* (Hale & Iremonger).

Martin, D. (1977), *Battered Wives* (Pocket).

Martin, J. (1983), 'Maternal and paternal abuse of children: theoretical and research perspectives', in D. Finkelhor *et al.* (eds), *The Dark Side of Families: Current Family Violence Research* (Sage).

Mason, S. (1986), 'Bristol on the move', *Men's Antisexist Newsletter*, no. 23, pp. 16–17.

Masson, H. C. and O'Byrne, P. (1984), *Applying Family Therapy* (Pergamon).

Masson, H. C. and O'Byrne, P. (1987), 'Making family therapy useful: the educator's task', *Social Work Education*, 7 (1).

Matthews, R. and Young, J. (eds)(1986), *Confronting Crime* (Sage).

Matza, D. (1964), *Delinquency and Drift* (Wiley).

Matza, D. (1969), *Becoming Deviant* (Prentice Hall).

Maxime, J. E. (1986), 'Some psychological models of black self-concept', in S. Ahmed, J. Cheatham and J. Small (eds), *Social Work with Black Children and their Families* (Batsford).

May, M. (1977), 'Violence in the family: an historical perspective', in J. P. Martin (ed.), *Violence in the Family* (Wiley).

Mayhall, P. D. and Norgaard, K. E. (1983), *Child Abuse and Neglect* (John Wiley & Sons).

Maynard, M. (1985), 'The response of social workers to domestic violence', in J. Pahl (ed.), *Private Violence and Public Policy. The needs of battered women and the response of the public services* (Routledge and Kegan Paul).

Messerschmidt, J. W. (1986), *Capitalism, Patriarchy and Crime: Towards a socialist feminist criminology* (Rowman & Littlefield).

Mettlin, C. and Woelfel, J. (1974), 'Interpersonal influence and symptoms of stress', *Journal of Health and Social Behaviour*, 15 (4), pp. 311–19.

Meulenbelt, A. (1981), *For Ourselves* (Sheba Feminist).

Miller, A. (1985), *Thou Shalt Not Be Aware; Society's betrayal of the child* (Pluto).

Milner, J. and Blyth, E. (1988), *Coping with Child Sexual Abuse: A guide for teachers* (Longmans)

Minuchin, S. (1974), *Families and Family Therapy* (Harvard University Press).

Minuchin, S. (1984), *Family Kaleidoscope* (Harvard University Press).

Minuchin, S. and Fishman, H. C. (1981), *Family Therapy Techniques* (Harvard University Press).

Montgomery, J. (1988), 'Children as property?' *The Modern Law Review*, 51 (3), pp. 323–42.

Moore, J. (1982), 'Like a rabbit caught in headlights', *Community Care*, 4 November, pp. 18–19.

Mount, F. (1983), *The Subversive Family* (Jonathan Cape).

Myles, et al. (1985) *Taught not Caught. Strategies for Sex Education* (Cambridge: Learning Development Aids).

National Children's Bureau (1987), *Investing in the Future: Child health ten years after the Court Report* (NCB).

National Children's Home (1988), *Children in Danger* (NCH).

Nava, M. (1988), 'Cleveland and the press: outrage and anxiety in the reporting of child sexual abuse', *Feminist Review*, no. 28, January, pp. 103–21.

Nelson, S. (1987), *Incest: Fact and Myth* (Stramullion).

Newsom, J. and Newsom, E. (1968), *Four Years Old in an Urban Community* (Allen & Unwin).

Nokes, P. (1967), *The Professional Task in Welfare Practice* (Routledge & Kegan Paul).

NSPCC, *Annual Report 1903*, unpublished source (NSPCC Archives, London).

NSPCC Inspectors' Directory 1904, unpublished source (NSPCC Archives, London).

NSPCC, *Stockton-on-Tees, Thornaby and District Branch Report 1893–4*, unpublished source (NSPCC Archives, London).

NSPCC, *Stockton-on-Tees, Thornaby and District Branch Report 1894–5*, unpublished source (NSPCC Archives, London).

NSPCC, *Stockton-on-Tees, Thornaby and District Branch Report 1899*, unpublished source (NSPCC Archives, London).

NSPCC, *Stockton-on-Tees, Thornaby and District Branch Report 1911*, unpublished source (NSPCC Archives, London).

NSPCC, *York and Mid-Yorkshire Branch Report 1899*, unpublished source (NSPCC Archives, London).

O'Brien, M. (1981), *The Politics of Reproduction* (Routledge & Kegan Paul).

O'Hara, M. (1988), 'Developing a feminist school policy on child sexual abuse', *Feminist Review*, no. 28, spring, pp. 158–62.

Ong, B. N. (1986), 'Are abusing women abused women', in C. Webb (ed.), *Feminist Practice in Women's Health Care* (Wiley).

Open University (1987) D211, Social Problems and Social Welfare, Block 3, Unit 17 (author, C. Cannon), *Images of Domesticity: the work of the Family Centre* (The Open University Press).

Osborn, A. F. and Butler, N. R. (1985), *Ethnic Minority Children: A comparative study from birth to five years* (Commission for Racial Equality).

Pahl, J. (ed.)(1985), *Private Violence and Public Policy* (Routledge and Kegan Paul).

Palazzoli, M. S., Cecchin, G., Prata, G. and Boscolo, L. (1978), *Paradox and counter-paradox* (Jason Aronson).

Palazzoli, M. S., Cecchin, G. and Boscolo, L. (1980), 'Hypothesizing, circularity, neutrality; three guidelines for the conduct of the session', *Family Process*, 19, pp. 3–12.

Parents Against Injustice (PAIN)(1986), 'A response to child abuse – working together . . . A draft guide to arrangements for interagency co-operation for the protection of children'.

Parents Against Injustice (PAIN)(1987), Lecture by S. Amplett at Pontefract Royal Infirmary, 24 November.

Parton, C. and Parton, N. (1989), 'Child protection, the law and dangerousness', in O. Stevenson (ed.), *Child Abuse: Public Policy and Professional Practice* (Wheatsheaf).

Parton, N. (1979), 'The natural history of child abuse: a study in social problem definition', *British Journal of Social Work*, 9 (4), pp. 431–51.

Parton, N. (1981), 'Child abuse, social anxiety and welfare', *British Journal of Social Work*, 11 (4), pp. 391–414.

Parton, N. (1985a), *The Politics of Child Abuse* (Macmillan).

Parton, N. (1985b), 'Children in care: recent changes and debates', *Critical Social Policy*, 13, pp. 107–17.

Parton, N. (1986), 'The Beckford Report: a critical appraisal', *British Journal of Social Work*, 16 (5), pp. 511–30.

Pelton, L. (1978), 'Child abuse and neglect: the myth of classlessness', *American Journal of Orthopsychiatry*, 48 (4), pp. 608–17.

Pelton, L. H. (ed.)(1981), *The Social Context of Child Abuse and Neglect* (Human Sciences Press).

Pfohl, S. J. (1977), 'The discovery of child abuse', *Social Problems*, 24 (3), February, pp. 310–23.

Phillipson, J. (1988), 'The complexities of caring', *Social Work Education*, 7 (3), summer, pp. 3–6.

Philp, M. (1979), 'Notes on the form of knowledge in social work', *Sociological Review*, 27, pp. 83–111.

Phoenix, A. (1988), 'The Afro-Caribbean myth', *New Society*, 4 March, pp. 10–13.

Pierce, L. H. and Pierce, R. L. (1984), 'Race as a factor in the sexual abuse of children', *Social Work Research and Abstracts*, pp. 9–14.

Pilalis, J. and Anderton, J. (1986), 'Feminism and family therapy – a possible meeting point', *Journal of Family Therapy*, 8, pp. 99–124.

Pimlott, B. (1988), 'Thatcher's aims do not help ease abuse of children', *Sunday Times*, 3 July.

Pitts, J., Sawa, T., Taylor, A. and Whyte, L. (1986), 'Developing an anti-racist intermediate treatment', in S. Ahmed, J. Cheetham and J. Small (eds), *Social Work with Black Families and Children* (Batsford), pp. 167–86.

Plummer, K. (1984), 'The social uses of sexuality: symbolic interaction, power and rape', in J. Hopkins (ed.), *Perspectives on Rape and Sexual Assault* (Harper & Row).

Pollock, L. (1983), *Forgotten Children: Parent–Child relations from 1500–1900* (Cambridge University Press).

Poulantzas, N. (1978), *State, Power, Socialism* (New Left Books).

Prochaska, F. R. (1980), *Women and philanthropy in nineteenth century England* (Oxford University Press).

Rainwater, L. (1974), *Social Problems and Public Policy: Deviance and Liberty* (Aldine).

'Reasonable punishment' (1987), *STOPP News*, 2 (6), summer.

Rich, A. (1977), *Of Woman Born: Motherhood as experience and institution* (Bantam).

Rights of Women (1984), *Lesbian Mothers on Trial. A report on lesbian mothers and child custody* (Rights of Women).

Rivara, F. P. (1985), 'Physical abuse in children under two: a study of therapeutic outcomes', *Child Abuse and Neglect*, 9, pp. 81–7.

Roberts, S. R. (1986), 'Examination of the anus in suspected child sexual abuse', *The Lancet*, 8 November, p. 1100.

Rochdale NSPCC Child Protection Team (1986), *Doing Networks and Case Conferences* (Rochdale Area Review Training Sub-Committee).

Rose, N. (1987), 'Beyond the public/private division: law, power and the family', *Journal of Law and Society*, 14 (1), pp. 61–76, spring.

Rowe, J. and Lambert, L. (1973), *Children Who Wait* (ABAFA).

Rowntree, B. S. (1901), *Poverty: A study of town life* (Macmillan).

Roys, C. (1987), 'Two reports on feminism and family therapy – with Marianne Walters', *Association of Family Therapy Newsletter*, 7 (3), p. 12.

Rush, F. (1980), *The Best Kept Secret* (Prentice Hall).

Sainsbury, E., Nixon, S. and Phillips, D. (1982), *Social Work in Focus: Clients' and Social Workers' Perceptions in Long-term Social Work* (Routledge & Kegan Paul).

Sands, P. (1988), Interview with line manager.

Satyamurti, C. (1981), *Occupational Survival: The case of the Local Authority Social Worker* (Blackwell).

Schechter, S. (1982), *Women and Male Violence: The Visions and Struggles of the Battered Women's Movement* (South).

Scott, H. (1987), *Case Records* (Kirklees Social Services Department).

Schur, F. M. (1963), *Crimes without Victims: Deviant Behaviour and Public Policy* (Prentice Hall).

Secretary of State for Social Services (1974), *Report of the Committee of Inquiry into the care and supervision provided in relation to Maria Colwell* (HMSO).

Secretary of State for Social Services (1988), *Report of the Inquiry into child abuse in Cleveland, Cmnd 412* (HMSO).

Sennett, R. (1970), 'The brutality of modern families', *Transaction*, 7, pp. 29–37.

Sgroi, S. (ed.)(1981), *Handbook of Clinical Intervention in Child Sexual Abuse* (Lexington Books).

Sharron, H. (1987), 'The influence of the Paterson factor', *Social Work Today*, 30 March, pp. 8–9.

Shorter, E. (1982), *A History of Women's Bodies* (Basic; Penguin).

Sivanandan, A. (1985), 'RAT and the degradation of black struggle', *Race and Class*, 26 (4), spring, pp. 1–33 .

Smith, D. (1987), 'Knowing your place: class, politics and ethnicity in Chicago and Birmingham 1890–1983', in N. Thrift and P. Williams (eds) *Class and Space: The Making of Urban Society* (Routledge & Kegan Paul).

Social Services Inspectorate (1986), *Inspection of Family Centres. A National Survey of Family Centres run by Local Authority Social Services Departments* (DHSS), November.

Social Services Inspectorate (1988), *Child Sexual Abuse: Survey. Report on inter-agency co-operation in England and Wales* (DHSS).

Social Work Today (1988), 'Anger at BASW conference over QC's view of social workers' role', 19 (30), 31 March, p. 3.

Spencer, D. (1982), 'Staying on helps blacks to exam. success', *Times Educational Supplement*, 8 October.

Stallybrass, P. and White, A. (1986), *The Politics and Poetics of Transgression* (Methuen).

Stark, E. and Flitcraft, A. (1985), 'Woman battering, child abuse and social heredity: what is the relationship?' in J. Norman (ed.), *Marital Violence* (Routledge & Kegan Paul).

Stedman Jones, G. (1971), *Outcast London* (Clarendon Press).

Stevenson, O. (1986), 'Book review of *The Politics of Child Abuse*', *Journal of Social Policy*, vol. 15, no. 1, pp. 119–21.

Straus, M. (1979), 'Family patterns and child abuse in a nationally representative American sample', *Child Abuse and Neglect*, 3, pp. 213–25.

Straus, M. A., Gelles, R. J. and Steinmetz, S. K. (1980), *Behind Closed Doors: Violence in the American Family* (Anchor/Doubleday).

Stubbs, P. (1987), 'Professionalism and the adoption of black children', *British Journal of Social Work*, vol. 17, no. 5, pp. 473–92.

Sutton, A. (1980), 'Child abuse procedures - are they worth the risk?' *LAG Bulletin*, May.

Taft, J. (1983), in N. Timms, *Social Work Values: An Enquiry* (Routledge & Kegan Paul).

Taylor, I., Walton, P. and Young, J. (1973), *The New Criminology: For a Social Theory of Deviance* (Routledge & Kegan Paul).

Taylor, I., Walton, P. and Young, J. (1975), *Critical Criminology* (Routledge & Kegan Paul).

Thane, P. (1982), *The Foundations of the Welfare State* (Longman).

Thatcher, M. (1988), Speech to the General Assembly of the Church of Scotland, 21 May, reported in *The Guardian*, 23 May, p. 38.

Thompson, L. H. and Pleck, J. H. (1987), 'The structure of male role norms' in M. S. Kimmel (ed.), *Changing Men. New Directions in Research on Men and Masculinity* (Sage).

Tolman, R. M., Mowry, D. D., Jones, L. E. and Brekke, J. (1986), 'Developing a pro-feminist commitment among men in social work', in N. Van Der Bergh and L. B. Cooper (eds), *Feminist Visions for Social Work* (Silver Spring, MD: NASW).

Tomlinson, S. (1982), 'A case of non-achievement: West Indians and E.S.N./M. Schooling', in G. K. Verma and B. Bagley (eds), *Self Concept, Achievement and Multi-cultural Education* (Macmillan).

Tonkin, B. (1987), 'A year of living dangerously', *Community Care*, 31 December, pp. 15–17.

Trepper, T. S. and Barrett, M. J. (eds)(1986), *Treating Incest* (Haworth Press).

Tung, D. L. and Koch, J. S. (1980), 'School administrators: sources of stress and ways of coping with it', in C. L. Cooper and J. Marshall (eds), *White Collar and Professional Stress* (Wiley).

UNICEF (1987), *The State of the World's Children, 1987* (UNICEF)

Valentine, C. A. (1968), *Culture and Poverty: Critique and Counter-proposals* (Chicago University Press).

Ward, E. (1984), *Father–Daughter Rape* (The Women's Press).

Warren, C. (1986), 'Towards a Family Centre movement; reconciling day care, child protection and community work', *Child Abuse Review*, 1 (3), summer, pp. 10–16.

Washburne, C. (1983), 'A feminist analysis of child abuse and neglect', in D. Finkelhor *et al.* (eds), *The Dark Side of Families* (Sage).

Waterhouse, L. (1987), news item in *Community Care*, 9 July, p. 7.

Waterman, J. and Lusk, R. (1986), 'The scope of the problem', in K. MacFarlane *et al.*, *The Sexual Abuse of Young Children* (Holt, Rinehart & Winston).

Waters, J. (1987), 'Spreading the load', *Community Care*, 4 June, pp. 22–3.

Webb, A. (1975), 'Co-ordination between health and personal social services: a question of quality'. Unpublished paper presented to European seminar on interaction of social welfare and health personnel in the delivery of services.

Weissman, H., Epstein, I. and Savage, A. (1983), *Agency Based Social Work: Neglected Aspects of Clinical Practice* (Temple University Press).

Wetherly, P. (1988), 'Class struggle and the welfare state: some theoretical problems', *Critical Social Policy*, no. 22, pp. 24–40, Summer.

Whitehead, A. (1987), *The Health Divide: Inequalities in Health in the 1980s* (Health Education Council).

Whitehorn, K. (1987), 'Cannibalism and other taboos', *The Observer*, 2 August, p. 39.

Wild, J. (1988), 'The male social worker and sexual abuse work: towards an anti-sexist framework', *Child Protection*, vol. 3, no. 1, pp. 3–6.

Williams, P. (1987), 'Constituting class and gender: a social history of the home, 1700–1981' in N. Thrift and P. Williams (eds), *Class and Space: The Making of Urban Society* (Routledge & Kegan Paul).

Wilson, E. (1977), *Women and the Welfare State* (Tavistock).

Will, D. (1989), 'Feminism, child sexual abuse and the (long-overdue) demise of systems mysticism', *Context*, vol. 9, no. 1, pp. 12–15.

Winnicott, C. (1964), *Child Care and Social Work* (Caldicote Press).

Wood, R. (1987), 'Raging Bull: the homosexual subtext in film', in M. Kaufman (ed.), *Beyond Patriarchy. Essays by Men on Pleasure, Power and Change* (Oxford University Press).

Wooden, W. S. and Parker, J. (1982), *Men Behind Bars, Sexual Exploitation in Prison* (Plenum).

Wringe, C. A. (1981), *Children's Rights: A Philosophical Study* (Routledge & Kegan Paul).

Wrong, D. H. (1979), *Power: Its Forms, Bases and Uses* (Blackwell).

Wynne, J. N. and Hobbs, J. T. (1986), 'Examination of the anus in suspected child sexual abuse', *The Lancet*, 8 November, p. 1100.

Wyre, R. (1986), *Women, Men and Rape* (Perry Publications).

Wyre, R. (1988), NSPCC Conference, London, 23 and 24 March.

Index